Return From The Wild

Return From The Wild
The Story of Lassie, the Collie Born in a Fox Earth

John Roberts Warren
Illustrations by Philip Snow

Michael Butterworth

First published in Great Britain in 2012 by Michael Butterworth

2 4 6 8 10 9 7 5 3 1

Michael Butterworth
michaelbutterworthbooks@googlemail.com

A CIP catalogue record for this book is available from the British
Library
ISBN 978-0-9552672-4-6

Printed and bound by CPI Group (UK) Ltd, Croydon, CR0 4YY

Design by dust, Sheffield
http://du.st

Foreword

THIS IS the true and original story of Lassie – a beautiful chestnut-red collie, born of a wild mother in a fox earth. Although totally devoted to me, she remained to the outside world a wild creature during her sixteen-year adventure-packed life.

Much has been said, both for and against, the possibility that Lassie was a hybrid fox-dog. Genetics disprove such crossbreeding between species – yet the facts which follow remain unanswerable.

Of the earliest period in Lassie's life – her infancy in the fox earth, and the events in the autumn of 1953 that led to her capture by James Cook, the then inspector of Macclesfield RSPCA – I know little, except what I have managed to learn in conversation with the people who witnessed a small but insignificant part of it. I have, therefore, had to reconstruct the first part of my story that deals with her capture, utilising these few details as well as my knowledge of the people and the area around Macclesfield, Cheshire, where Lassie was found.

John Roberts Warren
Monk's Heath
Nether Alderley
July 2012

Prologue
November, 1953

THE ONLY real chance the two men waiting in their makeshift hide had of seeing the killer dog were during the scant periods when the moon broke through the clouds and cast a pale silver light through the late autumn canopy. At such moments they stopped their quiet conversation and strained forward, trying to catch site of their quarry. But the heavy rain clouds returned almost at once, making the task all but impossible. Seasoned Cheshire farmers, they were used to such conditions, and above the intermittent noise of the rain striking the rough roof, or wind gusting through the treetops, kept up a laconical good humour, using the opportunity to indulge in small talk or the occasional important matter affecting their hard country lives.

Four or five hours earlier they had parted company from the remainder of the search team, consisting of an RSPCA officer and his voluntary diggers, also mainly farmers. The officer and his men had parked their van as close to the wood as it was possible to get, whilst still being able to monitor any expected events. Their engine stilled, they were nearly as intent as the two farmers, listening out for the sound of their quarry – or gunshots. As protectors of animal life this was not a job they relished, but it was better to work with the farmers and control the conditions under which any animals were killed, if only when absolutely necessary.

The lair had been staked out much earlier, in the bright of day, when the hide had been built – a rough square of strong branches covered over with tarpaulin, with lighter branches laid artfully on top and against the sides to act as camouflage. Their quarry was a little 'blue-merle' Border Collie of unknown breeding and history, a stray who had run her luck and was currently abroad somewhere in the night. The farmers knew she would have to return sometime to her present home in the wood, and hopefully before too long – and on their watch.

Many times, in lulls in the wind, they thought that a rustling in the undergrowth denoted her arrival, but the belaboured wood was only casting spells on them – some bough, taxed by the commotion of the weather, had sounded out its anguish; the track of some small resident, unaware of the men's presence, was making its way through the heaps of grey bracken and briars; or some phantom in their minds, trying to fulfill what it was they sought, projecting itself out into the blackness.

Their reluctant vigil on such a night was made necessary not by the ordinary motivations of paid men, but by something far deeper, that of protecting what was theirs. Farmers in the Cheshire hamlet of Moreton had become aware of this small interloper from the wild in the early autumn, when she had first come to live in the wood bordering their fields. No one knew where she had come from, but the farmers understood from bitter experience that a feral dog would be trouble. Shortly after her arrival their fears were confirmed when lambs had started disappearing, and the tell-tale traces of blood and patches of wool told them what species of culprit it was – nothing else was big or strong enough to drag such well-grown lambs away.

Once a dog has run after sheep, it will nearly always go back to them. In the wilderness, where truly wild animals avoid capture more easily, it is difficult for the less experienced domestic dog to resist the temptation of easy prey. Presumably, this wild collie had at first sustained herself on rabbits and whatever other wildlife she could manage to catch. Becoming bolder, especially with young to feed, she had turned her attention on the less troublesome lambs.

In just half an hour, a dog running wild can cause thousands of pounds worth of damage, and not just from the loss of lambs killed outright as food for the hungry dog. Ewes, in their panic, abort their young; stampeded cattle, in their fear, abort their calves. The little blue-grey collie had not been immediately blamed, though many farmers would have instantly shot her – as faithful and reliable as such sheep dogs can be, like any dog, they have the potential to turn on their subjects, especially when hungry. They thought at first that she was a working dog, belonging to a local farmstead, out for country runs. Even when the evidence continued to mount, the killings were not conclusively linked to her. But as the weeks went by the losses to their livestock, when added to likely future losses, became too high. As they had done on other occasions, the close-knit community of farmers acted together.

They mounted a search, beginning by combing the thick wood where they had established she hid during the daytime. There they had found her traces – more remains of the missing lambs – and the tell-tale tracks that led to her lair.

The two men stretched their legs as best they could in their cramped confines, vigorously rubbing their hands together for warmth. After the lively, wide-ranging talk of earlier, they were now largely sunk in their own thoughts, but still warily scanning the mysterious tangle of light and shade exposed whenever the moon showed. When it seemed as though the wind and rain would buck the forecast and last throughout the night, the clouds suddenly cleared, leaving the bright moon and a mass of stars to reveal the tangle with startling clarity. At first, this proved to be as much help as hindrance, for the wind continued, blowing freshly across the fields and through the trees, and former rustles now became visual movements as well. Fortunately for them, just before dawn that too died away, and the countryside suddenly became very still – as though a great hand had been waved over it.

Almost every detail in the wood had become clear. The trunks of the trees – rowans, ash, oaks and conifers – once invisible in the darkness, now stood out as stark silhouettes, limned by the steely-soft rays of the moon. Now, they could now not only hear, but distinguish, the different rustles of creatures that had not yet hibernated – the scuttling of little mice and voles, and the sounds of those consigned to spend the winter foraging for food to keep themselves and their families alive until the arrival of spring. The hoots of owls and distant barks of farm dogs, the rumblings of occasional steam trains moving their cargos of goods on the periphery of the night, the sharp smell of the dark vegetation – the night now seemed vibrant with a feeling of expectancy.

The two men became instantly alert, carefully exchanging just one meaningful look, afraid of making the slightest movement or sound in case they should miss the anticipated stealthy dragging noise made by the collie as she returned with her latest kill. Their loaded rifles were quickly and silently slid into position, safety catches off, protruding from the hide. Angled in the branches in the wall of the shelter were two powerful torches, ready to flood the area with more light. Should she be caught in this trap there would be little chance of her surviving. But they had to be careful. If they surprised her too soon, her very sharp canine senses would be alerted, and the night would be wasted.

A few short yards in front of them a large silvered oak trunk grasped upwards, growing age-worn and mossed from the dim mass of a sandy and well-vegetated bank. On a sunny spring day, the green slopes of the bank would have supported dozens of bluebells. Ivy also twisted there, and in the summer the honeysuckle would be in full flower around the secondary growth of smaller trees. Now, the roots of the great oak curled frozenly downward into the ground, disappearing from the view of the two men, down behind the dark mat of dead bracken and brambles. They knew well enough that behind the undergrowth, in the bank beneath the roots, lay the old fox earth – the end of the trail – in which the collie had made her home. It was so tangled and dense that it was hidden from sight even during the day. Only a small track, big enough to take a fox, or perhaps a badger, led through it to the lair at the back.

A long time passed, and the scene changed again. The moon had disappeared, and the stars were fading fast. Pale twilight was forming, miraculously changing hunched and crouching monsters into familiar trees and vegetation. As often happens to people who have been up all night, at that time of the morning they become drained of will, and feel themselves strangely at peace with the tiny bit of the world that surrounds them. Where before phantoms had appeared on the darkness, now, illusions of another sort tricked the two men. Images that they could clearly see, took on a more flexible nature. Bushes, frozen in the stillness, now appeared to move. Sounds, unnaturally sharp, leapt out, making them jump. Then the first real light of dawn broke, and the magical wood awoke. Uncertainly at first, and with growing confidence, the first robin began to etch its winter song on the still, slightly misty air. Magpies chattered, woodpeckers 'chikked' and the ubiquitous pigeons cooed, as ever.

Before the two men properly realised what was happening, a new sound, almost lost in the rising clamour of the awakening wood, came from somewhere near the edge of the wood. It was not the haphazard noise a blackbird or thrush might make, flicking over dead leaves beneath the bushes, or the fleet scurrying of a hedgehog, but a substantial sound made by a much larger creature – breaking its way slowly through the undergrowth! It was laden with purpose, and moving slowly toward them. Instinctively, they knew this was the collie, slowed down by dragging something obviously large and heavy towards her lair....

The snapping of branches and undergrowth grew steadily louder, exaggerated by the sudden ceasing of bird song, until finally her dim shape came suddenly into view, struggling backwards through the foliage. The tension heightened unbearably as the men waited, fingers on triggers, for the exact moment – they couldn't afford to get it wrong. Neither wanted another long night like this, in a hurry!

The dog dragged her catch labouriously forward, until she and her prey could clearly be seen. It became evident straight away she must once have been a magnificent working dog, but now she looked starved and exhausted. Her once luxuriant, tri-coloured coat – a mixture of blue-grey, black and white – was matted and rough, lacking the soft sheen it must once have possessed. Her body was animated, even afflicted, by a lean hunger that appeared to have taken hold of her like a disease. At intervals the exhausted dog stopped to rest for a few brief moments, without allowing her teeth to let go of the lifeless body she had in tow before, every muscle quivering with the strain, with head down and haunches raised, resuming her Herculean task. In the brightening twilight it was quite plain to see that her catch – a limp, woolen shape, collapsed like a rag and stained with dark blood – was one of the well-grown lambs from their fields.

The men were tensed unbearably, expecting at any moment for the collie to be in the right position for their guns, when their attention was distracted by a sudden movement from the direction of the lair – and the sight of five small, furry shapes creeping cautiously out of the bracken. The men quickly realised these were the collie's puppies, confirming what had made her turn killer, and the reason the RSPCA had been called in to help. The animal society had been asked to participate not to oversee the kill – which they are often asked to do – but because the number of deaths indicated that the collie might have a litter. Her puppies would need to be taken into care.

Yet something other than sentiment stayed the men's resolve for a moment longer, almost losing them their opportunity. By contrast to their mother's coat, the coats of these puppies, seen as they crept forward to greet her, were of a darker, more uniform colour. In the steadily brightening light, they appeared to be red, or at least, a sleek orangey-brown. Because collie pups are notorious for taking on the same characteristics as their kind, the men were puzzled.

Were these wild puppies really the collie's offspring, then? They looked strong and well fed, and, judging by their size and the way they moved, about ten to twelve weeks old. Although they were obviously quite hungry, and eager to get to the food, they did not rush to the collie as puppies of domesticated dogs normally do. Instead, they approached in silence, without wagging their short tails. Yet perhaps this odd behaviour – a wariness and an instinctive control over their feelings – was something to do with the hard lessons they had already learned from living in the wild?

Although they dared not risk even a brief glimpse at each other, all these thoughts rushed rapidly, almost simultaneously, through both men's heads as the collie continued dragging the dead lamb toward the lair. By now, the puppies were moving silently about the animal as she dragged it, closely following her with rapt attention.

At the very last moment the collie seemed to sense that something was wrong. Whether she had intended to drag the lamb into the fox earth, or not – whether the puppies were to have had their meal inside or outside – was never discovered, for she suddenly dropped the dead animal and threw back her head, uneasily scenting the air, her sharp eyes scanning the thicket that contained the men's hide. Although she couldn't see any movement the quivering mother knew instinctively that danger lurked there, and barked out a single warning – but was too late to save herself, for the two men fired and the bullets struck her almost at the same time. Her body shook briefly from the impacts, and then sank silently to the ground. Yet her warning bark had saved the pups, for within a split second they had vanished back into the earth.

The men's sure aim meant the collie's end was almost instant. She struggled only briefly with death, then her head fell back, limp, upon the crushed vegetation. By some trick of the light, or possibly the result of an exhausting burden lifted from both gunmen and prey, her lighter coat now looked smooth and shiny with health. And if it wasn't for the way her neck was unnaturally stretched out at full length, head back as it rested on the ground, she could have been asleep. After the echoing gunshots, and the many alarm calls of the birds reverberating shrilly through the air, had died away, the wood fell eerily silent.

The scene had a shocking intensity to it, and the farmers were more moved than they could have imagined. The collie, once domesticated but now virtually wild, yet for reasons unknown, had lived the only life she could have done for the sake of her litter. The men felt no satisfaction in killing what had once been a prime working dog. But they were at least pleased the ordeal was over, and climbed out of their hide, relieved to be able to relax, stretch their legs and wait for the arrival of the other men.

Hearing the shots, the RSPCA inspector soon arrived with his helpers, and began his work. Aided by the two farmers, both eager to indulge in some warming work, and explain as much as they could about the strange pups at the same time, they began clearing away the bracken and briars from the mouth of the earth, tossing them impatiently aside, before setting about the task of digging. All were stiff with cold, and glad to get into action.

The sandy loam was easy enough to move, but the work was made harder by the many tough and spreading roots of the large oak. The young puppies would presumably be living like fox cubs in the earth, and the men had to dig cautiously to avoid injuring any of them, should they come suddenly upon their chamber. A Red Fox earth can belong either solely to a fox or it may be shared with a badger. Possibly because both are targets of human persecution, the two animals will often co-exist together, and even breed in the same earth, or sett, and respect each other's young (although it seems to be first come, first served – the first to have pups will usually dominate, violently if need be, the complex). Or they will simply build separate chambers for themselves, but share a communal entrance run. When the earth is abandoned, as seemed to be the case with the collie's lair, it might be taken over by other animals in need of a ready-made home – such as rabbits, or members of the Mustelid family, like polecats and stoats, even otters, if only temporarily.

Most of the puppies' time would have been spent sleeping, apart from when they were being fed by their mother. At first they would have been given only her rich milk and, after about five weeks – if they were dogs, not foxes, which wean at about ten weeks – weaned onto solid food such as the meat of hares, rabbits and lambs. At about six weeks they would have started to play in their chamber – and even start the fight for individual dominance – still happily living all their time deep under ground.

After nearly two hours of hard digging, three snapping, snarling and completely terrified puppies were lifted from the earth. In the now bright morning light their coats could be seen to be variations of rich chest-nut red, instead of the grey-black-and-white of their mother. Surprised, even though already warned by the shooters about their unique colouration, they had little time to speculate, for the biting, scratching dogs had to be secured inside the boxes that had been brought to contain them.

Cursing the energetic puppies for the fight they were putting up, the men nevertheless soon had them secured, and recommenced digging, needing to extricate the two puppies that they knew remained. But they had scarcely started when a sudden blur of movement occurred amongst their forest of legs and feet. From the black interior of the half-opened earth a reddish form, not much larger than the collie, burst out, and before the startled men could think of halting its progress, had made clean its escape through the trees and out into the open fields. In its panic, the creature had collided with the dog boxes. As it had spun round to regain its bearings, the equally startled men caught a glimpse of the unmistakable features of a full grown, male Red Fox – the trademark tail, flash of white undercarriage, and glint of white teeth bared in a snarl of fearful hatred – before it shot off into the fields!

Perhaps if the fox had been a collie, the men might have retained their presence of mind and captured it as it made its difficult escape. But the suddenness, and the fact that it wasn't, had stymied them completely, and they immediately remembered the uncharacteristic colouration of the puppies' coats.

Their task momentarily forgotten again, the men stood talking, speculating on what this new sighting meant. The fox had been a dog-fox, they were sure, because of its size – only slightly bigger than the collie, whose body had already been placed in a sack and lay at the foot of a tree, waiting to be carried to the van. That it was a Red Fox – with its rich colouration, shorter legs, and unmistakable tail – there could be no doubt. Only two conclusions seemed possible: either the collie had taken up with the fox, the two had mated, and the litter of pups was their offspring; or the fox had moved in to share the earth with the mother and her puppies. The former seemed the most logical, for the latter did not take account of the distinct colour of the puppies' coats, let alone the improbable coexistence of an unmated fox and dog! Yet as farmers and animal workers familiar with the breeding of animals, they could recall no precedent. Besides which, a dog successfully mating with a fox was not meant to be possible! According to most researchers, all the Canids, such as dogs, wolves, jackals, coyotes, can freely interbreed – except for the fox, seemingly because it has now strayed 'too far' from the original genetic makeup of its (dog) Family into its own rather exclusive smaller sub-group, or Genus, and has far fewer chromosomes. If the puppies had been the offspring of domesticated dogs, they should have taken on their mother's characteristics. As it was, these looked and behaved more like foxes, though neither truly fox nor truly collie.*

The yipping noises and struggling of the pups in their boxes once more reminded the men of the work still to do, and they wearily returned to their digging, again putting aside speculations, at least outwardly. Hardly had their spades touched the earth when the sandy bank, already weakened, caved in with a dull thump. This was what the men had feared, and it was unlikely the two remaining puppies would now be brought out alive. Such proved to be the case, for they soon came across the still forms of the two puppies, asphyxiated by the sand. More cautious than their siblings, they had stayed deeper within the lair. Their flattened corpses, a little

---

*It is now known that foxes can breed with coyotes. As coyotes can breed with dogs, and all the other Canids including wolves, dingoes, wild dogs et cetera, and also breed with each other, they are probably all 'conspecifics'. (See the work of Dr Jean Lightner, who comments on a claimed coyote-fox (Vulpes) hybrid that appears to be reliable in Mammalian Hybrids and Generic Limits by Richard G Van Gelder, American Museum novitates, No. 2635, New York; American Museum of Natural History, 1977.) A common objection to including foxes into this well-known web of interbreeding has been their differing chromosome numbers to other Canids, but this is not a problem in other fertile life forms with very similar (or even very differing!) forms/colours et cetera, like ciclid fish, and others. (See the work of Dr Arthur Jones, et al.)

more ginger-brown in colour than the others in the clear light of day, and still warm to the touch, were brought out and placed in the sack with their mother, ready to be taken to the waiting van. When they were quite sure that no other puppies were left within the earth, the men began to pack away their guns and equipment.

The sun was now fully up, and the wood had long lost its magical quality. Satisfied with the night's work, the farmers began making their way back across the pastures to their farms. The RSPCA men, less happily, returned to their van with their boxes and shovels and the sack. The dead collie and her two dead pups would now be taken to the RSPCA incinerator.

Uppermost on their minds was the problem of what they could do for her remaining offspring, the three 'fox-dog' puppies. They had possibly inherited the full, free-ranging instincts of their wild Red Fox father – what their mother had only sampled briefly during her brief time away from men – and if they truly were of fox blood, as it was thought, it would be quite impossible to find homes they would accept.

Chapter One

MY STORY began later that morning. I did not know it, as I set out to the RSPCA centre that I had chosen the momentous day of the little blue collie's death. I suppose I must have looked a little incongruous, a painfully shy lad of only fifteen, tall, skinny, fair almost blonde hair, with greeny-grey eyes, yet dressed roughly in work clothes of hard-wearing trousers, muddy leather boots, a sweater and a jacket with leather elbows and cuffs. As always when I visited, I was in a state of high expectancy to see what the inspector, James Cook, might have for me. But little did I realise what that Sunday would bring!

I arrived at the small surgery of the normally busy rural practice just as James was returning with his men from the marathon vigil at the lonely fox earth in his old, rather battered dark-blue Morris van. I watched expectantly as the well-known van steered its way into the backyard and parked where the animal compounds – mainly for dogs – were housed.

My special love was for dogs, and I had already grown very attached to several belonging to my parents. But I loved animal of all kinds. I would go so far as to say that I preferred the company of animals to humans, and because of my father's twin professions of market and landscape gardener, it was no great difficulty for me to seek out such companionship. Where we lived, on the smallholding in the farming country outside Macclesfield, could not have been a better place for an animal lover like myself.

At the time, four dogs lived with us – my father's huge Alsatian bitch, Zena, who followed him faithfully wherever he went about the smallholding; two Pembrokeshire Corgis belonging to my mother; and Floss, a grey-and-white smooth-haired Border Collie cross inherited from my grandparents' farm. Zena had been acquired as a six month old, part-grown pup – the result of a pub bet – and had grown into an admirable guard dog. She was fierce and much larger than the average Alsatian, and very off-putting to strangers. She was a strange dog who obeyed only my father, and showed affection to no one else. The two Corgis, Rusty and Trixie, came from my mother's interest in breeding. Rusty was a brother to one of the Queen's stud lines, and sired many puppies that lodged with us for short periods before being sold. Trixie was one of two breeding bitches that Mother had grown especially fond of, and was now, with Rusty, kept as a family pet. The other bitch, Sadie, who I had grown terribly attached to, had recently died of old age. The loss had upset me terribly, and it was Sadie who had prompted me to fulfill a dream of owning my own dog. Her passing meant that there was also the room for another dog; until then, the farm had had a full quota; so as soon as possible after her death, in between schoolwork and farm duties, I had begun to make my search.

In those days – my mother's small breeding concern apart – there was not the money about to buy a new dog from a breeder, but even if there had been, I would much rather have accepted a stray, or a dog in need of a good home. I had decided that I wanted a collie, not another corgi. We had kept collies on my grandparents' nearby farm, where I had been born and raised until the age of twelve, and most of the farms round about us used them (mainly some sort of Border Collie), to work their cattle and sheep. As a breed they have a fine combination of intelligence, innate loyalty and friendliness, which makes them perfect working dogs. In my situation, as both dog lover and farm worker, able to give them all the work and exercise such energetic dogs needed, they seemed ideal.

It was not normally difficult to acquire dogs and animals of many kinds, from all the farms and countryside around us. There was never a shortage of lame, neglected, unwanted or stray creatures for those who were inclined to help, and because I had a reputation of being such a person, regular approaches were made to me by owners and other animal lovers. Often these were complete strangers, who knew my reputation and who, for one reason or another, wanted me to take their animals into care. Many of them were animal lovers whose pets had become too demanding. Others were owners who were just glad to be rid of them. Yet others, were people who had made the mistake of acquiring pets that they afterwards realised they didn't want – sadly, such creatures are often bought on a whim, or even, as in the famous 'Lassie' films, because they had become topical. But at the time I began my search, for some reason, there were no offers of dogs. And so I found myself once more on James Cook's doorstep.

The veterinary centre was a familiar place to me. I had been there on countless occasions, usually certain of finding something of interest. As a result of this I knew James very well indeed. He sensed I was truly interested in animals, and he was one of the few people I could talk animatedly to. He often phoned me up to tell me which new interesting animals had been brought in, to see if I could do anything with them. James had been the resident inspector at the centre for about ten years – as long as I could remember. For I had known him since the age of five, and had visited the busy offices regularly since the age of ten.

He was a tall, lean man in his fifties, with graying, receding hair, a thin, pointed face, and twinkling blue eyes, whose gaze I was never able to hold for long. His practice covered the town and the outlying farms, including our smallholding. James obviously had a special empathy with animals, a deep, very human love of them. When an animal was in danger he had no thought of his own safety, and had risked his life countless times saving animals and birds. One of the most dangerous jobs I ever saw him tackle involved crawling out on a ladder across a frozen pond, to rescue a young mute swan frozen into the ice. His deeds awed me! Unfortunately, he was part of a breed of inspectors who even then were dying off, steadily being replaced by careerists.

It was James who talked me into taking in animals, and he often brought them to me, especially the larger ones he could not himself accommodate at home, such as goats, ponies and donkeys that were usually old and unwanted, and everything else from kittens and puppies, to pigeons and jackdaws.

I spent many long and warm hours with James, talking about our mutual obsession. He used to say of these animals, "Oh well, John will always take on a bit of old rubbish!" He knew I was always a soft touch.

One day he turned up with two baby goatlings! They were so cute, each a pale fawn colour with white facial and leg markings, and large doe-like eyes. Under their chins they had two little white tassels, which I called 'bells'. The small creatures were so appealing I couldn't refuse them, and although knowing I risked incurring the wrath of my father, who objected to the many 'uncommercial' animals I attracted, I accepted them.

We already had one aged white nanny goat, and her two months' old kid. Our goats had always been quiet and unobtrusive about the farm, but changed a great deal after the arrival of these two newcomers. They quickly formed a small 'herd', and the three kids had great fun racing and play-fighting each other, much to the annoyance of the old mother goat.

As all goats do, these loved to climb, and their racing games soon became more elaborate. They had discovered that by leaping onto our Alsatian's kennel roof they could, with just one more leap reach a much more interesting play area. This happened to be the long, corrugated roof of a shed we called the Boiler House, which lay three feet above the kennel. The three goats would race to the kennel, bound upwards onto its roof, and just as adeptly jump up onto the corrugated sheeting. Now, the game really began as their young hooves thundered from one end of the roof to the other, just stopping short of the edges, making the most horrendous din.

One night, as my father prepared the pig feed in the Boiler House, the three young goats started their game by rushing across the roof. The clattering of twelve hooves on the metal, amplified enormously inside the building, caused my father to rush out in bewilderment. Seeing three cheeky faces looking down at us, and hearing the aged mother goat bleating frustratedly on the ground, quite unable to jump up to her youngsters, he had to laugh, but, overall, was not too pleased.

"Aye, very funny, lad," he intoned, "but if they do it again I'll 'ave their hides for rugs!" And I guessed he was not entirely joking...

Most of the little 'arrangements' I made therefore, had to be done in the strictest secrecy. Poor old Dad had the responsibility of managing the fine line between profit and loss for our business, and on the question of these animals, which constantly threatened to overload this equation, was forever rebuking me. Had he known about the sheer volume of 'illicit' animals that I had directly caused to be on the farm, he would have held up his hands in horror. He realised, of course, that extra animals somehow found their way onto the smallholding, but I never admitted to him from where some of them came.

For every animal that eventually stayed, there were several that did not. Over the years, many would come and go in greater or lesser numbers, and Father himself was not immune from popular trends in certain birds or animals, either. For instance, he once decided rabbits were completely unnecessary to the profitability of the farm, and a fruitless chore. My four black-and-white Old English Rabbits were, therefore, given an ultimatum to go. I decided to liberate them on a sandy bank on our land, north of the river, where there was already a large warren. Not only did the rabbits survive, but they began to breed freely, and I found it most interesting to note that the babies, born to the previously domesticated females and wild rabbits, were jet-black. But, of course, having been born wild they remained so, and bolted at the first sight of a human being. Wild rabbits do have a dark, often black or 'melanistic' form as well as the normal brown, or combinations of light and dark coats, as do many other lifeforms, from birds to fish to flowers.

The secrecy with which James and I worked served to strengthen our natural bond, and made our little deals all the more enjoyable, so when, on this clear sunny late autumn morning I found myself once again on his doorstep, I thrilled with anticipatory pleasure at what I might find.

Only the day before he had told me he "might have something" for me in the morning – if his mysterious night's work turned out as he imagined. But because his manner had been casual, and he and given no clues, I had thought little about his words. He knew I wanted a particular type of dog, and that was all. When James had seen me waiting there, even after his long ordeal of the previous night, he had jumped excitedly to life and invited me into his surgery. Now, as his blue eyes lit up brightly, and he moved one finger agitatedly in the air above his head his words of the previous day suddenly came back to me

"Ahhhh, John!" he cried. "Just wait until you see what I've got for you!"

In his mind, whatever he wanted to give to me, he had already given. Knowing he knew I was already irrevocably bound up to wanting a particular kind of animal – a dog – I knew it must be a dog, but what kind? I let him guide me eagerly through the surgery and back outside. It was now just a question of going through the formalities, I thought.

He led me to the open rear doors of the waiting van, where his colleagues were still busily unloading their grim cargo. The sack containing the dead mother and the two unlucky pups was taken away to the incinerator, and I deliberately looked away, guessing its sad contents. Left inside the vehicle were the three boxes containing the survivors, as I understood it from James's hurried explanation. Yet the boxes were quite silent. They gave no outward signs of their occupants – no tiny barks and yelps or scratching noises, none of the familiar signs ordinary puppies would be giving. They seemed empty. Momentarily I was nonplussed, and 'looked' a question at James...?

"Two of them, both dogs, have already been half-claimed, but this little..." he replied to my unspoken question, pulling one of the boxes toward the edge of the van floor; he partially opened it, allowing me to see inside, before continuing: "...this little one, she's a bitch, has no one to look after her. But you may choose any."

I peered inside and saw the small, quivering form of a still very frightened collie-type puppy. My unconscious reaction was one of delight – and shock. She seemed to me to be an agreeably vital little pup, and my heart immediately warmed to her, but the pronounced uniform reddish colour of her coat, strange amber eyes and the sharpness and vigour of her expression, shocked me. On the surface her gaze was innocent, but it held an intelligent hostility, mingled fear with threat, the like of which I had seen in no puppy before. But consciously I saw only that innocence, that purity, which somehow I knew was uncommon, and felt extremely touched, even privileged.

We looked at the other two puppies, which had the same amber eyes and same sort of foxy-coloured coats – but I had already set myself on having the puppy with the darker colouration, and reached down to pick her up.

"Careful..." I could hear James' voice, warning me, but it was as though I was detached, in a void, and absolutely fascinated by its unusual features. Too late! Scarcely had James had said to me, "Which one do you want?", and I had replied, "This one", and picked the cub up, than she sank her teeth into my hand. As the needle-like pain shot through me, I almost dropped her, but, helped by James, I managed not to, and got her back into the box. For the first, and not last, I had been made aware of her considerable potential for hostility.

"You'll have a bit of a problem with this one, 'cos she's a wild little devil!" James chuckled as he examined my hand that, fortunately, was not badly damaged, just pricked – a bit like my ego!

I had to admit I felt I had seen quite enough of the puppy for one encounter, and was glad to see her safely put away. But I felt that here was a really uncommon dog, and I stressed to James that I did want her. She wasn't quite what my parents had in mind for me, and as I pledged to accept her, knew that I was courting trouble, especially with Father. But I was caught by a reckless desire, seemingly beguiled completely by those strange amber eyes, and found it impossible to turn her down.

While we walked back into the surgery to attend to the formalities, James told me the whole story of her origins, the facts of which seemed to fit with the luxuriousness of that lovely fox-red coat and tail I had seen, firsthand – and which had so shocked me. As I listened, I became all the more convinced that here indeed was the dog that I had been waiting for; but the startling turn of events had made me almost mute.

"Oh, well," I said, casually nursing my fingers, after he had finished speaking, "we'll do something with her…somehow!"

I was still somewhat distant, having suffered my first emotional hurt from this dog, yet completely fascinated, when I set out, carrying her box on the long walk back to the farm. I departed, leaving James to tidy up and salvage what sleep he could, sure that I could tame her, whatever the difficulties – and they might be considerable.

When I arrived home with the new puppy the sky was already starting to cloud over again and spots of rain were falling, turning the morning grey and casting the land and buildings back into their usual damp condition – and also dampening my newfound confidence to tame both wild pup – and Father!

* * *

Our smallholding, which was more or less like a small farm, was situated in Tytherington, a small hamlet just on the outskirts north of Macclesfield, about twelve miles away from the little village of Moreton, outside Congleton, where my new 'collie' had been born. In those days, Tytherington did not have a shop or a public house, and was considerably more countrified, still surrounded by fields and woods, and threaded by the River Bollin on its long, looping way across the Cheshire Plain to Liverpool Bay. It had a rather grand old hall, and a few farms, but at the same time was so close to Macclesfield that it might have been an extension of it. The nearby main road continued on north to Adlington, through typical Cheshire towns like Poynton and Hazel Grove.

We were almost self-sufficient, selling salad-greens, vegetables, bedding-plants and dairy produce to towns like Macclesfield, which in the 1950's, was still a 'silk town', a working mill town. In other words, it was known as a woman's town – for the work that went on in the mills was in those days still regarded as being woman's work. The other main industry was farming, and small traders like ourselves, who all earned a living off the beautiful rolling foot-hills of the Pennines that give that corner of Cheshire its special character. This consists of a fertile mix of hill and farmland, rich in wildlife and beautiful water features – brooks, rivers, lakes and meres – with many fine trees, woods, and prosperous looking towns and halls, or 'stately homes'. This attractive countryside inspired wonderful work from one of the finest country and wildlife artists of all time, a local farmer's son, Cheshire born and bred, Charles Tunnicliffe, RA OBE – a man who studied his dogs and farm animals first hand, and even beautifully illustrated the advertising for the animal feeds we used.

My mother, as well as rearing Corgis, which she did mainly for pleasure, was also a hairdresser with her own business in Macclesfield. She was one of five children from a farming family, originally from Newark, Nottingham, but who now owned a large, 100-acre mixed farm called Pool End – The Big Farm, we called it – where I and my mother were born, and which almost bordered our acreage and smallholding, separated only by Tytherington Hall. In those days most farms were rented, and my grandparents must have heard that land further north was going cheap, so up they came and rented it. They arrived at Pool End in March, 1900, as eager newly-weds.

The Big Farm, which I remembered so well, had been taken over by new tenants four years earlier, when I was eleven, and my mind still teemed with the many happy memories of living there. With my mother's time taken up by her business, my early years had been spent in the care of my grandmother. I got on extremely well with both my grandparents, perhaps my grandfather most of all. He was the gentleman type of farmer, a good Christian and well respected by all around. When I knew him best he was in his mid-sixties, although he never seemed old to me. He had tremendous patience with livestock, and over the years I inherited much of my own love and knowledge of animals from him as well as gaining experience from many of his actual animals.

How well I remember being shown the nests of the various birds and being told by him exactly what each one was, of being told the names of the wild flowers – the difference between cowslips and primroses, the names of different violets and the many types of grasses – and where each grew. He inspired in me the courage needed to return to hand-milk a cow that had just badly kicked

me and knocked over its pale of milk. He also showed me how to respect the countryside, and not just country matters, but how to be charitable also. Thoughts of my grandfather were only happy ones. His sudden and unexpected death at the age of sixty-four, when I was six, five years before my grandmother finally sold up, came as a devastating blow.

Grandma was born in 1875, a Victorian in heart and temperament. She was always dressed neatly, and was never caught looking even slightly dowdy. In fact, she was still trussed up in stiff black crinoline and hoops when she first came north in 1898, to a grand ball in Macclesfield – and to meet her prospective in-laws. Her brother was already in the town, running the shop our family would long supply with farm produce, Burdin's, a well frequented, high-class grocer's shop on Mill Street. Her life had always been a hard one, so it was par for the course that she would rear her children, ably look after the big farmhouse, and take-in paying guests – all helped by the fact that she had somehow also fitted in time to be a governess in France! Pool End, about a mile away from us, was so large that Grandma always had someone staying there. And she still found the time to work on the farm, and laboriously turned all the milk produced into butter and cheese in a hand-churn. As a young woman, aged eighteen, she had been sent out to a specialist farm to learn the trade, which had to be paid for by her parents. As farming between the First and Second World Wars was in decline, and food at a premium, Grandma put her knowledge into practice, and turned the farm's entire milk yield into foodstuffs of one sort or another. This production of homegrown, farm food was still essential for the nation after World War Two, as the country tried to pick itself up. When the butter was freshly made, and the cheese mature, they were taken by Grandma in a pony and trap as far away as Manchester, although more often than not into the centre of Macclesfield, five miles away, to be sold at her brother's shop. What aromas the thought of that shop conjures up! Even now, if I close my eyes, I can still smell the freshly ground coffee beans that the shop also sold, amongst other rich smells of good, old-fashioned foods.

One fine spring day, aged five, I accompanied Grandma and her wares on her regular delivery into town. She was dressed, as usual on these outings, in her impeccable best. Today we were not only delivering to Burden's shop in Mill Street, but also visiting Byram's Cakeshop Café in nearby Chestergate, where we stopped first.

Byram's was very well known, and very old fashioned. The cakes and pies displayed on lace doilies in the windows always fascinated me. There were three 'Mrs Byrams', all sisters – Miss Grace, Miss May and Miss Bertie – who were all very proper in their ways. I could not come inside but had to sit quietly in the trap whilst Grandma chatted and had tea with them. Next, we left for Burden's, and after parking outside the shop Grandma dismounted and went inside, where once again I was left sitting on my own. For a while I watched the shop assistants offloading the heavy cheeses and carrying them inside where Grandma was attending to her business. But then, growing bored, I picked up the pony's reigns and foolishly flicked her back. Immediately, Fanny, for that was her name, swung into action, and swiftly drew away from the astonished faces of the assistants.

Fanny was a light-red chestnut trotter, with a mane and flowing tail of the same flame colour. In her younger days she had been raced in the trotter trials at Hazel Grove, won many prizes and held in awe by all who saw her. She was still very fast, although nowadays confined to the light trap, or 'dog cart'. Yet once started, there was no stopping her, and picking her long legs smartly up to her chest, as such ponies do, she headed straight for home! The most I could do was hold tightly onto the reigns, rather frightened as we swept along through the town towards the Town Hall – where the regular traffic policemen at first held up his hand, shouted "Stop!", then nimbly leapt aside! – then thundered on, through the market place, down Jordangate and on in to Beech Lane, where, in front of us, we came up upon a bus travelling down the hill. The omnibus was perceived as a challenge to Fanny, and at once she accelerated, drawing level with it, and finally overtaking it. The driver stared in disbelief at the sight of the racing pony and the small boy at the reigns! At the rate we were going we were were soon in Tytherington, and as we approached Blue Bell Lane, PC Ring, the local policeman, a severe looking man who when off duty was often to be seen standing at his garden gate, rushed out to try to stop the pony, but she was going too fast. Despite his valiant attempt, he was flung aside. She raced on, sparks striking from her pounding hooves, only stopping after we swept into the gates of Pool End Farm, before finally coming to a stop outside the farmhouse door. Fortunately, there was little traffic on the roads in those days and so the ride, though hair-raising, had been relatively safe. About two hours later, however, grandma arrived by bus, looking harassed and dusty and, accepting no excuse whatsoever, bent me down and caned my legs with her walking stick!

Even now, in my mind's eye, I can still see my grandparents leaving for church on a Sunday morning, Grandpa always wearing a dark suit with spats, bow tie, black bowler hat and white gauntlet gloves. The gloves were his trade-mark, and he never went out driving without them. Grandma would also look very elegant, in a full-length black dress and coat, a pearl choker at her throat, and hat trimmed with black ostrich feathers. Their handsome turnout, a Dennet gig – so-called because of the padded semi-circular sides around its seat

– was a plusher version of the trap. It was black and highly polished, with maroon leather upholstery and narrow yellow wheels, its open carriage suspended by leather braces to ensure a comfortable ride. All gleamed in the bright sunlight. Their proud red chestnut mare, her coat brushed until it shone like glass, would toss her head as she waited, impatient to be off – as I had personally discovered! Then, with a cheery wave, they would go, sweeping out of the driveway on their way to Prestbury church, two miles distant.

There was also the American Barouche – a four-wheeled carriage not unlike the horse-drawn landaus one sees on Blackpool promenade. Grandpa's had been bought from Ohio and was dated 1875. The Barouche needed two horses to pull it, and the whole family could fit inside. So Fanny was teamed up with Crystal, an Arabian palomino mare. But as the two did not agree, a long pole divided the horses in harness. The Barouche turnout was the height of Victorian fashion and greatly envied.

After Grandpa's tragic death, Grandma continued, with her usual determination, to run the farm. She had the help of her only son, Uncle Tom, an accountant and keen sportsman who liked cricket and boating, but though he also liked animals, never really took to the farming business. He tried hard to keep it going, but his heart wasn't in it, and sadly the decision was made to sell up. Grandma, deeply upset, knew even she was unable to keep the farm going unaided. Years later, Tom made one more attempt to return to farming, but was still dissatisfied with it, and eventually emigrated to Australia, where he achieved his dream of founding a large boat-building business.

Everything was sold by the auctioneer, except for a few items of furniture and a few animals that were bequeathed to us, including Fanny, who Grandpa had expressly stipulated in his will was to be retained. We also inherited a grand old carthorse, Samson, who came to us mainly to live out his life in tranquil retirement (though not the other grand old carthorse, who had once pulled Grandma's carriage out of a deep snowdrift, after we had slid into a ditch – and she had walked miles to bring back, personally, as I was too young to help in any real way!). Doughty Grandma, still showing that grand Victorian spirit, moved a short distance from the old farmstead into a pleasant cottage with two acres of land, taking the equally sprightly pony with her, and lived on in active retirement for many years, before dying at the age of eighty-one, in 1956.

By contrast, my father's large family (he had seven brothers and one sister) were market and landscape gardeners, and Macclesfield true and proper, local born and bred. Whereas my mother had been brought up a real farmer with a strong love of nature, Father had been in market and landscape gardening all his life. One of his best jobs was landscaping and terracing the sloping garden of the 'Pigeon House', Gawsworth, which featured in Tunnicliffe's popular book about east Cheshire pools and their wildlife, Mereside Chronicle, and where I later worked for a time. Perhaps it was for this reason that Mother had the most sympathy for my love of animals, and that I received from her greater encouragement than I did from Father, who was of a much more commercial and practical mind – and plants usually give far less trouble than animals!

I was an only child, rather withdrawn. I tended to prefer my own company. By a strange twist of fate I was also the only child of all four of my mother's siblings, so had no cousins. My shyness prevented me from making many friends and, unlike most other boys of my age, I had no interest in sport. There was no lack of the latter available, from swimming clubs to football, cricket and tennis, but I would have none of that. I got my exercise 'naturally', in work and the countryside. I liked town life even less. Early school years had been OK, if only because I knew I could escape back to the farm as soon as classes ended, and ride, bareback, my beloved pony, Suki, through the woods and fields, or track animals, and similar pursuits. Later, whilst attending King's School in 'Mac', I would daydream of the smallholding or, my favourite pastime, draw caricatures, despite getting into trouble for 'doing' the staff! Then, in my teens, when I thought about experimenting with a more conventional lifestyle, I briefly attempted to play sophisticated social games, like dancing and dating, but quickly retreated. The possibility of hurt and confusion was just too great! Although these were thrilling times outside the farm, with post-War prosperity seeping in, I just knew I preferred the reliability and peace of animals and the natural world.

I did not know why this should be; nor did I attempt to question how I was. I could not say whether my love of animals was as a result, or a cause, of my being a loner. It was not a simplistic thing; the animals were friends in themselves, not friend substitutes. Unlike many so-called human friendships, theirs were sincere, totally reliable and constant, as any dog owner knows. I genuinely cared for every animal that I took in. With me, they lived their full lifespan, and I never got tired of caring for them as some children will do once they have lost their passing interest.

Thanks to my grandfather, I knew every inch of the countryside around the farm. I almost knew every blade of grass, all the flowers, where different birds were nesting, and their names, and much more. I was aware of the seasonal changes and their effect on the land, and on the lives of the people who worked there, rather than local darts tournaments, or the problems of which car to buy or what type of house to go after. Respect of the countryside is a very strange thing. It is not something that can be taught at school, but some intangible quality that one grows up with, that cannot be shown but only felt. Very fortunately for me, I had been born with it.

Our house, which my father owned, together with twenty-two acres of land, was a nice detached building on a level with the main road, but the main part of the farm – as we grandly called the smallholding – had a rather low-lying aspect at the bottom of a hill, which resulted in its dampness. Its glasshouses, the farmyard and other outhouses, all sloped downward toward the River Bollin. In winter time and in cold weather the air down there was chiller and often damper than at road level, and though sometimes very beautiful on early summer's mornings when the river mist would writhe and coil softly in the air, shot through with pearly sunlight, at most other times it seemed drab and dank. It often seemed to be in a basin of mist or damp all its own, and I never liked this much. By contrast my grandparents' farm, only a short distance away, was much higher, and I enjoyed the early days I spent there far more.

But on the momentous autumn day, in 1953, when I returned with the little 'collie', I was too preoccupied with my own thoughts and excitement to consciously bother much about this gloominess, and immediately rushed into the garden. My haste was partly excitement, but I also wanted to have the chance of acquainting myself more with the puppy, in the hope of calming her down before introducing this strange 'fox-dog' to my parents. I had seen, on my approach, that the large garden surrounding the house was deserted – Father was probably working down near the river, and Mother cooking lunch up in the kitchen. It seemed an ideal opportunity to start our friendship, and so, arriving out-of-breath in the garden I set the box down on the grass. Squatting down beside it, I opened it, and, more warily this time, gathered her up.

I had her trembling, almost prone form in my arms for less than a few seconds before suddenly, once more, she showed her aggression. I was still not fast enough for this frightened little puppy from the wildwood. Before I could get a safe grip on her, she twisted furiously and once more sank her needle-like teeth into my hand, this time with such force that I dropped her instantly, cursing out loud! Darting like an arrow down the garden towards the yard, she quickly took cover beneath our old turkey verandah, causing a few moments of concern within, but the wily old birds soon settled down again.

The verandah was an open-fronted hen shed with wire-netting sides and a wooden, slatted floor. It was freestanding and raised some twelve inches above the ground to keep the turkeys from being harmed by contaminants in the soil, while allowing them to enjoy plenty of fresh air and sunshine. Once the puppy was secure under that narrow space, it was quite impossible to get her out, though I tried for half an hour or more. Fortunately I had no school that day, but that didn't mean I had no work to do. I had my usual farm chores, and so had no choice but to leave her there for the time being. Both irritated and concerned, I went about my jobs, returning to the yard as often as I could in the hope that she had decided to come out. Even the rich, drifting smells of our traditional Sunday lunch failed to tempt her – and even me – out of our respective 'shells'. And she remained in hers all day.

When evening then fell, and the fiery pup had still not emerged, I left a bowl of bread and milk, and went to bed feeling morose. Already, her wild displays were making it difficult, if not impossible, to cover up for her. I had to tell my parents of the new dog, of course, and they merely commented negatively on her strange behaviour, deflating me further. My mother, always the more sympathetic, had at least noticed my anxiety, and had helped me try to coax her out; but Father simply told me to "stop messing about", and get her out, one way or another. He did not want any disturbances during the night.

I was still lying awake, tossing to and fro, long after I should have been asleep. I thought only of the strange little fox-coloured dog. In my thoughts I pictured her lying there alone in the dark, rolled into a shivering ball, when only a few short hours before she had been wrenched away from the only warmth and security she had ever known, with her strange family in a fox earth. The early winter was uncommonly cold, and though the last few days had been more kind, the temperature might still drop and become far too cold for the thin fur and small bones of a very young puppy. I wondered too whether she would be able to defend herself adequately from the fierce Brown Rats, which nested in abundance in our grounds. The older dogs and the cats spent most of their spare time hunting them down, which possibly explained our rats' greater aggressiveness.

Most of all, I wondered whether I would still find her at all when I awoke, alive or dead – whether, in her desperation, she might already have made the fatal mistake of creeping from the security of the verandah, and running away into the unknown countryside. More than once I ran through the events of the night before as the concerned vet had described them, trying in my imagination to reconstruct her life in the wild. I saw the dark trees in the wood swaying and heaving with the rain and wind, the damp night fields and the desperate mother searching for food, and then pictured the peace and quiet of the warm earth where the puppies waited, sleeping and playing, sometimes on their own, and sometimes with the wily dog-fox – the wild creature that had chosen to be, or had somehow become, their father.

Thus my thoughts turned constantly, turbulently, and several times I was reduced to wondering whether the experienced vet had been right, after all. He had warned me that I might be taking on more than I could cope with, and in my determination to bring her into the domestic atmosphere of the farm, perhaps I already had.

Still I did not sleep and, thinking that I would never see the puppy again, at 5 o'clock, in pitch darkness, I hurriedly dressed and went straight out to the verandah to see if she was still there. To see to the back of the recess I had to lie on my stomach on the concrete surface of the yard. In the cold of the morning, I peered into the blackness, sweeping my torch across the back wall for any sign of her. For a long moment I could see nothing. Then, my heart jumped. The torchlight struck the motionless form of the little dog, her head raised from her crouched position, pale yellow eyes flashing wildly. I was beside myself with joy. She was still where I had left her, and in a mixture of relief and sadness at what we humans had inflicted upon her, I imagined the poor pup had not slept either, but had lain awake keeping a dreadful vigil, too frightened to move yet too frightened to stay.

To my further joy, I noticed that the bowl I had left her had been licked clean – a very good sign. She had at least moved enough to do that.

To me this was a most heartening sign of encouragement, for it meant that I had established some rapport with her – and an animal that does not eat is usually a very bad sign. I immediately renewed my efforts of the day before, to woo the little red puppy out. As I lay there, feeling the dampness creep through my clothes, I called softly to her.

"C'mon, Lassie," – for that was the name I had decided to call her, – "C'mon, girl. C'mon, I won't hurt you."

I clicked my tongue to reassure her. I have the not uncommon countryman's habit of clicking my tongue to call any animal, whether dogs, cats or poultry, and so tried this with her. But after half an hour or more, I realised my efforts were meeting with the same resistance as they had the day before.

Patiently, I tried another tactic. The morning was again breaking quite mistily, and by the half-light I went in search of some long poles to try gently to push her out. My father was up by the time I returned, and still concerned about the predicament this new puppy had put us in. He decided to help me try to dislodge her. Together we tried to encourage Lassie to leave her hiding place. Part of my mind was still on the task, and part now on what Father was making of it all. But we were unable to reach deep enough inside, for she had hidden as far away as possible, out of range; behaviour that, I would come to know, was typical of her.

I did not want to frighten her too much, and so we abandoned the poles, and I reverted to coaxing her out with speech and gestures, more as a display to my father than a realistic expectation of getting her out. Father eventually left with an emphatic, "Humph!, followed by, "Well, I've told you lad, just get 'er out, one way or t'other!" I remained, coaxing her on and off until it was time for breakfast, and school. I prepared another bowl of bread and milk, pushed it underneath, and resignedly left her to it.

At school I was very tired, and felt almost as uncomfortable as I had during the long, long night. I felt very low indeed at having to leave so small a dog to the unpredictable happenings on the farm. But my mood was tempered with a slight sense of triumph, however small....

Chapter Two

A WHOLE two weeks went by, during which Lassie remained beneath the turkey verandah, even with all the gobbling and kerfuffle above. During school time I was unable to give her the attention I wanted to, further frustrated by the evenings drawing in. At the weekends I still had the farm chores to do, but at least had more time to spend with her. Whenever I could I kept her company, talking to her, trying to coax her out and learn to trust me. Progress seemed interminably slow, but I was determined to win her heart. Each day I pushed more food under the slats.

One evening, when she thought she was unobserved, I caught her emerging from her retreat. One of my jobs was to clean the eggs that I had collected on my rounds. At the end of the day I would stand washing them in the kitchen sink, from where I had a clear view of the verandah. I was, as usual, automatically dividing my attention between the eggs and the turkey house, when I was surprised and delighted to see the small form of Lassie creeping out from under it. The verandah stood between the house garden and the farmyard, and she slunk out cautiously, carefully looking this way and that. Noticing that the yard was empty and quite silent, except for the occasional splashing of running water coming from a natural spring, she crossed the cobbles and took a drink. After she had finished, she looked about uneasily before returning to the verandah.

After this she got into the habit of venturing forth at dusk, but never during the day, and she was ever ready to dash back under the safety of the verandah at the slightest noise. Naturally I was overjoyed, but even basic progress was taking far longer than I had imagined. My busy father had by now begun to feel tricked, and was, as I feared, becoming increasingly hostile to her. He did not like the idea of having to care for a wild puppy, especially as we already had the three other domestic dogs to contend with. He was convinced, like I, that Lassie was of 'fox blood', as he called it, and thought she would prove to be a worthless killer if kept. Her prolonged reticence only served to bolster his feelings. I already knew he wanted her gone. He even as much told me so: "Look, lad, I know how you feel about your animals, but this one, well, she's just not worth it – why don't ye just cut your losses, an' give her back to James, or... oh, I don't know", and went off shaking his head at my stubborn look. It was, I realised much later, a tacit admission of my important role at the farm and his grudging acknowledgement that my many animals were usually helpful – he was giving me more time, if unwillingly, to prove him wrong about Lassie.

During those early weeks I felt bitterly alone, and fought all suggestions to have done with her. Even my mother, who was normally very easy going about my wishes, increasingly wondered whether I would be able to make Lassie into the dog of my imagining – the dog I so desperately wanted her to be, and was still convinced she was, beneath all those insecurities. Nevertheless, Mother was still the sole light in my dilemma, and between the two of us we usually managed to talk Father into allowing the puppy a further provisional stay. I wished, more than ever, to prove my father wrong, and I hoped this latest small reprieve would allow me the time to gain Lassie's confidence.

Some moral support also came from James Cook. Never one to forget an animal once his official responsibility for it had ended, he paid a visit shortly after Lassie's arrival to see how boy and dog were faring. James arrived in his old RSPCA van, and wearing, as usual, his formal uniform – a long, dark blue raincoat and flat police-type cap. Being a friend of the family, he was invited into the house for a chat and a cup of tea, even though his real concern was to see how I was faring with the little wild dog.

When I told him about Lassie's antics he was amused, and told me she would learn to trust me – providing I continued to be patient. But he also brought sad news. Lassie's brothers – the two other survivors from the original litter – had died within a few days of one another. They had been unable to bear their captivity, it seemed. Though I was saddened, strangely enough I was not at all surprised by this news, and I felt a certain pride in my decision to leave Lassie be. I felt, as well, a huge sense of relief that she had been delivered into my care, and not into the hands of others. The owners of the other two puppies had tried to teach them the rules of domestic dogs too soon, probably too harshly. The poor little things must have died of fear. So I felt justified in my instinct to allow Lassie to express her wild nature, despite the ongoing heartache her untouchability gave me. She too might have gone the same way as they, had she not escaped beneath the verandah – or had I listened to my father, and taken the stricter measures he had demanded to extricate her and keep her under control. Of course, I think that her survival might not have depended on my devotion, but simply on the fact that she was still essentially free. But whatever had kept her alive, she was now, apart from her roaming fox father, the sole surviving member of that fateful fox earth.

I think I was able to relate to Lassie – and know what was best for her – because of my love of the wild and my own loner status. Domestic animals are easy companions, but I have a greater awe for the wild ones who have to pit their wits against all dangers – food shortages, weather extremes and danger from man – and have no loving, all-providing hand to fall back on. I did not realise just how special Lassie was; I simply knew she was very much more interesting than other dogs. I wanted her, wished her, willed her, to survive. Ultimately, that would mean training her, I knew, but I was determined not, as I saw it, to let her down, and wanted to prove wrong those people who seemed to wish to dash my hopes.

After that first sleepless night, and the knowledge that she had eaten the food I had left her, my initial confidence started to return. Despite the sad news about the other pups, it never occurred to me that if I tried to tame Lassie she would ultimately pine away for her wildwood, and die. The special relationship I thought might develop between us reinforced a secret feeling

I had that she would be the one to survive. It might be said – and my father had intimated this to me with characteristic bluntness – that, out of respect for her wild ways, the kindest thing would have been to put her to sleep. But, apart from a natural reluctance to kill any animal unnecessarily, I felt that it was right to make the attempt to train her – she had no say in her unusual genesis, after all. Anyway, she was rather beautiful, and who could resist any puppy?

And I, rarely interested in the doings of the human world outside our gates, had endless time and patience, and spent many hours each evening, coaxing and talking to Lassie, where she still huddled under her retreat. As usual, I lay flat on my stomach whilst she, crouched at the far end of the verandah, watched my every movement with those glittering yellow eyes, seemingly listening intently to each word. I placed food in her bowl twice each day, and though she always ate it, she would still not touch it while I was near, or visibly watching her. Although by this time winter had set in, in earnest, the cold did not seem to worry her, and so this rough living beneath the cramped conditions of the old turkey verandah went on for almost three months.

Strangely enough, the resident turkeys continued not to appear bothered by her presence, probably because they were well used to dogs about the place and she didn't have that strong foxy smell. That was the sort of information I was constantly gathering about Lassie, especially concerning the pros and cons of her strange heritage.

During this time, Lassie only ventured forth to explore the farmyard at dusk. She would dart back beneath the verandah if surprised by anyone close at hand, but if the intruder was further off, she would simply run away into the darkness, out of sight, and disappear.

My visits to the verandah with her food soon became a ritual, and I was wondering how this relative calm was going to break when, one fine morning, I found I had my answer. Until Lassie's arrival, my first job of the day, at 7 o'clock, just after rising, was to milk our dairy cows. These were short-horn crosses, of several colours. But my first job now was taking Lassie her bowl. Arriving at the verandah, as usual I called her name, but this time there was no response. With mounting dismay, I called her name several more times. I rose to get a torch, and soon returned, shining it into the darkness at the back of the verandah. But the recess was empty. I wondered whether, running off into the darkness of the previous night, she had decided to stay out, and was late returning. The thought almost encouraged me, for she might have decided at last to come out of herself. The only obvious alternative, that she had actually returned to the wild to stay, was too bleak to contemplate...

I placed the food in its usual place, and promptly started a search of the farm. A feverish quarter of an hour or so was spent looking in all the sheds and under the cotes, but when I still could not find her I began to grow disconsolate. The nagging fear that she had run away, steadily grew inside me. I looked frantically for her, endlessly calling her name, and extending my search to the fields. The growing hopelessness of ever more fields to search, extending outwards in virtually every direction, beyond river, road and railway embankments, drove me back to scour the farm buildings again. I was on the point of resigning myself to the fact she had gone – when a slight movement from the top of our old Dutch barn caught my eye. The barn was a favourite retreat for the animals, but I had not looked there, thinking that it was too high for a puppy to climb. At first I thought that one of the cats was lying up there, but some instinct made me look more closely.

Lassie!

My heart jumped for joy.

"Lassie!" I could not help shouting out, "Lassie, girl! You're up there!"

She did not move when I called, but simply continued to survey me, as though coolly bemused by all the fuss. She had seen me searching frantically for her, yet remained aloof and distant the whole time – although, of course, it soon occurred to me that it was only I who had thought her lost! The pioneering pup had merely found a new home.

The barn was probably about fifty yards downhill from the house, at the far side of the yard among the outbuildings. It was a very tall structure, standing on its own. Half of it was hay bay, consisting of four wooden pillars roofed over with corrugated metal sheeting, with the hay bales piled between the pillars. The other half was a barn as such, with walls of wood and metal, which we used as a store. The hay bales were stacked nearly twenty feet above the ground inside the structure. From this lofty vantage point, on top of the hay, Lassie had a panoramic view of the whole farm without being too visible herself. It was the reason she had chosen it, of course.

I knew better than to rush up to her, and so, containing my excitement, climbed cautiously up to her. As I neared the top I extended my hand toward where she stood, all the time talking softly. But as before, my attempts to get close to her failed. As soon as I came too near she backed away to a safe distance. It wasn't her way to put her hackles up. Instead, she backed off, arched her back and looked rather hunched – not in a menacing way, for she was more frightened than angered, but in a way that made it clear that she would run off if I approached further. I decided to stay my ground. Her pale, lemon-coloured eyes flashed at me, something she especially did, I came to realise, when she was nervous. Those magnetic orbs seemed to vary between pale lemon to deeper amber, depending on mood or light, whilst the dark iris often looked – or was it just my imagination? – smaller and more vertically flattened than a normal dog's (like a fox's!). But I continued to talk to her, consolingly, and was eventually rewarded. Her expression altered, visibly relaxed, and for the first time she began to look attentively at me. I thought perhaps that she understand some of my words. At the very least, was she beginning to see that I posed no threat to her? I did not push my luck but jubilantly climbed down, and left her, and ran off to do the milking, now terribly late and hoping my absence would not be noticed.

From then on she made the hay bales her home, apparently deciding that this was a safer place for her to be. It was certainly more congenial. Growing quickly, she would jump from one bale to another to get right up to the top. As well as the farm, from her new position she could see a little of the main road that ran by the side of the house, and with only a small movement of her head, watch the trains coming and going on the embankment along the south-eastern edge of the farm, opposite; or by looking more or less straight ahead, down to the river at the north end of the farm. She could not see much further than her own land, though. Because of the farm's situation in its long, almost rectangular hollow, with a tall bank behind us on the Macclesfield side too, the wildwoods and the farmlands beyond remained hidden from view – and perhaps that was another advantage to her survival, confining and circumscribing her new home to a natural, if domesticated, 'basin'? Perhaps having both wild and domesticated worlds so serendipitously combined, and with clear boundaries – at least initially – was a big plus in her development? I cannot really say, only that I was very, very pleased with her 'settled' choice of home, even if she was still largely unapproachable.

Many has been the time I have been asked the question why I called her Lassie, and I honestly do not know. I had decided to name her during that long first night when I had lain awake in my room, concerned for her safety. I had seen the film *Lassie Come Home*, of course (I did not completely shun 'civilisation'!), which was then all the rage, but I cannot say whether it had any influence on me. The hero of the film was a pedigree Scots Rough Collie, tall and elegant, with a long muzzle and flowing reddish coat, not the working type of Border Collie, which are usually smaller, and black and white. Also, generally speaking, I was not that influenced by popular sentiment. I was not usually fond of films, preferring, when I had the time, to read books

– but for some reason I never got to read Eric Knight's book, on which the picture was based. I chose the name partly because of a policy my family had of never using a name more than once. The name Lassie was, of course, common enough for a dog, both before and after the film made the name a household word. Perhaps I picked it for no other reason than one would have named a dog Blackie, or Shep (another name 'high-jacked', this time by a popular song) – and, unconsciously, because the famous Lassie was also reddish…? Whatever the reason, I felt that 'Lassie' was just right for her, and would not have had another name.

I continued talking to her in the mornings, and each evening when the day's work was done I climbed up into the hayshed with her supper. I was able, eventually, to get within twelve feet or so without her moving away, but if I tried to move closer she instantly jumped up and widened the gulf between us again. On the surface, I never tired of this courting, for what I was trying to do could not really be calculated in time, or in weariness. I enjoyed what I was doing, and did not try to force the pace, though a deeper part of me remained disappointed at the lack of progress. She was still too nervous to trust me fully, although cautiously beginning to investigate more of the farm, and then only after dark and quickly retreating to her domain when discovered. Her reticence continued to hurt me, but I took heart from another small gain: when I talked, she would seem to regard me ever more intently, with those bright eyes and raised ears. But never once did she show the slightest trace of pleasure, or any other strong emotion, except fear. Never once did she wag her tail. And that finally made me succumb to the rising despair I felt inside. Because, as the months went by, and there was still no acknowledgement of my efforts, I succumbed to feelings of negativity once again, and contemplated the awful thought that those negative voices were right; inherently, she was no good, and I could do no good for her.

Chapter Three

NOT LONG after Lassie came to live with us, the newspapers got hold of her story, and she was featured in the local and national press. Through this media attention came the first of many animal experts interested in the controversy surrounding her birth. Had I allowed this sudden public attention its fill, Lassie's instinct to shun humanity would have turned out to be well founded! I too, for the most part, was 'against' this world of humans, at least as it existed outside the farm, and so viewed the first interest shown in Lassie from that quarter with indifferent suspicion. I believe zoologists and naturalists have an important part to play – I am as much interested in their work as any animal lover would be – but was worried about the affect their examinations might have on Lassie. From the beginning, I saw my role as minimising the publicity, and keeping the curious at arm's length.

The first reporter who came to see me was from the Macclesfield Express. He had been sent by the paper's editor, Clifford Rathbone, himself very well known locally as a writer of country articles, who in later years signed himself, 'The Stroller'. At the time of the mother collie's death near Congleton, and then again after Christmas and the January sales, there were few good news stories about. Checking with the RSPCA to see whether the centre had anything of interest to act as a gap filler, Clifford had been told the story of the collie and her puppies. He ran the story in his paper, and was now, in the New Year, keen to follow it up. Making a fresh enquiry at the RSPCA, he was told that one of the puppies had been given into my care, and sent a reporter round to see me. I showed the reporter a fleeting glimpse of Lassie, and told the man what I knew about her history, and so the pup's story, together with a photograph of myself, appeared that week. From there, her tale found its way into the Manchester Evening News, and then into the News of the World. Each reporter told the full story (although often, annoyingly, with variations and the inevitable errors), and it was not long before I began to receive enquiries from the animal experts.

Among the many people who first came to see the 'fox-dog', as Lassie was now popularly labeled, were two well-known zoologists who wanted to examine her and carry out a blood and a chromosome count. The main difference between a dog and a fox lies in the number of chromosomes, the 'strings' that carry all the DNA, dogs, wolves, jackals, coyotes having almost twice as many as Red Foxes, which is thought to be why they can all interbreed – except with Red Foxes. It has to be said, that several other kinds of fox do have almost as many chromosomes as dogs, so the whole question is far from conclusive. However, the 'count' was the only evidence that science was prepared to accept that Lassie was a hybrid. The very idea of these requests quite horrified me. The experience of being caught and handled by strangers – when she would not even allow herself to be handled by me – might terrify Lassie and send her the same way as her two luckless brothers, and I flatly refused to have her examined.

Most of the experts declared the idea of a fox-dog hybrid to be impossible. Of the two zoologists who came to see her, one – Gerald Iles, the then curator of Belle Vue Zoo – thought that the hybrid theory was, on the face of it, improbable but not impossible, and the other – Brian Vesey Fitzgerald, well known internationally and in Britain popular for a television series about dogs and how they should be trained – slammed the whole idea. But they, and others, including the farm's two (large animal) veterinary surgeons, Drs Wright and Monroe, readily agreed they had never come across such an unusual case. Since then, I have actually heard of several such cases – but, although also attested to by experienced country folk, they too have never been scientifically investigated. Any such evidences are derogatively labeled 'anecdotal'.

I tended to believe what I could see and know of Lassie, and was content to rely on the visual evidence. I believed emphatically that she was of fox origin, and though I put this visible evidence to the experts – the strong fox characteristics that Lassie bore – they remained aloof. They were unable to tell me why this dog came to be so unique, insisting only on seeing clinical proof.

I did, of course, take a good deal of consolation from this fame of Lassie's. The attention served to increase my pride in her. Most satisfyingly of all, it seemed to impress my father slightly. After the appearance of Clifford Rathbone's newspaper article, Mother and Father had been pleased for me, but had soon forgotten about it. When the article developed into a controversy, they were genuinely surprised. My mother was openly approving. Father, as usual, kept his feelings close to his chest, but I knew he was the more surprised of the two. He had been consistent in his opinion that I would never do anything with Lassie, and was perhaps afraid of losing face – especially should I now manage to tame a famous, wild 'fox-dog'! As he was a man who could never be seen to be wrong, I had to accept that he could not be more forthcoming than he was. And, of course, he was also concerned for my feelings, should Lassie prove untamable or go wild – or even meet the same fate as her unfortunate mother.

Lassie's first spring was, for her, fraught with dangers. For the rest of us, it was our usual hectic time to prepare for the main selling season in the autumn, when most of the farm's revenue came in, so were very busy with all the details of breeding, propagating and planting. It was a hard, if sometimes beautiful time of the year. The swallows returned to nest in the farm buildings, particularly the barn, their favourite nesting site, which they had vacated at the end of the previous summer. Amazing to think they had flown all the way to Africa and back! After the drabness of the winter months, their return was a great tonic, and we were also greeted by a welcome blaze of colour from the great number of trees about the farm, especially the early spring-flowering types like almond and cherry, which grew there in abundance.

In 1954 bad weather extended well into the New Year, making our work extra difficult. After a long spell of cold dry-ish weather at the end of the winter, the year had turned unpleasant, wet and chilly. We were repeatedly flooded by the river, which was in spate for most this period. Between the floods and the rain, the farm was turned into a quagmire. In these sorry conditions that year, many flowers, vegetables and other crops eventually rotted or failed on us.

Our trade was mainly in eggs, poultry, potatoes and salad crops, but also flowers, potted plants, vegetables and other crops grown for sale on the busy market stalls, which needed supplying three days each week. We also grew various fruits, but these were never commercially viable, so kept for ourselves. We were not quite self-sufficient, and had to buy-in some of our produce, such as butter and cheese.

The fields, which had been ploughed in the autumn, had to be ploughed again at the beginning of April, then tilled, and finally sown. Work in the greenhouses had been ongoing since Christmas, and many of the seedlings now had to be transplanted outside. To add to an already large compliment of laying hens, there was an influx of new chickens to look after. These were brought in batches of five hundred when they were a day-old, and then reared in brooders, which in those days were still heated by paraffin, entailing even more work and attention, and smelly at that! The little goslings and ducklings from our farm stock were also hatching, soon to be incubated with the brood hens. It always amused and pleased me to see how many different creatures would bring up other's young, even if they looked quite different, a natural tendency that certainly helped our sort of business.

Then we had the turkeys and guinea fowl. These were also brought up in the 'normal' way, hatched by free-range hens, but the turkeys, being prone to illness, were very difficult birds to raise. We had none of the modern day antibiotics and preventatives, therefore the baby turkeys had to be looked after extremely well, and constantly watched for signs of the dreaded disease known as 'blackhead'. They must, as Grandma had told us, on no account be left out in the rain to get wet, so at the slightest sign of a shower everyone dived-in to put the turkeys under cover.

The turkeys had to be segregated from the other fowl on account of their susceptibility, and could not be allowed to roam about quite as freely as the other young birds. Catering for their diet was equally time consuming. I well remember the seemingly endless chore of chopping up dandelion and dock leaves that they needed as food supplements. To raise turkeys was quite an art. Today, the Pure Whites have replaced the original Bronze breed, and are intensively reared in vast numbers in scientifically controlled conditions. Nevertheless, it did occur to me how well they survived out in the wild just fine....

The pigs, too, needed a great deal of attention. By now they were having litters and needed help to give birth, which meant all-night vigils with paraffin lamps. Although there was electricity in the main buildings, the wiring did not extend everywhere, and we used those pressurised Aladdin lamps. It was my job during the short, dark days from November to April, to prepare the lamps each evening, a task I hated doing because it was so fiddly and unrewarding. We had six lamps in total, and each one had to be filled with paraffin, have its mantle checked, and be primed and pumped-up, ready for use. I used two of the lamps to give the poultry their late feed, and the others to light the pig cotes. After birth, the young piglets had to be watched to make sure they were not crushed by their mother's weights – again, how on earth did they manage so well in the wild! I was always concerned about the health and happiness of our assorted livestock, so this sort of occurrence gave me food for thought on how we could improve things, or try to work out what we breeders might be doing wrong.

During all this activity there was hardly a moment that one could properly call one's own. This was both a blessing and a curse. It was productive, but it meant that I did not have the time to give serious life matters their proper attention. And this was a very important year for me. I had reached school-leaving age, and needed to think of my long-term future, but I failed to do this adequately. I reasoned that the farm would provide me with a steady, life-long career, and made the ill-advised decision to allow work to take precedence over my O-Level exams. I could be with Lassie more, I told myself, even though the extra work prevented me from spending all the time with her I would have liked. Perhaps this was a good thing with Lassie, being the way she was; my feelings for her were forced to take second place to the relentless schedule imposed by the farm. This amazing dog clearly needed very careful handling, and it might well be that I had accidentally stumbled on the right approach, precisely because I had only limited time for her. Too much fuss and rush, and Lassie might not have survived. Whatever, I could not spend as many hours as I would normally otherwise have spent in frustrated brooding and wondering – and just threw myself wholeheartedly into full-time employment. I never took the O-Levels.

All the while the work steadily increased until June, the peak of our labours, and the busiest time of the year. Throughout, whenever I had a spare moment I continued to woo Lassie over to my 'side'. Unlike us, she was impervious to the weather. She had a warm, dry place to sleep, up on the hay bales, and continued to lead a serene existence, seemingly detached from the hard realities of life. Her wild origins, somewhat aloof nature, youthful energy and sharp, acquisitive intelligence allowed her to live her own dreams, 'naturally', a princess among dogs.

I often wondered at her 'self-education', and just what she made of all the animal activity spread out below her throne. It must have been very intriguing to her. Thankfully, she still showed no 'foxy' inclinations to slaughter it all!

She was now seven months old. She was still gangly, and about eighteen inches tall, her coat still very straight, flat, and chestnut red, but was growing fast, her face becoming more elongated and pointed and losing its puppyish looks. She still seemed to treat me as a cypher, a part of her strange new environment that she regarded, possibly, as harmful, and I was still not permitted to get closer to her than a few yards. She had enjoyed no puppyhood, as such, and never played or romped (apart from briefly back in the fox earth), or barked, as normal puppies would do, and received practically no affection other than my talking to her in the evenings. Dogs crave affection from their masters, but Lassie was different.

Every ounce of her energy was taken up by watchfulness and self-defence.

She did, however, have two rather special friends – Beauty, a snow-white but deaf female kitten, and her little sister, Sandra. The two kittens had sadly been abandoned at only three weeks old, when their mother, Jane, acquired by my father with the smallholding, suddenly vanished, never to return. Somehow, this unlikely threesome became firm friends. They had a definite code of communication between them, as all animals who get on as friends seem to do. Lassie would allow the kittens to visit her lofty lair amongst the hay bales, in return for which they showed her great affection, something she obviously needed, if not from me, but from other creatures. As she lay down, both kittens would snuggle up alongside her, purring loudly, and gently kneading her flank with retracted claws. I was quite surprised to see that they had no fear of her. She never became aggressive with them, and even allowed them to share her food, although she would turn away the older cats that made an appearance in the hayshed. She showed no jealousy when I handled the kittens, in fact no outward response at all. The kittens were the only animals able to get close to her, and she otherwise remained wild and mistrustful.

Apart from the kittens, there were other daily visitors who were more or less accepted – if not welcomed – to the hayshed. I kept, probably, a couple of hundred poultry of my own, which ran freely about the farm, and among these were a number of Old English Game bantams. Each morning, resplendent in black-and-white polka dot plumage, several of them would fly up to establish nests amongst the hay. A proud little game-cock always accompanied them, and would crow loudly whilst they laid their eggs. There was also an old black-and-white Muscovy Duck, Jemima, who had for years made her nest, each springtime, at the highest point of the barn. She lined her nest with white down, before laying up to sixteen large, creamy eggs, which she would incubate for almost five weeks. The duck had been brought in by my father, and proved herself to be such a good mother that she was allowed to make her nest wherever she chose. Another compelling reason why she was given such independence was her temperament – like many Muscovys, this large and dominant dock was a real bruiser! And along with her strong personality, she could fly. Unlike other domestic types of duck she could move anywhere about the farm, and would not be deterred in her aims. We usually let her be!

This year the old duck made her nest in the hay-shed as usual, even though this was only a few yards from where Lassie slept. To get to her favourite position, the growing 'fox-dog' had to pass her frequently, and as she did so the duck chided her and ruffled her feathers angrily, as she would with any other creature. Though Lassie did not like this, there was nothing she could do. She seemed to know that it would be useless to attempt to oust Jemima, and decided to ignore her. This went on until the brood was hatched.

Because the baby ducklings were hatched far above ground, I often wondered how they could possibly get down without injury, as they obviously had been doing for several years, although we had never discovered how. One morning, as I was tending to Lassie, I learned the answer. First the mother flew down to the ground, then, with an encouraging 'purring' sound, which only a Muscovy can make, summoned the baby ducklings to follow suit. At this signal, one after another, the little ducks fearlessly launched themselves into the air and plummeted down onto the ground! I watched, puzzled, until I realised that because the ducklings were practically weightless, the impact on the hay after their long fall did them no harm whatsoever, even though some landed upside down or actually bounced. I should not have been surprised, though, for the young of many wildfowl could do this, from tree-nesting mallards to Arctic Geese – which regularly jumped hundreds of feet without harm! I had learnt wonderful facts like this whilst working on the breeding of the rare Hawaiian Goose, during a brief stint at Sir Peter Scott's Wildfowl & Wetland Trust, at Slimbridge, just before Lassie came on the scene. Incidentally, I had also been chided for not bowing to the Queen, when Peter Scott was showing her the rare geese!

My father was still largely negative toward Lassie, and warned me that she would eat the eggs, or even the baby ducklings, when they hatched, but happily was proved wrong one morning when the old duck appeared on the farmyard with her new brood of fourteen strong ducklings. Lassie had touched none of them.

During the daytime, she remained high above all on the hayshed, but each evening, as dusk approached, she would come down, first making sure that she was well out of range of any humans. So far, my parents had not seen much of Lassie, for she ran away whenever either of them came toward her. My father, to give him his due, would call Lassie, wanting to stroke her, or get her involved, but she continued to ignore him. One day she did eat some eggs – but ones he had freshly collected and put in a dish on the ground, and he became annoyed. Such behaviour only served to confirm his prejudices! I did try and excuse her by pointing out that Lassie associated dishes with food, but it was a black mark against the mysterious 'fox-dog' as far as Father was concerned. Again and again, he told me that she was too wild to be of use. But she never harmed anything – chickens or even smaller animals – so he could not justify her expulsion from the farm.

Eventually, I began to see that he would grudgingly tolerate Lassie, providing she didn't go too far, and my anxiety began to recede. But I was too young to understand his wish that all animals should pull their weight. When he lectured me about this, his words washed over me like water off a duck's back. We continued to have arguments over Lassie's 'usefulness', as well as over other things, and though I listened to his reasoning about productivity, I never let him win. As well as continuing to love and believe in Lassie, I had, after all, abandoned any academic dreams, for what they were worth, and thrown in my lot with him and the business, and was a hard and irreplaceable worker. In a way, I was doing Lassie's share! Nevertheless, his remarks were a great source of irritation. I knew that I had to continue to work hard, both on the farm, and to win Lassie's affection, before an incident arose that antagonised Father so much he would insist that she leave.

Meanwhile, a kind of status quo was achieved, whilst we got on with the hard, everyday work on the farm. The situation remained like this throughout the long summer months, until, one October evening, I had another major breakthrough with Lassie. She came down from the hayshed rather earlier than usual, and for some unknown reason entered the Boiler House where I cooked the daily potatoes for the pigs. Such dirty, labouring jobs were usually mine, and this one, tending to the needs of the pigs, was no exception. Once a day I would put the potatoes into wire mesh buckets, immerse and shake them in a trough of running water to take off most of the soil, and then throw them into the boiler. Noticing where Lassie had gone, I stopped what I was doing, got down on my hands and knees and crept quietly up to the doorway.

"Hello, Lassie," I said softly, warily – for I did not know what I would face, whether she would bite me, jump at me, try to rush past me or launch herself over my head as I made my approach.

Instantly she swung round, agitated and annoyed with herself for not having heard my approach, desperately looking for an escape route. This time there was none. I had moved completely into the doorway, barring her only way out, so she froze, as though turned to stone, standing motionless, ears flattened, whilst her breathing grew sharp and her startling eyes flicked too and fro, instantly alert to my every action.

"Come on, girl," I said, "I won't hurt you – let's be friends."

Inching forward, still on hands and knees, I slowly stretched out my hand and gently caressed her forehead. I felt her trembling beneath my touch. Her fur felt unbelievably soft, possessing a vitality that sent shivers of delight through my body. But I was so surprised that she had stayed there that I did not have any further thoughts, as my mind, like my breathing, stilled, and was entirely in the moment. Her pale, amber eyes flashed strangely, and she could at any time have snapped at my hand. We stayed together like that for several very long seconds – she motionless, and I fondling and stroking her coat – before the spell was suddenly broken. As though unable to bear my caress any longer, she made one terrific leap over my head, and raced out through the open doorway.

Once outside the building, at what she felt was a safe distance, as I called out to her, she stopped running, and turned round. It was a blustery autumn day, with leaves and straw blowing about the yard. A few poultry were scratching about, unconcerned about the drama going on. She stood quite still, a gust ruffling her rufous coat, calmly watching me with those large, bright eyes. She would allow no further approach. Each time I came closer to her, she quickly stepped away, increasing her distance with each attempt I made. Finally, she turned, ran to the barn and with three graceful leaps, reached the top of the hayshed, vanishing from sight.

I went to bed that night feeling elated. At long last, this was the breakthrough with my precious wildling dog I had waited and hoped for! I had touched her, and she had not attempted to bite me in return. I was now sixteen, and bursting with the mixed feelings and thoughts of that important milestone, made all the more significant for me by Lassie and the prospect of leaving school. It had taken almost ten months out of that emotionally exhausting year, talking and coaxing her, to reach this stage. Exhausted from all this excitement, and my full day's work on the farm, I slept soundly.

Chapter Four

THE WINTER of 1954 was another unrelentingly cold one, and was followed by one of the wettest summers that I can remember. Day after day, week after week, the months rolled by, bringing with them endless, heavy, grey skies and relentless rain, making life and work on the low-lying farm difficult and unpleasant. Often, only the thought of that special 'fox-dog', calmly observing all our waterlogged efforts from her 'throne' at the top of the barn, kept me going.

It amused me to think of her watching us in the hollow in which we were 'marooned'. That's how I often thought of it, with three ascending boundaries completely hemming-in the little farm, and the wide, fast-flowing River Bollin, which then went eastwards under the bridge on Beech Lane, describing its northern limits, although the rest of Father's acres were on the far side of the river. Because the only access to the smallholding was down the narrow, bumpy track that ran along the side of the house and off Beech Lane, we frequently became our very own Noah's Ark, quite isolated in a quagmire of mud and water.

Undeterred by the weather as she always was, Lassie, growing ever more adventurous in exploring further and further away from the farm buildings went off on increasingly longer roams as often as she could. This was quite a shock when I first discovered it, but there was little I could do, apart from somehow locking her up, but that would have its own problems. I just had to accept it for now. She had one set route for leaving the farm, climbing the railway embankment and crossing the track, north-eastwards, to the fields beyond. Usually, she did this particular route each evening. I discovered her exit route one day just before dusk, after I had finished closing the poultry houses, and noticed Lassie walking along our boundary fence. She was uneasy, and clearly did not wish to be seen leaving, so I feigned indifference, fiddling around with several unnecessary tasks and trying to watch her from the corner of my eye, until, eventually, she left the farm by way of the embankment. Using my best tracking skills, gleaned from years of careful nature watching (and several classic adventure stories!), I managed to follow close enough behind to see her cross the railway, and run down into the fields.

Even in the semi-darkness I could see that Lassie looked and acted very like a fox. Her cautious movement, the way she paused and scented the air at regular intervals, and the litheness of her form, reminded me of a creature from the wild. I set out down the slope after her, but quickly lost her as she gathered speed, easily outwitting me in the undergrowth and hedgerows. It was a bit upsetting to see how easily she had punctured my conceit of invisibility!

I was not surprised by her choice. The river was usually flowing too fast to swim across, at that time, and, to climb the hill behind, she would have to pass close to private houses. She never tried the road because, for a reason I could not establish, she was terrified by traffic. Even the noise of traffic coming from afar would visibly upset her. Perhaps, on one of her nocturnal wanderings, she had ventured onto the road and been frightened; or perhaps the world of speeding cars with aggressive horns and exhaust fumes was simply too alien for her refined sensibilities to cope with. I learned later that, when she did have to use roads, Lassie was extremely careful or crossed very rapidly.

She would leave the precincts of the farm in such secrecy that usually, not even eagle-eyed me would see her go. Each morning, to my huge relief, she was home again, lying quietly atop the hay bales. More often than not, when she returned from these wanderings she would bring back a freshly-killed rabbit, which she would deftly skin and then eat. That was another 'foxy' shock!

The first time I saw this was early one morning. Moving purposefully and briskly towards the farm, quite the opposite of her cautious movements when leaving at dusk, she ran past me as though I was not there, the dead rabbit in her mouth, and jumped up to the hay bay. Quickly, I ran after her, climbing the ladder impatiently to see what she would do. The morning light enabled me to see her quite clearly lying down on the hay, the rabbit held between her front paws. Keeping the creature firmly in place, she deftly skinned it with her teeth, and then began eating it, crushing its bones. In less than ten minutes, only the skin remained. She had not stopped to acknowledge me, and I was surprised how unconcerned she was by my intrusion.

Well, I was both pleased and concerned! As she had grown away from the bread and milk I gave her, and no longer liked tinned meat, and had always despised dog biscuits, my precious 'fox-dog' was simply doing what her wild fox father would. With greater frequency, she began to look for her own food, usually a rabbit or, occasionally, even a Brown Hare (even though our Cheshire Brown Hares are some of the largest in Britain, up to eight pounds in weight, and very strong, fast and agile, with a vicious kick). During these dining operations not even the two kittens, Beauty and Sandra, were allowed near her. At a warning growl, they knew to keep their distance until her meal was over.

My father grumbled more than ever when he realised that Lassie now ate only raw flesh, which she caught herself, disdaining the food we gave her. Though her outings were actually a small help to farmers, in that they kerbed the rabbit population (even ours, for not all of her rabbits came from afar), the development made him even more convinced that one night she would harm domestic animals – and like her infamous mother, eventually be shot. But his warnings had stopped worrying me, and anyway I was somehow convinced otherwise, particularly as Lassie never went out during the day when there was most chance of her meeting such an end. She was always back at dawn with her catch, and through the day she rested safely on the hay bales, or – to my astonishment – occasionally followed me about the farm.

Although Lassie had been probably following me for some time, I only gradually became aware that she was following me when, as I went about my jobs, I began to feel her eyes on me. At first I would just see her sat immobile at some convenient viewpoint, watching me, but then she definitely started to follow. She would remain at a distance in clear view, looking very uneasy, but for some reason drawn to my progress. She would do this at any time during the day and would keep it up for about an hour or so, until her attention wandered elsewhere. Another welcome breakthrough!

Despite my father's fears, there was, in fact, no anxiety locally about Lassie. Several farmers had mentioned to me that they had seen her on their land, but said no damage had been done. Of course, I begged them not to harm her, and promised to keep her in, to allay any fears. But I knew I could not keep my promise. It would have been impossible to keep Lassie imprisoned. I had to keep my unwavering trust in her that she would do the right thing. So far, so good!

As the wet summer wore on, the gangly, long-legged puppy began to change into a slender and very beautiful dog. Her coat had grown longer, and instead of being straight was now pronouncedly wavy, and an even richer chestnut-red. Her carriage was good, cultivated no doubt by fierce, wild pride, though when frightened she would still instinctively cower and cringe away. Even so, there was always an air of fierceness in this, as one sees in wild Canids like foxes, or even a crouching lion.

Lassie remained firm friends with the cats, and tolerated Jemima, the Muscovy Duck, but was indifferent about the dogs. She got on well enough with the Corgis and Alsatian, Rusty, Trixie and Zena, at least tolerating and acknowledging their presence, but never frolicked with them and never included them in her wanderings. As for Flossy, my grandmother's old farm dog, she spent most of her time resting, excluding herself from most activities.

Lassie did not get on with strange dogs at all. Any occasional visitor to the farm was considered to be hostile, and when, rashly or otherwise, they approached her, she would engage them seemingly out of pure aggression, motivated by a natural feeling of superiority. She began by encircling the caller, barking. This was itself unusual, for Lassie, like her wild 'cousins', very rarely barked, but when she did it was strange and high-pitched, quite different to the barks of all the other types of dogs that I had heard. After circling, if the visitor appeared nervous, Lassie would sense it and continue, but, cannily, if they were calm, or showed annoyance, after her initial alarm was over she would creep away, honour apparently satisfied.

So she was not completely a 'free' dog, in spite of her obvious desires and sense of superiority. By keeping herself aloof she was able to maintain her shaky 'top dog' status, but she also had to conform to the social pressures exerted by the other dogs. Like most other animals, male or female, bitches have a particular pecking order. The last-born, or last to arrive into the group, find themselves at the bottom of the pile. As one leaves, or dies, the next one automatically steps up. At this time, it was the little Corgi, Trixie, who was the senior dog. Next in line was Zena, the Alsatian, then the retiring Flossy. So Lassie had no choice but to be at the bottom. Rusty, the other Corgi, being male, was the only one without a hierarchical position. If a dog finds himself living in a colony of females he will not exert his dominance, but be respectful, and give way to their demands. True to this natural code, Rusty was reserved and gentlemanly. It was his way of avoiding being involved, and retaining his independent status. I often thought of a parallel with some men's behaviour.

Lassie's status was further complicated by the attention I gave her. The dogs naturally sought out my attention more than my father's, because I was the one who most often took them out for walks. Whoever exercises dogs will soon win them round. Rusty, Trixie and Zena instinctively knew that Lassie was my favourite – I could not have hidden the fact – therefore, although Lassie was technically at the bottom of the group, in another quite real sense she was also at the very top. And so they were jealous, resulting in many minor incidents and snappings at feeding times, although fortunately, nothing very serious.

Lassie's character as well as her looks was developing. She had grown much more certain of her surroundings, and her fine intelligence had more opportunity to express itself. Shortly after beginning hunting for rabbits she began to show great prowess as a ratter. In this role she even earned the grudging respect of my father. Brown Rats can be exceedingly costly to farmers, and the fewer there are of them, the better. Keeping down their population is, of course, the main reason farmers keep as many cats and dogs as they do. Because of our closeness to the river, the smallholding was plagued with families of river-dwelling rats (not to be confused with the harmless Water Vole, unfortunately given the title 'Ratty' in Kenneth Grahame's *The Wind in the Willows*), attracted to the livestock, particularly the small chickens and ducklings. The oft-quoted fact about rats' diets – that they prefer to eat corn – is largely pure myth. Rats like high protein, and preferably blood, and they will always get it if they can.

We were lucky enough to be able to control our rat population, but had our fair share of casualties. We would discover these while doing our rounds, usually in the early mornings, either coming across the feathery remains of chicks, or the tragic living survivors, floundering about with their legs chewed off. When they could not get at the chicks, the rats would climb on the feedbags which contained the corn, and chew holes in them. On farms specialising in cattle, attacks on the grain store can prove costly. Once the grain bags have been contaminated with excrement, the cattle will not eat from them, and the corn has to be thrown away.

Fortunately, we had a fine ratting team, comprising both cats, the three older dogs and, soon, Lassie. Trixie was the best catcher. Her method was to 'mop up' after the rats had been flushed out of their hiding places. Despite her short legs, she was incredibly fast! As soon as the Corgi had killed one, she would kill another, and because she was so small, could shoot into places where bigger dogs could not follow, and pursue her prey to all corners of the farm. She would hold them down with her paws, and rip them up with her sharp, little teeth, so that they were literally eviscerated from top to tail. Her intentness was amazing to watch, and she was always there, wherever or whenever my father or I were flushing them out.

Beauty, the white cat, had a lower score, but for all her smaller size, still did very well. Her method was to sit patiently, hour on hour, by the side of a rat hole until the animal eventually had to come out. When it did so, she would pounce and hold it in her paws until one of the dogs came along to assist her by finishing it off.

Rat holes were everywhere. They would appear overnight, so there were plenty of the pestiferous rodents to keep us busy. Lassie began, in her usual cautious style, by carefully watching the other dogs and cats, then eventually having a try herself. To begin with, all dogs are unsure about catching any prey item, but usually learn how after their first attempt. If they do not, then they are in for a hard time – rats can bite, severely!

Lassie needed only the one lesson. One morning after feeding the chicks, passing the barn where the rats often hid, Father and I were stopped by Trixie, the six-year-old Corgi, excitedly running to and from the open doorway. She ran into one of the two stalls and began sniffing and scampering amongst the hay, and then ran back to us, and then back to the hay, to attract our attention. We knew she had smelled the presence of rats and, as the tireless Corgi was not often wrong, decided we had time between our regular tasks to get rid of these particular ones. As soon as she realised our intention, Trixie ran delightedly to take up her position outside the barn entrance. We entered the building, picking up a pole each, and began beating at the straw. Very soon squeals and rustles began to issue from amongst the bleached stalks, and we knew that Trixie had been correct. From the noise, I could tell that there four or five big rats – about an average catch – running ahead of our poles, and I was suddenly doubtful that Trixie could handle them all. Rusty and Zena were in the house and, though my father had given them a call, had not yet arrived to help out. Imagine my surprise, therefore, when, looking out, I saw Lassie standing there in their place! She must have been following us, hanging well behind, out of sight as usual, and missing nothing. Good girl, I thought! Perhaps sensing Trixie's excitement and sensing that the other dogs had not heard my father's call, she had moved up to the Corgi and cautiously held her ground there, in front of the open door.

Yet Lassie stood there a little uncertainly, slightly nonplussed, not really sure what to expect, and I felt sorry for her. I was only able to catch this fleeting glimpse of her before the rats, deciding that they could resist the poles no longer, burst out into the daylight to make a run for it. There were four, and they set out rapidly in four different directions. Immediately, Trixie shot forward and cut one of them off almost before it had left the barn. With a sudden shrill squeal the first rat was dead, and she turned and was immediately off after the second. The third rat sped off to freedom. Had Lassie been experienced, she would have had the time to catch it, but now found herself fully occupied with the remaining rat. In its blind panic it had aimed itself almost directly at her, and she was forced into a position from which she could not with any dignity retreat. But the thought that the rat had the temerity to attack her was more than she could stand, and her uncertainty soon changed to anger. With a sudden, sharp growl she launched herself at it. However, the rat had not wished to attack her. It was intent only on making its escape, and changed trajectory. It was not fast enough for Lassie who, quick as a flash, blocked off its route. Several times the rat changed direction, and each time Lassie, always ahead of it and facing it, followed suit. Eventually, they were so close to one another, virtually face to face, that the rat had no option but to jump over her head. With its legs extended and tail held out straight behind it, it looked more like a long brown lizard as it flew through the air. Although caught unawares by this surprise move, Lassie still managed to twist back her head and take a snap at it, but missed. By the time the rat hit the ground, the novice ratter had regained her balance, twirled round with great speed and precision, and, confident that she had it at last, stood over it, holding it down with her paws as she had seen the other dogs do. She was reaching down, with her jaws prepared to snap it up, but as she did so the terrified rat suddenly wriggled free, jumped up again and this time sank its teeth into her conveniently positioned nose. Her angry fluster now turned to outright fury! Amazingly, without letting out a cry of pain, she quickly got the rat off her nose with her paws and crunched it in her jaws. Then, leaving the dead animal on the ground, she tried momentarily to tend to her bloody nose, before running up the hay bales and out of sight.

I knew better than to run after her, so cried after her instead, "Good girl, Lassie!", and hoped that she heard and understood my loving and gratified praise. I felt sorry for her, but I was also flushed with pride, aware that my father had witnessed the whole occurrence. "Aye, well done, Lass!", he boomed, before awkwardly ruffling my hair and with a perfunctory nod, wandered off back to his usual tasks.

After that one lesson, Lassie never allowed a rat to get the better of her, not even for a moment. The pain she must have felt, spurred her on to kill more and more, and she set to, with a vengeance. It was as though she was determined to prove that never again would she suffer such humiliation at the hands of so tiny a foe. Now that she had found a farmyard role to play, rather than join in with the dogs, she struck up a working partnership with Beauty, whose company she preferred.

The Lassie/Beauty team worked perfectly. Beauty would find a hole and, whilst she waited, Lassie would either wait with her, or keep an eye out from a distance. When the rat emerged, she would let Beauty pounce, hold it, and then bound over to finish it off herself. When the mood took her, Lassie could wait all day by a hole, and always caught her quarry in the end. Trixie and Lassie became our best ratters. Between them, and Beauty and Zena, they succeeded in almost completely ridding the farm of rodent vermin.

Bit by bit, Lassie entered into farm life, but on her own terms, not ours or those of other animals. To say I was pleased, if regularly mystified by her 'hybrid' nature, was an understatement. One day, an incident occurred in which she revealed another side to her developing nature – her first, uncanny instinct for what was right and wrong. I had tried to teach her this, as any owner conscious of his dog's welfare will do, but I was never successful. The incident showed me that she could not have formed her moral code directly from me, but from her own observations and deductions. A young, stray cat was trying its best to sneak a chick away from a harassed mother bantam. The bantam was hampered by having a large, newly-hatched brood to attend to, and was trying to keep them safely together. Time and time again, the brave little hen attacked the cat, while the chicks scattered in panic. The cat was worrying the mother rather than attacking her, just threatening to attack, but its ploy, if it was a ploy, and not inexperience, was working. The hen was tiring, and sooner or later the cat was bound to succeed.

Lassie must have been watching the battle from the hayloft, and quite suddenly she descended and ran into the fray, snapping at the cat, which fled away; whilst the mother hen, clucking angrily, reassembled her family, and peace was quickly restored. I had been cooking potatoes, and witnessed the event through the Boiler Room doorway, and although I had been on the point of intervening, Lassie had been thinking ahead of me. And from that day on, Lassie found another role for herself, as self-appointed peacemaker to all the farm creatures!

Astonishingly, Lassie's 'rule of law' insisted that complete harmony must reign on the farm. There was to be no infighting between any animals or birds, and if any fights or bickering started, she was always quick to put a stop to them. The decision-making was quite remarkable on her part. When I think of animals possessing such intelligence and social intent I think of wild animals – including foxes – not domestic animals that, generally speaking, have grown so dependent on mankind that they passively allow their former wild animal ways to be trained out of them, and human ones installed in their place.* Because Lassie had no mother to teach her, and would not learn directly from me, I can only assume that this noble instinct for ordering was natural to her. It came from the wild.

It was now late summer again, and autumn was approaching. Lassie was almost two years old, full-grown and astonishingly beautiful. She had a majesty about her, and an air that suggested she was well aware of this. Smaller than the black-and-white sheepdog we see so often in the countryside, and with a glorious fox-red coat, heavy mantle and a long, bushy tail that almost swept the ground when she walked, Lassie was clearly different. Her face was pointed like a collie's, but her eyes, still pale yellow, were quite unlike those of any dog I had ever seen, either then or now, many years later. At times they could look strangely savage, belying her well-kept appearance and recalling her mysterious origins, as if I could ever forget them. Generally, she was still slightly off-hand, but appeared to be quite happy, though easily put into moods. She would get quite cross if too many

*Some of John Warren's observations about 'passive' domestication of wild animals, have now been scientifically demonstrated in Canids like Silver Foxes, which are just a colour variant, or 'morph' of the globally widespread Red Fox (*Vulpes vulpes*). Both behavioral and physiological changes from their wild forebears have been bred out of them, in as little as three generations. Russian researchers, by just initially breeding for 'tameness', discovered that the foxes are friendlier to humans, have shorter legs, flop their ears down, develop curly tails and even wag them when happy, and have begun to vocalise and bark – all like domesticated dogs, but not like wild, or even normal, farmed foxes. They have also developed a wide range of color patterns like domesticated dogs, from white to black and every pattern in between, and have even lost their distinctive musky 'fox smell'. Thus, researchers have concluded that humans breeding Canids for tameness seem to 'automatically' 'force' them to retain juvenile characters of 'cuteness' – exactly, they say, as we have done with domestic dogs, from wolves! All of this information, especially regarding the virtually identical dog-like domestication of Red and Silver Foxes, adds weight to the author's claim of Lassie's 'fox-dog' status. Reported in *The Secret Life Of Dogs*, BBC2 Horizon, 01/2010; also online in Wikipedia.

attempts were made to win her round. Her eyes would flash and take on their savage look. When happy, she had a relaxed mellow look about her face, like a smile, which was perhaps more the domesticated dog in her. But she still never wagged her tail like other dogs, or showed any obvious sign of emotion. Or indulged in any jumping about. No playing like a normal puppy or young dog. None of that exhilarating racing in circles or figures-of-eight around 'beloved master', for instance. She was far too serious and sophisticated for that. You could only tell how she was feeling by looking into her eyes. I was often strangely moved by Lassie's exclusivity, and the unique insights into the wild she brought me – but, as a more typical local farmer might have said to me, "Thee's got a reet queer dog theer, John lad!"

Despite her growing maturity she was unable to take the biggest step of all, as far as I was concerned. She still would not allow me, willingly, to touch her. She would come if I called her name, but would do no more than stand quietly, regarding me from a safe distance. During the day she continued resting most of her hours away, up in the hayshed, only coming down to join Beauty for ratting, for instance, or if she felt called on to quell some farmyard disturbance. I still could not say that she was 'my' dog, which I was aching to do! Lassie stayed of her own free will, and if she had chosen to leave I could not have prevented her. If I stopped to think about it, as I tried not to, she held my heart in her hand...or paw, in her case.

The agonizingly slow development did give me some confidence, though most other dog owners would have long given up on her. In my fondness for her and her ways, I was reduced to savouring the smallest improvements. The incident with the rats, for instance, had surprised and delighted me in a way that I could not properly explain.

Then, one evening, Lassie came down from the hayloft earlier than usual and attentively followed me around the fields, keeping her distance as I tended the poultry units. Egg collecting, feeding, and cleaning out the hutches was the main evening job, and in the winter months I had to start early in order to finish by dusk. She had never ventured so far with me before, or stayed with me so intently. Such was my pleasure as I worked that I could scarcely concentrate on what I was doing. I tried to keep her there, exactly at that distance, by pretending not to have noticed her, in case she ran away. She stayed with me almost until I had finished, before leaving quietly. Like a powerful light going out, I suddenly became aware that her gaze no longer hung on me. She was not in her hayloft when I returned to look, and I could only suppose that she had sneaked off into the approaching night.

To my great delight, she followed me in the same way again the following night, and the night after that. Gradually she allowed the distance between us to diminish from forty or fifty feet, down to only a few, until to an observer it must have seemed as though we were man and dog in the true sense of the word, inseparably bonded side by side, though they would never have guessed that I could not touch her. Her presence on my poultry rounds became a ritual that she seemed to look forward to as much as I did. I felt that an enormous breakthrough had been made.

Emboldened by this new sign, I decided to follow her over the embankment one evening to see where she went. Though I had known for months the path she took to leave the farm, after my first attempt to follow her, when I had quickly lost her, I had not tried again, if mainly because of my fear of trespassing on the railway line and the other farmer's fields beyond. There were several public footpaths I could use but, naturally, Lassie rarely used them. After the first attempt I had been warned off going there by my father, and had to endure months of frustration watching Lassie leave the farm, but being unable to follow.

That evening, from the corner of my eye, as she accompanied me, I kept a close watch on her for the slightest sign of restlessness in her manner that would indicate she was ready to leave. But there were none. As though at the beck of a distant call I could not hear, and without any visible announcement at all, she suddenly left my side and was off like a rocket towards the hill and up to the embankment. Taken unawares by the speed of her departure, it took me a few moments to respond before, flinging down my work tools, I chased after in hot pursuit.

It is practically impossible to keep up with a dog, especially one like Lassie. She climbed the embankment quickly, scented the air to check that she was alone, looked to see if there were no trains, then crossed the tracks and broke into a fast run. The countryside on the far side was open, and little inhabited, except for the occasional farm, and she soon lost me completely in the dimness and maze of small fields, hedges and woods.

Hidden from sight in the far distance, lay the Kerridge Hills, a dramatic upsurge of sandstone cloaked in green and topped with the famous 'White Nancy' landmark, where I suspected she hunted for some of her rabbits. I had been told that a red 'collie' had been seen there at nights, swiftly crossing fields and lanes in those prey-rich, Pennine foothills, so was prepared to believe that was her goal. But it took some believing, as the hills were about three miles distant and quite a trek for such a young dog. As I stood at the summit of the embankment, deciding whether or not to follow her any further, clouds that had hung heavy and chill all day chose that moment to release a fine soaking drizzle, drenching the long grass and foliage. It was a mad decision to make, but in the rain and failing light, in the forlorn hope of finding her, I ploughed on down the far side of the banking.

At the bottom of the slope the land flattened out into a cow field, where the shapes of our neighbour's cattle were sitting, lazily chewing. I strained to see to the limits of the field, and was rewarded by seeing Lassie still making her way between the cows. Just as I looked, she disappeared through the far hedge and into the field beyond. So there was another aspect of her 'foxiness', or at least uniqueness, for when stray dogs enter amongst cows, the first instinct of the cows is to bunch together for protection, or even attack (especially if they have calves), but these cows had not so much as turned their heads to regard her, but continued contentedly chewing. Obviously, they regarded her as a regular visitor and, furthermore, here was evidence she had obviously never harassed them.

Pausing only for a moment to get my breath, I set off along the side of the field up the slowly ascending ground, and arrived, puffing and panting, at the hedge where I had seen her disappear. Without thinking, I forced myself through nettles and thorns into the next field, and ran on. But by now she had disappeared completely, and I had to admit defeat. In a foul temper at my own foolhardiness, I began the journey home in the gathering darkness, stung, scratched and soaked right through.

After Lassie had left the farm her old instincts had taken over completely. She had reverted to a wild, wily and cautious, creature who shunned all humans – even me, my bruised ego just had to admit! My temper was made worse by the fact that although she had sniffed at the air to check that she was alone, she had almost certainly seen me. She had set off more swiftly than usual, in a deliberate and obviously successful attempt to evade me – to let me know, in her own way, that the 'outside' world she inhabited was hers, and could not be violated by any human.

Lassie was prepared to give me only so much of her friendship, and not the close affection and companionship I really craved. Quite decisively, she seemed to be saying that I was not to share in this wild, secret side of her life.

Chapter Five

I STILL shared with Lassie a general distrust of humanity, and in fleeting moments of wild hope, thought she might just recognise this intimate bond we had. But at low moments I could not help feeling that I was being allowed her favour because I happened to live with her – and she could not very well throw me out! This strange, fox-red 'dog' tolerated me, I thought, in the same way she put up with other people or creatures on the farm, presumably because she felt it would have been bad not to show any sociability at all. At the same time, sharing her mistrust of the world of men (although I was able to deal far better with it, of course, and easily retire when it all got too much), I could well imagine how deeply ingrained, and well deserved, Lassie's caution was. Her very first impressions of humans had been devastating, after all. Quite apart from that, she was completely different to any other animal in my experience. I was still thoroughly convinced she was part-fox. I had no choice but to hope she would someday 'understand' how I felt. Repeatedly, I let myself believe that the final breakthrough had been made – only for my hopes to be dashed yet again. Yet the frequent bouts of despondency were offset by equal bouts of joy at the signs of improvement. These painfully gradual indications were my one consolation.

I began to learn when she was ready to leave the farm on one of her night runs, solely by feeling. Although she gave no visible signs of wanting to leave, I would suddenly strongly become aware that she did not want to remain, or me to be with her. This reluctance became more obvious when, quickly finishing up my usual chores and attempting to follow her, she began gathering speed, putting a greater distance between us. I would attempt as well as I could to keep up with her distinctive, flickering red form, but she would cleverly use bushes and hedges as cover – and in the end I would always lose her. Damn!! She's done it again…

Yet, I carried on stubbornly attempting to follow her, and on the few occasions I did manage to see her at twilight, or even in the night, would call out cheerily, "Lassieee, Lassiee-eeeeee!", sure she would recognise my love for her, not see it as interference. But, as always, she ignored me, and quickly vanished from sight. During these nightly journeys away from my presence she clearly developed considerable hunting skills, and when I finally managed to actually glimpse Lassie the Hunter in action, her accomplishments came as another shock!

For the time being, the only rabbit skins I found were up by her hay bed in the barn, usually amounting to one per day. Bearing in mind that rabbits are easily able to outrun dogs – only a greyhound can reach the speed required to directly catch one, in open pursuit – Lassie must have been applying great skill. And she did, as I saw for myself when finally managing to catch her in action. She was truly amazing. But although they can run very fast, rabbits are not very bright and, when chased, tend to run in circles. Lassie had obviously observed their tendencies well and acted accordingly. To get the rabbit going, as I later saw, she would initially chase it, and then suddenly arc off in another, rapidly-calculated direction, and approach the rabbit from the side, just like a Golden Eagle, or so I'm told. Invariably, the veering rabbit would simply keep on going, and run straight into her!

When she caught the rabbit, she would quickly kill it with one swift bite. Then, to skin it, as I had seen her do in the hayloft, and with the rats, she would hold it down with her front paws, and with sharp, white teeth, drag the whole skin upwards, her head straining back. The skin would come off completely, whole. Then she relaxed, and gnawed the rabbit, sometimes for several hours, efficiently removing all the meat from the bones – then crunched the bones and ate them, as well. In normal dogs, rabbit-bone splinters can cause internal bleeding, and so are considered to be dangerous, therefore I was at a loss to explain how Lassie was able to cope without mishap. But cope she did, perhaps by chewing them properly – in the manner of foxes, which also eat the bones of their prey? Let the 'experts' disagree – I knew what I saw, and what they had not! I oft recalled an old Cheshire saying, "An ex is an 'asbeen, and a spurt is a drip under pressure!" Although I would probably never be able to prove, categorically, Lassie was a 'fox-dog', or 'Dox', another name for the likes of her, I knew what I knew.

I felt privileged that it was I, by following and observing her so closely, even if 'interfering' in her wild ways, who was able to discover and understand this wild side of her nature. I sincerely believed that if I was to achieve a proper, lasting friendship with her, I had to use every opportunity to understand her world, and not 'miss a trick' – even if it meant having to explain away my regular, scratched and muddy absences to concerned parents, and accept Lassie's potential danger in a countryside where gamekeepers still used deadly gin-traps, and left out poisoned baits for foxes, badgers, stoats and the like.

Back in the early 1950's, many parents might well be concerned about their youngsters getting up to very different sorts of tricks at night! Those post-War years were times of increasing social change, with the traditional ceremony of the new Queen's Coronation tempered by the exciting conquest of Everest, or the horrific explosions of the first hydrogen bombs – events that we witnessed briefly on our new little black and white television set, in moments of rare relaxation, but which I forgot about as soon as leaving the house to re-enter my special world of nature.

Thus our 'relationship' carried on, although I often felt, when observing her considerable hunting prowess – but only from a distance, the measurement of which was strictly controlled by her – that I was watching someone else's dog. As her wild ways won out, as seemed to be happening on these nocturnal roamings, I would despair of ever taming her. Yet each dawn she returned faithfully to us, and that surely proved where she regarded her true home to be?

My eventual aim was to put confidence into Lassie through handling her, the approach I would take with any dog. The thing I most desired was for her to be 'constant' to me – as I was to her. To teach this to a dog, you have to give it love. But love has to be given mainly through touch. Since that one brief fondle when she had been cornered in the Boiler House, I had looked in vain for another opportunity. It was as though she was determined she would never let that happen again...

All who saw Lassie were utterly awed by this beautiful, independent dog. For a start, none knew of any other completely red collie, as Lassie was – Welsh Border Collies, especially, were always red and white, some other Borders, black and white with a little reddish brown on the head only. Many ordinary people were convinced, as I was, that she had fox-blood in her veins. These included several local farmers, real old 'country characters' as I called them, whose opinions I respected greatly. One was a grand old chap called Tom Bailey, a short, fat, friendly farming neighbour, originally from nearby Staffordshire, who regularly helped others out when needed, and who was always ready to share a job with us. More importantly, to me, he not only had a great deal of general knowledge about dogs, in particular, but all animals. I remember once buying some hens off him, only for one to die about a week later. The next time I saw Tom, I said, "Did you know one of those Sussex Hens died?", and he replied, quick as a shot, "Why, 'as it bin in the paper?!"

Another real farming character, friend, and fount of animal knowledge, was Frank Nixon. Our family kept in touch with him even after he left to take up a new career on the railways. I had long relied on him for remedies, for poultry in particular, and like Tom he knew about all kinds of country matters. They both knew of many ordinary dogs that had 'gone wild', but these cases had only become feral – this meant that they had not been able to cope with the wild completely, and still relied on mankind or, like Lassie's mother, had to be shot. These men, who had lived on the land all their lives and gained a wealth of knowledge – where badgers dwelt, or Honey Bees were swarming, why Brown Hares 'boxed' in the Spring, where the best Field Mushrooms grew – could both sense in Lassie the unique qualities that enabled her to live in harmony with both the wild and mankind.

So why did Lassie 'need' to keep returning to the farm each morning? Sometimes, I felt sure that somewhere in her wayward heart she must have harboured a little affection for the boy who tried so hard to gain her love, and for the place, however alien, where she had spent her formative puppyhood. Perhaps that was what she was feeling on the occasions she did seem to pay attention to me, even to listen, when she came creeping back in the often misty dawn, sated and relaxed, from a successful hunt? In those slack, quiet hours, she often seemed to regard me differently. She would appear to take notice of what I was I saying, or lie there waiting to see what I might do.

One such early morning, in the Autumn of 1955, when we had been together nearly two years and I was eighteen years old, Lassie returned home looking hungry, and I guessed she must have had a rare, unsuccessful night's hunt. I was just finishing my first tasks of the day, and noticed her at the Boiler House door. Because we kept the boiler running most of the time, it was always a warm place, with the omnipresent smell of cooked potatoes and other foods. Many of the animals, including the cats, were attracted by the warmth and aromas, and congregated inside – and now Lassie had crept up, almost unnoticed.

Sensing that an opportunity to make contact had presented itself, I began to talk especially soothingly to her. At the same time I slowly picked up a piece of raw meat and bent down with it. Cautiously, I held it out to her. To my amazement, she came boldly forward and snatched the morsel from my hand! Now on my hands and knees, I offered her a second piece, then a third, all of which she accepted. Putting out my hand, I then stroked her head. A nervous quiver ran through her entire body, although she didn't immediately recoil. Lassie's inborn fear of man had been overcome by hunger – temporarily. As instinct once more took over, she backed away. However, I was delighted with that second brief moment of contact!

'Independent', 'wild', 'sophisticated', and several other words that summed up this self-sufficient dog – all rushed through my mind. They were words I regularly brought to mind to describe her. And now another word, 'Trust', joined them. She had let me touch her again – a blissful sign that she was warming towards me. Not for the first time I was made to feel that I was actually making progress, slow step by step. But she still refused to trust any other human. If my father was around, or if other visitors called, however regularly, she still immediately vanished from sight.

Her second birthday passed uneventfully. Then came the usual celebrations of Christmas and New Year, made even happier for me this year by Lassie's 'progress', before we were all too suddenly plunged into the hectic growing season. But the 'spell of progress' was rudely broken. An event occurred that initially brought that long-feared threat of banishment from my father. As well as turkeys and various other fowl and animals, we kept a good flock of geese. Although nowadays many people prefer to eat turkey for their Christmas meal, perhaps because the meat is whiter and there is a more of it on the bird – or simply because it became at one time fashionably American to eat turkey – in the mid-1950's, geese were still at the height of popularity on the Christmas table. They were, after all, very traditional British Christmas fare, stretching back through Dickens' day and beyond, and massive 'Goose Fairs' and country-wide goose 'droving' were still fondly remembered by some.

When our large, mainly white Domestic Geese started laying, in late February, the old gander who ruled the flock would become very aggressive indeed to any who approached too close to his cote. At first, he would threaten the intruder with a loud hissing sound. Simultaneously he would put his head down and stretch out his neck, and slightly droop and rustle his wings. If this impressive display did not work, or he was in a particularly bad mood that day, he would fly at you – and bite! With neck held straight out, the big goose would propel himself towards his target. Geese, unlike ducks, have a hard-edged, serrated beak and can give a very serious bite – and he could get a good hold and hang on grimly, until, pulled too far (by the victim's frantic retreat!) away from the cote where his precious female's eggs lay. Fortunately, I always knew when he reached this stage because the wing-flapping would reach such a mad intensity!

This is why, when out egg-collecting from my poultry, I usually carried a stick, to fight off any attacks. Most of the birds, if they feel like attacking me, will note the stick and not bother – unless, of course, they realise I had forgotten it. This quarrelsome old gander would not bother me when I had my weapon of defence, just threaten. But on this early summer morning in 1956, because it was reaching the end of the long laying-season, which lasts from March to June, I rashly came without my stick, and he really went for me. I had sadly misjudged his terrible temper!

Even though I had always feared an attack, I still acted with surprise, and became flustered. I could only wildly swing the bucket of eggs at him, and try my best to dodge and weave away from the nasty thrusts of his flailing beak. So I was on the losing side and even losing heart when Lassie, who had witnessed the whole affair, suddenly appeared. She stepped nimbly between us, thinking to break up the mêlée in her usual way – but the maddened gander now turned on her. Rapidly lunging out its pincer-like beak, it grabbed the surprised dog's fur and held on tightly, while it battered her with its outstretched wings. Lassie appeared to be momentarily non-plussed by this vicious assault, but then quickly lost patience. Her leg-hackles and neck erect, and lips drawn back to bare her teeth, she looked more ferocious than I had ever seen her! Effortlessly, she sidestepped the next assault the goose made, then, with a lightning flash of those white teeth the gander lay fluttering on the ground in its death throes. To my surprised eyes, it only appeared as a snap, but it was a fatal one. Phew! I could barely believe what I had seen, for it was hard to credit that she could have killed such a large and powerful bird as quickly and effortlessly as she did.

Very fortunately for Lassie, even Father had had a bad experience with the old gander, and clearly regarded it as a 'difficult' bird – so the dog was not entirely blamed. It was also fortunate that we had already reared the season's batch of goslings, so a replacement could easily be reared in time for the following year. It seemed to me that my wildling knew instinctively how far to go – knew exactly what she could, or could not do. After his initial anger and threats, Father gave Lassie another 'last chance' – with his usual sighs and much head shakings, that is! Mother, fortunately, saw the event far more sympathetically, even praising Lassie as the hero of the piece (at least when Father was not around!).

Next to the geese, the turkeys were the most hazardous creatures on the farm. It was under their special mesh-bottomed 'verandah' that Lassie had spent so much of her infancy, in poor imitation of her old fox earth. The turkeys needed this custom-built, aerated house with the slatted floor to guard them from illness, and only came out of it in fine weather, or when the other fowl – potential carriers of disease for the delicate constitutions of turkeys – were not about. We had four laying-hens, and one enormous turkey cock, or 'stag', which weighed about thirty pounds and had been with us for over five years.

This impressive turkey cock spent the warmer days of high summer parading around the yard, displaying his fine tail to all. Like the gander, he was very jealous of his territory, and, although normally accepting of our family, would readily attack any strangers on sight. He would also take offence at some object or other, like a bucket, or something bright or colourful. He was so aggressive to strangers, in fact, that we had taken to reading our own gas and electricity meters, for no official meter reader would dare to come down the track and face the bird!

Lassie and the big 'stag' had their agreement, for when she was around he knew very well not to jump at me, or at anything else. There had been many little instances when the turkey had threatened, or tried to attack, and Lassie had effectively intervened. But even the faithful 'fox-dog' couldn't be everywhere at once, and if she was out of sight, the turkey's good behaviour vanished instantly. His favourite, sneaky trick was to attack from the rear, and I had once dropped a whole bucketful of eggs – expensive, as well as very annoying and even painful! – when caught unexpectedly from that position. More usually he was forced, by my deliberate manoeuvring, to attack from a more visible position. With his great bronzed wings down, and impressive tail raised and fanned in that ostentatious and famous display that turkey's make, he would parade noisily at my side, then sprint quickly to try and match my increasing stride, and begin running in circles around me, all the time making the distinctive turkey 'gobbling' noise. Finally, if I didn't reach shelter quickly enough, the enraged bird would stand his ground directly in front of me, glare straight into my face from his madly, red-wattled head – and launch himself upwards, forcing me to take prompt, evasive action. But his wild displays could go too far.

Late one afternoon, while I was washing and grading

eggs, the peace was suddenly interrupted by a loud banging and bumping noise coming from the direction of the farmyard. I immediately stopped my task and went to investigate. I was met with an astonishing sight – Sidney Clegg, an excellent family practitioner who had been my grandparents' doctor, had parked his car in the yard whilst seeing to some minor ailment of Mother's. The car was black, very shiny – and brand new – and the turkey cock was savagely attacking his own enraged reflection in the doors, causing the horrendous noise! So fierce was the assault, that the two new door panels were already badly stoved-in!

I rushed over and tried to attract the manic turkey away, before more damage could be done. And at that exact moment, Sydney returned, and became incensed at what he saw happening to his car. In those days, a new car was an especial luxury, and quite rightly he was just as enraged as the turkey! Of course, once he had calmed down and been assured that the farm would meet the cost of repairs, all attention turned to the miscreant – and this time, thankfully, it wasn't Lassie. She had probably quickly weighed up the unusual situation and, as no creature was threatened, had decided not to try to intervene in this particular bit of farmyard hullabaloo. When the estimate came in for the replacement of the two brand new door panels, we decided that the cost far exceeded the value of the turkey, and so another tyrannical bird's reign came to an end.

Lassie, although nearly three years old, was still very mistrustful, and her 'inbuilt' fear of man persisted. After the second time she had allowed me to stroke her, I had hoped she might allow more, but she was still too nervous. What she was increasingly doing, though, was using me as a confederate in her 'watch' over the farmyard and animals, especially to hunt out vermin. She actively sought my help in driving out rats hiding in, or below, some inaccessible place. During the night, for instance, rats often moved in beneath the 'rearing arcs' out on the fields, where they would try to get at the little chickens immediately above them. It became Lassie's first morning job, when she returned from her hunting, to go around the arcs, checking them to sniff out any rats. If she discovered any had rats beneath them, she would come to get me to carefully lift up the arc by its handles, so that she could shoot in fast and grab any rat before it escaped. Yet I never taught her this method – she effectively taught me. On the other hand, if I heard a rat scratching about beneath the cotes, or saw one, I would call for her and, as I flushed it out, she would rush over to finish it off.

We were halfway to being a team, and I continued daily to coax and talk to her in the hope that I could get us to do more. Most of my attempts were still futile, although she flattered me by appearing to pay close attention, cocking her head to one side and listening for ages, if need be. After more time went by, on the odd occasion – especially if she was hungry – I did again manage to stroke her, but these moments were very rare. She would suddenly let me stroke her head or pat her side, leading me to think she had finally overcoming her reluctance. But the very next day, all might be reversed, and she would keep her distance, indifferent to all my entreaties.

James Cook still called regularly to see me, and to

hear the latest gossip about Lassie. Lately, on seeing him, Father had got into the habit of saying, "We don't want any old rubbish today, thank you!" 'Rubbish', of course, being James' own term. Father was saying, in the friendliest of warnings, I don't want you offloading any more questionable animals onto my son, thank you very much! Usually, James had only praise for Lassie and encouragement for me – the third 'gun', as it were, against my father in the ongoing battle to keep the famous red dog (which, of course, he always felt some kind of responsibility for). But, after hearing about the death of the gander, he was less sure.

"Lassie might be untrainable, and forever wayward," he told me sadly, even though my father had not taken too much exception, and thought Lassie might remain. "You just might have to think about getting rid of her, John, even after all these years – but, no, I don't know where she might safely go...."

Like my father, he shook his greying, old head as he left.

Had things between Lassie and I not been going well, I might have felt great despondency at this, but because of the improvement in our relationship, and my certainty that she would never kill a farm animal again, I was not badly affected. My confidence had increased, and these comments from 'outside', like my father's regular warnings, even from someone like James, no longer mattered. I felt more sure than I ever had done that Lassie's confidence – and affection – could be won. I no longer cared about the length of time I would have to wait, feeling that one day she would come through for me. I just instinctively knew it.

Chapter Six

LASSIE HAD entered into her third summer, and by now I had entered fully into the regular rhythms of full-time work on the smallholding. Although I had always enjoyed working with animals her presence was extra special, giving everything I did an extra meaning. The long hours were tempered by the thought that she was there. The knowledge that she would soon join me in some of my daily tasks always buoyed my spirits.

The salads – cucumbers, lettuce and other greens – were grown indoors in several large greenhouses; hardier crops like peas, beans, potatoes and rhubarb, outside. The poultry and pigs were largely sold to the trade at auctions in nearby Chelford, a well-known live-stock market and general farm, but some were home-killed for sale on our own, town centre market stalls.

We had four stalls in different towns – Congleton, Sandbach, Leek and Macclesfield. The market at Macclesfield, a mixed one, under canvas is still operating today, and nestles on the square below the '108 Steps' up to the higher town. It is not that dissimilar, at least in outwards appearance to the famous painting of it by C F Tunnicliffe. As well as these, I was allowed to set up my own stall, a trestle table arrayed with wares, on a parking area opposite the house. I operated this on

Sunday, and sold mainly to passing motorists. It brought in extra money, that I was allowed to keep for myself, and doubtless was a 'freedom' which my calculating father permitted as an incentive to do the extra farm work. He would certainly have had to pay more for an outside worker!

The market stalls were attractively set out with vegetables, salads, dressed poultry, eggs, cheese and other general farm produce. Apart from the cheese and butter, most of it was our own, although we sometimes bought in extra items for variety. At this time, we owned only one cow, kept as a 'house cow' for our own use, with any surplus milk being turned into home-made butter for the benefit of the stalls. Our customers were mainly locals, ordinary 'salt of the earth', working people, including a wonderful mix of characters, some of whom regarded Market Day as Funday! It was not unknown, especially after pub throwing-out time at 3 o'clock, for the men's greetings, virtually always friendly or sarcastic, to become even more extravagant, and maybe even their purchases. Some of the women could have 'drink taken', too. One old biddy regularly staggered noisily home past our house, two steps forrard, one sideways, either into any unfortunate passer-by – whom she promptly cursed for bumping into her! – or out into the road. It was a good job there was little traffic about in those days!

Most women round about were both sober and friendly, of course, on our Cheshire side calling me 'Love', if from Staffordshire 'Duck' (if you included Derbyshire, three counties met nearby at the beautiful 'Three Shires Head' landmark).

My father always insisted on politeness, so between him and the need to impress our clients I acquired good 'customer relations', as it would now be called. There would always be a bit of a pleasantry offered with their change. I learnt to recognise customers, greet them with a smile and ask how they were. If relatives or friends were ill, I would remember to enquire after their health... or if someone had recently bought a car (not as commonplace an event as it is today), ask how it was 'running'. Some still rode their horses into town or, like my Grandparents had employed, the odd pony and trap. I would remind customers of the other things we had on the stall, selling both myself and ever more produce – on a good day! The retail work was probably a good thing for me, as my existence back then was rather narrow by 'outsiders'' standards, as I still usually talked to animals in preference to my own kind!

I was quite happy in my daily farm routine of fairly hard work, which rarely altered. Each morning I would rise early to milk the single cow, attend to the poultry, then sometimes help Father with the pigs. The fifty or so breeding 'cells' for the pigs, when added to the large volume of poultry, added up to a tremendous work load. During the day I could also be working on the stalls, as well as the farm, and cleaning out the animals and feeding them in the evenings! There was still no time for television, had I wanted it, and still didn't, and I still rarely went out, not as other young people did, into pubs or the town. Although I did have smart clothes for 'best', I was usually more comfortable kitted out in tough tweeds or cords. The only media I listened to, later in the evening, was the radio, or even more rarely, a collection of '78' rpm records that I played on a mono record player in my bedroom. These were mainly the current pop songs of the day, by 50's stars such as Frankie Vaughan, Shirley Bassey, the Beverley Sisters or the singing cowboy, Tex Ritter. But all this came second to work, and especially work with animals.

I was often looking for an excuse to go out into the fields and woods, the other side of my love of country life. As much as I enjoyed the farm work, the need for some rest and quiet away from it – though still in Nature's realm – had not decreased since going full-time. Although, in all the years of working together, my father and I never really exchanged a cross word, he was not easy to work – or live with (as mother well knew) – and was also often away. He had the other side of his business to attend to – the landscape gardening – sometimes leaving me working on my own. Since Lassie had come on the scene, the temptation to roam had increased, and I wanted to join the wildling on her wild walks, after work, or, if not, have my own solitary walks with the heartening thought that she was somewhere near!

Since leaving school days behind, there was less opportunity to slip away. But between the end of each day's work and the start of evening duties, I usually managed to escape to a little wood about a mile northward over the fields. The walk was a delight, as these fields still had nesting Lapwings, or Curlew flying over with their cascading calls, and the hedgerows were stuffed with nesting songbirds, small mammals, flowers and their essential bees and butterflies. I had known the wood since my childhood, when in fantasy I imagined myself its owner, and affectionately named it Laurel Wood.

The wood, as the name suggested, contained many

large trees of that kind, grown large since they had been left to nature and quite unlike the neat little laurel hedging one sees in suburban gardens. The land was originally part of the estate of Tytherington Hall. * During the Second World War it had been commandeered for the war effort by the Home Guard, and eventually inhabited by American soldiers. Cheeky local kids used to ask them, "Have you any gum, chum?!" The grand old house had fallen into disrepair, and in the mid-1950's had sadly been demolished. It was to be the sad fate of many 'stately homes', then and later. Times had changed! No longer did so many country dwellers have to tip their caps to the landowner, or lord of the manor, for many large estates were selling up, their farm lands divided-off. That is exactly what had happened to Tytherington, its lands parcelled up and sold, mainly to surrounding farmers (including some acres to Father), but the wood had largely survived in its own wild way, unattended yet beautiful to the eyes of rare visitors like myself.

The mature laurels grew around the perimeter of the wood, intended to act as a windbreak for the more delicate 'specimen' trees within. This dense canopy of foliage rendered the edges of the wood very dark, and rather forbidding, but as one pressed further in the trees changed to a pleasing mixture, mainly of beech, oak and mighty elms, sprinkled at one end with elegant Scots Pines. Towering above them all was a huge, lone Monkey Puzzle Tree, quite majestic in its isolation, which Grandmother had told me was planted at the end of the 19th Century when the estate had been a splendid

*Not to be confused with Tytherington Old Hall, a little further north, that was traceable back to Elizabethan times.

place. She remembered it well, having come to live right next door when it was at the height of its Victorian splendour, importing, like many others, magnificent trees and plants from all over the British Empire.

Although the house and grounds were only a memory, the wood still covered about three acres and was largely unspoiled. It certainly appeared very large and dense to the child in me, and I had spent many long hours revelling in the tranquil aura of unspoiled beauty, although latterly without my beloved childhood pony. Some of the best moments of my young life had been spent in the very centre of the wood, where there was a clearing that sloped down to a large pool. Stretching right across this pool, reaching from bank to bank, an enormous beech tree had fallen, and from its silver-grey trunk I used to enjoy fishing for large Mirror Carp, or the occasional goldfish – survivors from the days when the pool had been stocked by the estate. The tree had been fallen some years but still remained in remarkably good condition, very smooth and wide, and it was easy, whether sitting or lying on it, to just close my eyes and conjure up visions of the estate's forgotten past, especially from Grandmother's vivid descriptions of life in late Victorian times and on through the two wars.

Unlike History, which I had often neglected at school, the pool was crystal clear, fed by a sparkling little stream that never diminished, even in the driest months. The stream ran above ground through the trees, and was full of large, smooth stones over and around which the water danced and tinkled on its way to the pool. The magical waters passed through it, leaving by some unseen subterranean exit. During high summer when the pool was at its best, its mirror-calm waters usually reflected the brilliant blue of the sky, or the slowly sailing galleons of peaceful white clouds. From July onwards, pink and white Water Lilies flowered in the deeper water towards the pool's centre, whilst Yellow Flag iris, bulrush and reedmace grew in the shallows, offering ideal nesting places for waterfowl.

The wood abounded with unusual flowers, some of which, unlike the common ones around the farm, I could not name. Possibly some were not native, planted by the pioneering Victorians. But it didn't really matter, for in spring especially, it was our familiar British blooms that lit up the wood absolutely radiantly. After the cold grip of winter came the welcome white groupings of the usual two species of snowdrops, and the broken carpets of yellow Lesser Celandines. Then, flowering in quick succession, came the daffodils, primroses and various violets, to be followed everywhere by a literal sea of bluebells. On the west side of the pool and completely confined to that particular area, grew a white variety of bluebell, quite unlike the wild, or cultivated, garden types. These seemed wild, although I was never sure if theirs was a true 'variety' or if their colour had been altered by some characteristic of the soil where they grew, in silent snowy beauty.

As few people ventured there, it was a perfect sanctuary for birds. Nesting in the trees, shrubs and even on the ground, were many kinds – blackbirds, both types of thrushes, robins, chaffinches, greenfinches, linnets, various summer warblers, and the shy little wren, with its amazingly big song. Bigger birds too, like endlessly cooing Wood Pigeons, the essential lullaby of drowsy summer woods, or their smaller, now rarer cousin, the Stock Dove, as well as pheasants, magpies and woodpeckers – and at night those spooky serenaders, the Tawny Owls, 'kerwicking' and 'wooing' the dark hours away. The pool had its own typical avian denizens, like the vociferous Mallard, solitary Grey Heron, and one of the most evocative of all waterbirds, the Moorhen, the name actually a strange distortion of 'Mere-hen'. These reed-loving birds rarely, if ever, live on open moors, and have a rather ordinary metallic cry, and when heard echoing through the early morning mistscape of any pool raise the hairs on the back of my neck. The pool was a fisherman's delight...

Once inside the wood, I never felt lonely, and could soon lose track of the outside world. Its timelessness had a healing effect, for I never felt rushed or hurried as I often did at the farm, and parental squabbles (sadly, a not uncommon feature of home life), faded away. My problems could be distanced and thought over in peace, and a proper perspective brought to bear on them. I returned home with a clearer mind, recharged and refreshed. Nothing ever seemed as bad once I had reached its sanctuary. I spent many hours turning around the negative thoughts put into my head by Father, even by my respected vet, about little Lassie. That was how I often spent the peaceful hours awaiting sunset, strengthening my convictions about her, whilst waiting, if I was lucky, to see those shy and retiring creatures, a badger family. Although I was rarely rewarded, when I did occasionally catch them drinking, the effect of seeing the delightful grey-and-white creatures was like a tonic, and I skipped back to the farm with them firmly fixed in my minds-eye – side by side with the mental image of a wild 'fox-dog', sharing and bridging both our worlds.

One day, I discovered that I was not the only one drawn to the wood's magic. Lassie, too, growing older and widening her wanderings, and needing far less rest during the daylight hours, increasingly found her way to 'my' little wood, especially in fine weather. The clearing in the tree canopy above the waters created a natural suntrap, and she would lie-up on the fallen Beech, drinking it in. With resplendent ruby coat gleaming above the bright ring of water below she looked like a regal princess crowning an enormous jewel. On the occasions I discovered her there, I would sit spellbound with her, enraptured by a scene made even more beautiful by her special presence. And when I realised she knew that I also went there, and didn't object, the wild secluded pool became the symbol of our bond, known only to us. How perfect! Yet, back at the farm, things between us were still not properly resolved. It was now nearly three long years since I had acquired her, and the struggle continued only as an unsettled truce – the distance, her distance, was still there for most of our time 'together'.

Unwisely, perhaps because of Lassie's continued independence, I was persuaded to accompany Mother on a short, three-day holiday. She often went away to her various sisters' houses. This year it was to Auntie Lillian, in Birkenhead, on the Wirral peninsula, on the opposite bank of the River Mersey to Liverpool. Even though this was a glorious hot summer, in contrast to the disastrously wet one of the previous year, I was unable to enjoy myself. Neither the majestic steam ships on the bustling river, nor the seaside resort of Wallasey, packed with happy crowds, nor the art galleries, shops or parks, could hold my wandering attention for long. I was far more worried than I had imagined I would be. Where was Lassie, what was she doing, was she getting into trouble? I had thought of taking her with me, of course, but did not see how I could overcome the problem of transporting her, let alone settling her into a complete stranger's tiny suburban garden!

On our return home I went immediately to the hay barn, but was dismayed to find her absent. Neither was she to be seen anywhere about the whole farm. My father told me, offhandly, "No, I haven't seen her since you left, come to think of it." On hearing that, I was devastated! I could only think that she had run away. Where was she – and what had happened to her in my absence? I knew I shouldn't have gone! Angry with my father because he had not even bothered to think of Lassie after promising to 'keep an eye on her', I quickly set off further afield to look for her.

As the evening was warm and sunny, my first instinct was to try Laurel Wood. I hoped desperately that she had retreated to 'our' pool. Yet as I ran swiftly across the normally beloved fields, oblivious of the happily chattering flocks of rooks and jackdaws heading for roost, I did not have much confidence I was right. Lassie might have concluded that I had abandoned her, the sole, tenuous link with our farm – me – apparently broken, and was now gone for good. She would have known well that my father had no sympathy with her, even if he would not have actually abused her – his negativity was quite enough. Alternately running and walking, it took me a good twenty minutes to reach the familiar dark perimeter of Laurel Wood. Climbing through the barbed wire fencing and pushing unheedingly through the wild tangle of dense summer undergrowth of bracken, Wild Rose and bramble, without a care for myself, I eventually reached the pool, scratched, panting and sweating. And there, above its shimmering, sunset-reflecting waters, on her usual beech 'throne' – lay languid Lassie, calmly watching me! My shock was quickly brushed away by tears of joy and relief. She obviously knew I was there, having heard my noisy approach from a long way off, calling her, and would have known it was me, for she would otherwise have abandoned the trunk. She just lay there, seemingly indifferent, yet watching me closely, keenly.

I couldn't help myself, but cried out, "Lass! Hullo Lass!", and, "Come on girl, I'm back!"

Instantly, she sprang to her feet and with a few effortless bounds around the pool margins, was by my side, looking up into my face with those strange yellow eyes, their dark-gold centres actually appearing to smile a welcome, although there was no other outward sign of affection like a wagging tail. It was the biggest sign of her affection I had received from her, and I was overwhelmed by emotion. My fear that she might reject me was forgotten as I instantly dropped to my knees, to be even closer to her – and she didn't flinch away. Speaking quietly to her, I slowly extended my hand and gently caressed her beautiful, red head. This time, no shudder of fear passed through her. She allowed my gentle stroking for some minutes. Then, just as suddenly as she had arrived at my side, Lassie leapt away into the thick undergrowth, and was gone.

This time, thoroughly trusting my instincts, I knew just where she had gone. I was elated. My dog knew I was home again, and she too had gone home. I stayed by the healing pool for some moments longer, silently rejoicing, yet utterly shaken by the power of the grip this little dog had on my emotions, taking me into both the depths of despair and the heights of rapture. Would I never simply be content with her, would I never just be able to rely on her, let alone take her for granted? Even now, after the closest contact this perplexing 'fox-dog' had ever allowed me, she had departed abruptly, without ceremony. Slowly but surely I was getting to know her, and was learning to go beyond normal modes of communication, attuned instead to something finer, much deeper, and invisible. Yes, there was clearly a strong bond, even if on her terms. Yes, I had been right to persist!

By that time it was growing dark. I picked up my jacket, brushed myself down and ran swiftly home, reaching the farm in record time, and quickly climbed up into the barn to see if my happy hunch had been correct. It was! There lay Lassie, contentedly, in her usual bed of straw, as though she had never been away. Next to her were her two feline companions. Now fully grown, Beauty and Sandra were lying beside her, purring loudly and gently kneading her rich, red fur with extended claws. More emotions flooded my bursting soul. I continued kneeling there for some moments, happy just to observe the beautiful scene, which became clearer as my eyes adjusted to the semi-darkness. Moving cautiously, talking gently all the while, I slowly crept towards her, reaching out my hand to pat her sleek side.

My loving gesture was quickly rewarded with a sort of softening of her eyes and face. She made no resistance, but lay there and allowed me to continue stroking her. Automatically, I put my head down to Lassie's, and was again rewarded as she nuzzled my hair with her soft, warm, moist nose and mouth.

I was about to put my arm around her, for a lingering 'good-night' hug – when suddenly the spell was completely broken. In the near distance a vixen screamed, and Lassie was immediately on her feet, ears pricked towards the unseen source of the howl, her whole being a-quiver. The fox screamed again, and it was obviously more than Lassie could endure, for with head thrown back, she emitted a long, terrible cry of her own! I was absolutely startled by this shocking noise. It was fox-like, but sounded even louder and more forceful in our natural amphitheatre, and not just because it was coming from my own little dog, right by my side. Lassie seemed once more oblivious of me. Foxes usually only scream like that in their mating season in the late autumn and early winter (with their cubs being born in the spring), and I was absolutely horrified. I could only shrink back, even after our groundbreaking intimacy of only a few moments before, and desperately yell at her to stop! But she continued howling, and before I could properly grasp what was going on, Lassie had descended from the barn with a few swift leaps, and disappeared into the darkness of the oncoming night.

Chapter Seven

AFTER THAT alarming, mid-summer evening when the vixen called, Lassie abruptly stopped visiting her regular haunt of the pool in Laurel Wood. I had to accept that, just as she had done in the past, the enigmatic 'fox-dog' had the habit of frequenting one place or the other for a period, then temporarily or permanently abandoning it before appearing somewhere else. After several evening visits to the wood without finding her there, I could only assume she had been drawn to another of her haunts, and it was one unknown to me. I knew she still went further afield to hunt, especially near the sandstone quarries of the Kerridge Hills, or in the Bollington fields between them and our farm, where she caught most of her rabbits. Yet I could not forget her reaction to that vixen, and uneasily admitted to myself that Lassie's sudden absence from Laurel Wood – a place of outstanding attraction to her – and the fox's eerie call, were connected.

But she still faithfully came home, every morning, so her latest mystery would just have to remain that, a typical Lassie mystery, at least for the time being. If I could not accept the wild side of her life, I would be on tenterhooks all the time – that was the price she asked, and although it was high, I could only acquiesce. I was usually glad to!

Now that she was getting older, other characteristics not apparent in puppyhood, revealed themselves. The strangest of all, frequently overlooked in the excitement and trauma of her life so far, was her avoidance of motherhood. By this time any normal, three year old bitch – even a fox – could have conceived several litters of pups. The main explanation for this lack, and one I tended to accept at the time, lay in her fox heritage. She was a hybrid, and most hybrids were barren.* Therefore Lassie was probably infertile. In the rare settled times of our relationship, especially recently, I had looked with increasing interest for any signs of motherhood, but found none – yet, that was hardly surprising in one way. For she certainly wouldn't allow any 'normal' dog

*The infertility or not, of 'hybrids' is still not completely understood. The classic case is of a horse and ass/donkey producing a mule – and 'mule' has become the synonym for any cross between similar 'species' of life. Yet mules are not always barren, even if, in breeding, they can only go 'backwards', and produce asses or horses. It is now known that other creatures as seemingly diverse as camels and llamas can fertilely interbreed, as can tigers and lions, False Killer Whales and dolphins, Capercaillies and Black Grouse, and even possibly Grizzly and Polar Bears, which have certainly bred together in the wild. (Many of the above 'hybrids' are the result of our own zoo experiments, or in the case of plants, horticultural experiments. It is well known that 'hybrid vigour' in plants actually produces increased fertility, or at least, fecundity.) And regarding fish; the massive variety of very different looking cichlids in certain African lakes, for instance, can all usually interbreed, even when having large differences in their DNA. It is this great potential for different 'recombination' of DNA that accounts for the huge variety we see in living things, yet with clear genetic boundaries usually at the 'Family' level.

near enough! Lassie had long accepted their presence, as she had with many other domesticated creatures, but very much on her terms as unofficial 'top-dog'. Correct distances, or 'terms of engagement', had to be followed. Then I had never actually witnessed her being 'on heat', or in season, although her distancing herself might have precluded that. At first, unexpectedly, I discovered I was not worried by her barrenness. On the contrary, it was actually another sign of her uniqueness. I found I was happy for her to display these unique signs of her individuality, as long as she stayed with me. Less easily dealt with was the fear that now she had undoubtedly reached adulthood, she may decide to permanently abandon the shelter I had provided for her, and return to the wild where she was born. And to the Red Foxes that apparently shared the other half of her life....

I had not dared mention to Father Lassie's response to the vixen, as this might well have led to further arguments about her unsuitability for the farm (and I could at least see he had a good point there!). The vixen's scream had been uncomfortably close to home, from no more than a field's distance away. But the awful thought that she might be attracting foxes right into the farm, I had already dismissed, as I had seen no proof of that, and neither had Father – for it would, of course, have provided the perfect piece of ammunition to get rid of her. The three of us seemed to live in a permanent, uneasy truce!

I felt I had to try and find out where the nearest fox's lair currently was. Casually, I enquired of several neighbours, and was told they were usually to be found at 'Black Wood'. Black Wood! Of course – I had completely forgotten about that dark, forbidding place, an almost lifeless coniferous wood that lay about a mile and a half away from the farm, beyond the railway and canal. It was, I felt, an auspicious place that lay conveniently between us and the Kerridge Hills. My interest aroused, I decided to go there as soon as possible. But first, I had to make the time.

For there was another minor revolution in my life. For three days a week I was now having to take part-time outside work, looking after poultry in nearby Prestbury. This mainly came about because Father was in one of his 'phases', winding down or starting up different lines of business on the farm. Sometimes he would become enthusiastic about keeping more hens, or pigs, or fewer cows, or turkeys, or the like. In addition, he had his own outside work of landscape gardening to deal with. I wasn't too disturbed, as it meant I still spent most of my time on the farm – and with Lassie, if on her terms – but I had to be more thoughtful how I planned things.

It was therefore a full week after hearing about the fox demesne that I managed to set out, taking the three dogs, Zena, Trixie and Rusty, for company. Lassie was nowhere to be seen at the time, although she often watched us setting out like this from her high 'throne', seemingly unconcerned. The weather was fine, and I remember feeling well and relaxed, wearing only a short-sleeved shirt, light cotton trousers and walking shoes. The dogs, naturally, also loved long walks, and raced on ahead as we made good time on the trek across the fields, alive with young Lapwings and curlews and the odd, loping Brown Hare. Fortunately, the dogs were well behaved, and curbed their natural desire to chase one, or the frequent rabbits, even if needing a stern "Heel!" to enforce it! In the distance, below the Kerridge ridge, I could already see the tops of the serried ranks of Black Wood, which like Laurel Wood, had been christened by me – that was not its real name. I often put my own names on things, because I thought it seemed more apt. Laurel Wood was diametrically opposed to Black Wood, lying towards the west, where the sun set (and near where my beloved grandparents had lived). Black Wood, to the east of the farm, always appeared to lie in darkness (at least in my 'secret world', cultivated over many years of solitary rambling) – hence its name. I had visited it only once before, as a school child and its dark impression had never left me. Because it was a pinewood, little except countless, identical conifers grew there. The undergrowth was dead and dank. Even the lower branches of the closely planted trees were leafless, and the canopy overhead so dense as to shut out most light. Whereas Laurel Wood was often ablaze with bird song, Black Wood was usually deadly silent – another 'black' mark against it. Most birds did not like its darkness or denseness, which interfered with their ability to fly and manoeuvre freely about, and except for a few conifer-loving birds like the Goldcrest or Coal Tit, rarely seen or heard, there was virtually no other sign of animal life. I had also remembered the wood as being vast – a huge area of regimentally aligned trees, probably planted between the wars for vital timber. Inside it, everywhere was a replica of itself, and it was easy to lose orientation.

The early evening was still fine, but not sunny. The hedge banks adjoining the fields were alive with various butterflies, and azure-blue harebells (also known as Scottish Bluebells) – typical late-summer flowers – and draped with ripening blackberries and other colourful, fruiting plants like the bryonies or nightshades. After a good hour's meandering we crossed the last of the cow fields, each well grazed and dotted with tufts of grass growing through the innumerable cow pats, and came in full sight of the wood. It looked immense and forbidding as our little troop drew closer, and we soon stood at its dense perimeter, contemplating the best place to enter. As the dogs slipped easily underneath, I climbed through the wire and immediately felt depressed and uneasy; there was no wind, and everything inside was deathly still, as though holding its breath. I certainly was! The forest appeared utterly dead. Overhead, the closely planted trees formed their own dark canopy through which little of the now overcast daylight could filter. The wood was living up to its name....

As we moved further into the gloom, the grasses and bracken which formed much of the perimeter vegetation, gradually disappeared, to be replaced by a spongy mass of yellowing pine needles through which little could grow. No flowers, no plants – excepting the odd, spooky-looking yellow or red fungus – other than the endless ranks of tall, thin trees, clawing their way upwards in the battle for light. Worst of all was the deathly quiet, and I shivered in the dank desolation as we walked. I could well imagine that foxes would like it here! They might well travel long distances for this sort of seclusion, away from where we humans wanted to be. But we pressed on – the dogs, of course, loving it, as they did anywhere in the countryside – and here and there, often led by them, I did find the odd clue indicating wildlife of one sort or the other. And after what seemed like hours of aimless wandering, we abruptly came upon a solitary fox earth beneath the upturned roots of a fallen pine.

The light, sandy soil, which spilled out over the matt of needles, appeared freshly dug, indicating that the animals might be in residence, but of the animals themselves there was no sign. We walked all around the spot, searching for signs of other earths or fox presence, but there were none. The dogs should have been madly barking and excited, sensing the near presence of a fox, but no; they were as keen as ever, but little more so than normal. Unnerved, disappointed, and tired, I reluctantly reached the conclusion that they had been present, and recently, but that we had arrived on the scene too late – and there was no sign, either, of Lassie. I decided it was time to leave, and start the long walk home.

It was then that I suddenly realised that it was too dark – and that we were lost! Oh dear, for we had obviously made the mistake of setting out too late. The end of summer daylight was fast fading, making it darker than ever within the wood. In the confusing maze of uniformly planted trees, with no westerly, sunward glow to guide me, it was quite impossible to get any bearings. A small twinge of panic flashed through me, as I set out walking in what I hoped was the right direction. At least I had the dogs to accompany me, although they were oblivious to my worries, still happily snuffling about at whatever they could, relishing the long walk. But after twenty minutes or so, I realised we didn't appear to getting anywhere, and were probably walking in circles! I stopped. All the trees looked the same…

It was some moments before I pulled myself together, trying to think clearly through the problem, and set off once more. This time, I decided to steadfastly follow one of the tree lines, soon helped by the presence of a small, dyke-like cutting that also ran along the line – hoping and wishing that if it remained straight, it would eventually lead towards the edge of the wood. And with a huge sigh of relief at the lightening scene before us, it eventually did, and we emerged triumphantly onto familiar fields – on the right, westerly side of the wood, which had certainly lived up to its name! But it was now well into the evening, and with no time to relax and celebrate, we set off briskly for home, before my parents really had time to worry (and Father complain about having to do some of my jobs!).

Making good time, we left Black Wood well behind. What a terrible place! I vowed never to go there again. Appropriately, in the distance I heard a dog fox call, distinguishable from the vixen by its deeper tone, and his cry was at once answered by the shrill shriek of a vixen, though further away. Yes, there were foxes hereabouts all right, and more than ever I wondered if Lassie knew them, or had encountered any of them on her regular wanderings near Black Wood? As ever, her secret life occupied my thoughts as we hurried on, the eerie sounds casting up unwelcome thoughts of our very own 'Hound of the Baskervilles'! Or in our case, 'Hound of the Brocklehursts', after local landowner, Sir Philip Brocklehurst!

By now the moon had risen, casting a pale, ghostly light across the countryside as I hurried on, over the canal, then the railway, cursing myself at the late hour. The dogs, of course, were well used to foxes, so simply pricked their ears before trotting on contentedly, happy to be included in such an extended romp. At length we reached ever more familiar landmarks, and knew we were near home. Then the final two fields, and the road which would shorten our journey by a good ten minutes. I knew Father would soon be getting mad at me if I didn't hurry, for it was late by our standards, and as well as evening chores I had to be up early in the morning for the market.

Walking into the final field, I found it was full of cows peacefully lying down and chewing the cud. They were used to me, and the dogs using the field, and didn't bother to rise. On we hurried, past them, until we were about three-quarters of the way across – when there came an awful bawl – the unmistakable bellow of angry bull. Though I couldn't see him I could sense he was rather close. Quietly, I urged the dogs to stay near, and tried to quicken our pace. Then suddenly, in the dim moonlight, I saw a huge shape tearing with its hooves at the hedge bank, and panic really gripped me. The bull gave his frightful bellow again, all the while tearing up clods from the banking. Although I shakily recalled that not all bulls attack walkers, something had clearly upset this one! He must have scented us downwind as we approached, a stranger and three dogs 'trespassing' on his territory, and with the hour being late and with the unfamiliarity of the situation – although it was regularly used as a footpath – had taken exception.

Before I had time to gather my senses, the vague, bulky shape materialised into a huge, black-and-white Friesian bull, clear now in the strengthening moonlight, heading straight for us! The field belonged to neighbours, and I recognised the beast as theirs, and not one I had ever considered bad-tempered or dangerous before. But then I had never seen it untethered before, and wondered vaguely if, and how, it had escaped, or if the farmer had turned it out for the night? All these thoughts jumbled through my head in seconds as instinct kicked in, and I found myself yelling at the dogs to, "Go home!", and running at full pelt. Yes, that was a stupid thing to do in the circumstances, especially for someone like myself who prided himself on his country knowledge – for it doubly drew the bull's ire down on me, rather than the dogs, which could much more easily dodge it, especially Corgis that originated as cattle dogs. There was nowhere for me to hide, and all I could do was race as fast as humanly possible for the still distant road fence. Behind me came the awful thundering of hooves, straight out of a cowboy movie, but now hideously real and intermingled with the furious barking of the dogs, amidst a panicked vision of cows rising to their feet and milling around in confusion. But as fast as I was, and desperation sure increased my speed, I was no match for the bull, and suddenly he was upon me and I was knocked viciously to the ground from the sickening impact of his massive head between my shoulders.

Though feeling extreme pain, I quickly turned over on to my back in a vain effort to avoid another attack. The agonised cry that came to my lips died away as my head swam with the effort. Then, as if all that was not bad enough, the great beast dropped onto his knees and straight down onto my chest, crushing my ribs, and literally squashing the life out of me! The sickening stench of his breath was right in my face as I attempted to somehow brace myself, at the same time as avoiding his goring horns, and vainly pushing at his face with my jelly-like arms. To add to the mayhem, the Corgi bitch, Trixie, was barking furiously and snapping at the bull's head from the side in a brave attempt to turn him away from me – of the other two dogs, there was no sign. The Alsatian, despite her great size, had apparently fled, as had the other Corgi, and I felt helpless and desperately alone.

My senses reeled, and just as I was passing out from the acute pain, facing certain death – a tornado of fury flew through the darkness and grabbed the bull's flailing head, and grimly hung on. With yet another terrifying roar, this time literally washing over me like some exploding torpedo, the irate bull lurched to its feet and violently shook his head in an attempt to dislodge the dark furry creature from his nose. Yet as soon as it was viciously flung to one side like an old towel, the sinuous object sprang back at him and renewed its assault, grimly hanging on. Although it was quickly sent flying again, it still leapt back at the bull for a third assault! And again, and again!

For what seemed like an eternity, battling with unconsciousness and searing pain, I just could not understand what the 'dark, furry object' was. Then finally, in my confused state the penny dropped – it was Lassie! Of course, who else?! My little darling Lassie had come to save me! For the next few moments, all the while battling to stay conscious, I witnessed the most terrible battle between the ill-matched pair – the huge bull, ever more maddened by the little 'fox-dog', tossed her through the air again and again. But she would not give up. Time after time she savaged the raging animal's nose, holding on determinedly, whilst the Corgi bitch snapped at the bull's feet. Reluctantly, turning my head away from the furious mêlée, I tried to raise myself, but could not, pain screaming from what seemed like every part of my body, and so started crawling desperately towards the road and its still impossibly distant boundary fence.

A new outburst of furious barking and bellowing made me turn my head, just in time to see the bull lumbering away but still with the valiant dogs snapping at its heels – then the world began to spin in earnest, and I blissfully passed into complete oblivion.

Meanwhile an agitated Zena had returned home alone, trailing her choke-chain, quickly followed a few minutes later by Rusty. At this unusual sight, my parents were quickly shocked into action, and Father, pausing only long enough to grab a shotgun and torch, rushed out to look for us. Dad did not have far to look – for, after rushing up the road, in the very first field, an amazing sight met his eyes. In the middle of a large circle of about forty milk cows lay an immobile object in the grass, which looked like a human body. The whole scene was periodically and bizarrely floodlit by the headlights of passing cars sweeping across that side of the field. As he rapidly walked towards the object, he first noticed the panting Trixie, dishevelled and besmirched with mud, and bent down and gave her a rapid inspection, and a distracted pat.

Then as the cows reluctantly parted to give him a better view of the scene, he suddenly gasped – for there, in the strong beam of his torchlight, lay the apparently lifeless form of his son, battered and blood-soaked on the ground – and by his side, Lassie, the 'fox-dog' he had never fully trusted! Yet, whatever he may have thought at first, Dad was remarkably quick on the uptake, and rapidly deduced what had happened. It was obviously none of the placid, cud-chewing cows that had done the foul deed, for he knew they only ever attacked, usually dogs, when they have calves. So his thoughts quickly settled on the bull, which he knew well, although it was nowhere to be seen at that time. He quickly realised that Lassie was actually guarding my 'body', for when he approached too closely she threatened him, snarling fiercely, her amber eyes blazing in the torchlight.

Just at that moment, another man, attracted by all the noise and light, came running down from the road, and father urged him to, "please go and phone for an ambulance as quickly as possible!" With great relief, from my stertorous breathing, Dad realised that I was only unconscious not dead, and so reluctantly decided to leave Lassie standing guard over my limp form, for the time being. For what seemed like ages, he just stood there, regularly mouthing soothing platitudes to her and the Corgi, feeling like a helpless spectator, as Lassie continued to snarl if he approached too closely.

Just as he was deciding that he really would have to try and do something about her, the man returned, yelling that he had called the hospital, and an ambulance would be here "in a very short time". Father then rushed back over to the wooden fence and ripped a short section of it down, certain in the knowledge that the ambulance could only take minutes from the big Macclesfield Hospital. And so it was. The vehicle actually drove across the field to where I lay, still unconscious, and only with the added presence of the vehicle, and yet more lights and strangers, did Lassie reluctantly melt away into the darkness.

I came-to in the hospital, to be greeted by the worried faces of Mum and Dad, who had travelled anxiously in the ambulance with me. The events of that terrible evening, only a short time before, flooded over me. I relived them as best as I could for my parents, in ghastly detail, still vividly real – the huge bull's head goring down on me, its dreadful sour-green breath, the agonising pain as it knelt on my chest. I could still feel the pain, even more literally, as the great creature's head had almost caved in my chest! And one leg, too, was obviously badly injured. Even through the drugs that had obviously been administered, an overwhelming feeling of pressure and deep pain was present, although the sharpness had been taken off it, and I felt like I was floating in thick, warm mist. Yet the pain still swamped everything, and I could not avoid or forget it for one minute. Even so, my next coherent thoughts were not for my concerned parents, or even for myself. Almost as soon as the real world swam back into focus, I was gripped by a panic that overrode any other thought.

"How's Lassie?!" I slurred, "Has she been hurt?!"

"Don't worry, Lassie's just fine," Mother assured me, but I could tell from her expression that she was naturally more worried about me, and might not be telling the truth. And how could I be convinced until I had seen my little wilding for myself? Then I blacked out again.

After that, it was just a question of lying there, helpless, until I healed. My chest was full of sharp pain, as was one leg, in plaster, and various other parts also hurt like hell! Something, probably the persistent pains, told me that I might take a long time to mend. As soon as visiting time came around (at almost any time, in those first few days), my parents wanted to know about me. But I wanted to know about Lassie. Egged on by my urgent questions, Mother and I quickly managed to piece the whole story together – and she related how "your Father" had found Lassie standing guard over me in the field. The tears rolled down my cheeks as I realised I owed my life to that special dog. Her long battle with the massive bull, her refusal to give up, the way she had risked her life to save me from certain death, the thoughts just rolled endlessly through my head, like some film drama. But soon, Father realised that my injuries were not actually fatal, and was predictably far less soft with me – and chastised me for being so thoughtless! Had I no idea what he and "your Mother" had gone through?! Did I not realise that I should not be walking on farmer's fields, especially neighbours, at that time of night?! His words, as so often before, meant little to me, and I scarcely heeded them, for my main thoughts were on Lassie. Could he not tell me anything about what finally happened to her that night?! How did she look?! We both knew that many animals were capable of suppressing tremendous injuries, when they were preoccupied with their duties – far more than any human could. Did she look as if she was injured, I asked? Did he see any blood? When he just fudged the answers, if understandably in the dark and confusion of it all, I tried to explain what had happened, and in my preoccupation with the outcome for Lassie, hardly heard his concluding remark.

"Well, m'lad, it's a jolly good job that Lassie was there," he said in his practical way, "or you would have been killed!"

My feverish worries came to an abrupt halt – had I heard aright? Father, for the very first time, had admitted, and without his usual tone of reservation, unreserved praise for Lassie! From somewhere deep inside came a huge wave of pleasure. My father had eventually come to realise that Lassie was of some use, was even a life-saver. Perhaps my awful ordeal had served a purpose, after all. At these thoughts, I started to lose consciousness again. The neat hospital ward with its white-garbed doctors and nurses, and my parent's relieved faces, slowly blurred as I sank peacefully, smiling, into a warm, deep sleep.

Chapter Eight

I HAD three broken ribs, one broken leg, a dislocated finger and severe bruising in several places from the momentous run-in with the bull. It was a very high price to pay for the folly of my visit to Black Wood. But for Lassie, it seemed that it might well have been an even higher one, and I owed my very life to her. Yes, the hospital had looked after me well, but it was she who had actually saved my life. I couldn't possibly have survived much more of that crushing weight on my chest....

I spent two long weeks in the hospital, and thought about little other than my brave dog. And when my parents, either singly or together, came to visit, I always first asked – had they seen her at all?! But they couldn't tell me anything about her whereabouts, just mouthing the usual platitudes, like "Oh, she'll be alright, she knows how to look after herself", or, "You know how independent she is...", or "She's perfectly capable of feeding herself", and so on. They said that she must be still around, and thought someone had seen her, briefly, once or twice, hanging about at a distance, "... but you know how secretive and fast she is." Their words held little conviction and, when questioned further, couldn't actually recall who the 'someone' was.

When I returned home, on crutches, the first thing I did was to hobble down to the barn and look for her. I couldn't climb up into the hayloft, so had to content myself with standing below and lovingly, patiently repeating her name. But there was no answer, no appearance of her at all. Downheartedly, I admitted to myself what I had been refusing to believe, and feared so much, until faced by the actuality. The cats did come running, also looking a little lost, but I'm afraid I had little time for them. My condition prevented me from searching much further afield, and after an abortive search of the other buildings, I dejectedly limped back up to the house. Only then did my parents fully admit what I suspected, that she had never actually returned home at all, at least not that they knew of. No one had seen her since that black and fateful night in the fields.

Unashamedly, I wept for Lassie, convinced that she must have crawled away to die, quietly and bravely by herself, as many animals preferred to do – but she was not just any animal! I would not be consoled by my parents and, as the weeks crawled by, leg encased in heavy plaster, breathing still painful, I grew ever more sad and depressed. The pain of this depression was far, far worse than anything I had ever suffered before. I felt certain that she was gone forever. And the cruel irony of this, that she had gone just as my father was finally accepting her, was a double blow. In the very depths of my despair, I felt that it had all been for nothing. All those years of endless, selfless dedication, had been wasted, just like that. Yet my main grief was still for her possible pain, not mine.

Nothing happened to the bull. At nights it was still put back into the same field. The farmer, well known about the area, and a friend of my fathers', didn't even apologise to me. The incident was my fault. In fact, he complained about the injuries that Lassie had inflicted on the bull's face! We had no cause to find fault – even though I could well have been killed!

At this unhappy juncture in my life, I was nineteen years old. Lassie – if she was still alive – would be almost three. My part-time job at the poultry farm had to go on hold. Before the injury, I used to cycle the six miles or so round trip without any problem, three days a week. The remainder of the week I had been working, as always, with father on the farm. That now had to be severely curtailed. I had already been told that I needed to be on sick leave for 'several months', depending on how fast I healed. But I knew that leg breaks usually required about twelve weeks, all told, to mend. My ribs were healing faster, but my chest was still painful if I exerted myself too much. Not that it was going to stop me doing small jobs, when I could. Being idle, was not in my nature – and of course only encouraged more depressing thoughts about Lassie – so I limped around collecting, washing and packing eggs, and attending to other light duties.

And I really needed to keep occupied for other reasons, for 1956 was depressing in more ways than one. Long before Lassie came on the scene, the most-beloved individual in my life had been Grandmother – and she had just died, suddenly. Dear Grandma, who had brought me up and granted me the freedom of Pool End Farm, and continued to teach me the old country ways after Granddad had gone, had now gone, too. She was such an integral part of the whole lost scene that

I now mourned. I saw her passing as symbolic of the decline of everything around me that I loved, and I felt even more alone.

Even Grandmother's strong will could not go on forever, and after falling ill she had been persuaded by Mother to leave her cottage and come to live with us, "for a little while", where she could be more easily looked after. Unfortunately, after only a few weeks at the farm, she suffered two strokes, and died quite quickly, aged eighty-one. We had still been close, right up until the end, for I had visited nearly every day in her nearby cottage before her move to us. Yet even in death, Grandmother's strong Victorian spirit made its presence felt, as it had in life. In her will she made the unusual request that she be drawn to the grave on a special little conveyance – pulled by Fanny – the still lively pony who had served the family so well for thirty-three years. So that was how she was taken to rest, in Prestbury Church graveyard, and although it was naturally a very sad funeral – she sure knew how to go out in style! But there was very little in my life to smile at.

Fortunately, during that long, sad, autumn, a late spell of fine weather helped Father get the heavier work done, which he had to tackle by himself. I did attempt some of the less strenuous heavy jobs, even though I should not have done, but often with spectacularly disappointing results. Trying to carry heavy buckets of water, for instance, only to tip them over; or staying on my feet too long and exhausting myself. And walking almost any distance was tiring with the pain, and heavy plaster on. For the first time in my life, my heart just was not in it.

Somehow, we managed to get the newly harvested produce from the summer months into storage. We bagged potatoes, and put the beetroot into 'clamps' – that's where vegetables are placed neatly together into a long ruck and then covered with soil, ending up looking something like a long, narrow hummock with sloping sides, where they can be protected until needed. There was also the usual, later fruit harvest, like apples and pears, to attend to, though only enough for our own use. New pullets, acquired during the summer and now reared, were put into our two large laying houses for the winter, where they could be easily fed and protected during the colder months to come. Turkeys, and a few geese, were being fattened up for the Christmas Market, not that far off on our calendar. The pigs, which bred year round, had to be given their usual attention, as were the dozens of other creatures, whether clad in fur, feather, wool or hide, which shared our busy life on the smallholding.

At length, my leg was healed sufficiently to hobble around without the use of crutches, and I happily discarded them for much of the time. After being handicapped for what felt like an age, it was marvellous to be able to walk freely again. Yet I still could not do too much to help my father, and each day, after exerting myself as much as I could, I had no option but to retire to the house and lie around reading, or listening to records. I still had little outside social life, although a few old friends did call to try and cheer me up – the incident with the bull was not widely known outside a very small circle.

I also tried to go out on short walks, but the other problem was that everything around there, or everywhere I looked, reminded me of Lassie in some way! That was the worst thing, for I was genuinely trying to make the best of the predicament I found myself in, only to fall apart at regular intervals. I would imagine her old, silent and comforting presence behind me as I collected eggs; expect her to suddenly bound out and settle some farmyard disturbance; or, while tending potatoes in the boiler shed, be reminded of the time when she first let me stroke her, or feed her. At each memory my heart would almost burst with a sharp, unbearable pang, and I would be almost physically sick until once more losing myself in work. When left alone without work, or at the end of each day, I would think about her for hours on end, going over and over in my mind the events of that fateful night, searching for some small and important point I might have overlooked which might lead me to conclude she had survived. But it was hopeless – surely, surely, if Lassie were still alive she would have scouted the farm to check whether I was still here or not – and have been seen by someone? And if she had not seen me, then, surely, she would have returned again to make certain? She surely would have missed me, in her own peculiar fashion? I recalled her return after my brief holiday in Birkenhead – but then I had gone to look for her, first, hadn't I? Questions, questions, but no real answers, and I still expected her any time. And when she did not come, I would then fear the worst, again – she must be dead. But the very next hour or day I would be scanning the horizons once more, sighing as I turned sadly back to this task or that, only to realise that I had not completely given up hope.

I began to long to reach my old haunt of green bowers and 'spiritual' solace, Laurel Wood, before the winter set in completely, even though it would inevitably remind me of the special little 'fox-dog' – and who knows, she might just be there?! But I barely dared hope that openly to myself. Being thoroughly irritated and bored one afternoon, I decided to slip off unseen, without telling anyone. My leg felt almost ready for the ordeal, and although I knew my parents would not approve, I set off across the fields as surreptitiously as possible, although wisely taking a crutch with me in case I needed support.

The early late autumn weather had unexpectedly held fine, the sky blue and the sun quite strong. A light breeze, laden with warm autumn scents of dead leaves, newly ploughed fields and the distinctive odour of mushrooms and toadstools, helped to keep my spirits high, focussed on the coming peace of the pool. But the wood, which had always seemed just a few happy steps away, now appeared impossibly distant. My left leg, as it now did if I put too much weight on it for too long, was already aching abominably, bone-deep, and I soon grew exhausted, despite using the crutch. Several times I was on the verge of turning back, but could not accept yet another defeat. Perhaps I was urged on by the knowledge that life would soon close down for the winter, and the urgency of experiencing the last of autumn, much of which I had missed that year, before it did so. Probably, deep down, scarcely admitted, was the wild hope that once more I would find the one object of my love...

Determinedly, I struggled on, and eventually staggered up to the perimeter fences, clambered untidily through them – and once I had negotiated the straggling laurels, was rewarded by the usual, delightful atmosphere of the wood, and once again, amazingly in my circumstances, it pulled its old trick. Utter peace and calm fell on me. My pain was banished, and I was soon immersed in the rich late autumn colours, of reddening brambles, golding bracken, and the bright orangey leaves of beeches, especially, which were protected from the high winds often needed to shed them. All around me hung the last leafy vestiges of warm colours, above the carpeted woodland floor, all set against the rich, deep greens of the conifers and laurels. The unusually strong winter sunlight pierced down through it all, turning it into a jewel-like display that took my breath away. I realised at once that the long weeks of confinement in hospital, followed by the enforced stay at the farm in its misty hollow, had taken their toll spiritually, as well as physically, and my soul was almost depleted.

As I gratefully adjusted to the sort of peace I hadn't felt for months, I detected the faint scurrying of various little mammals in the undergrowth: mice, voles, shrews; perhaps even stoats and weasels, hedgehog; or a Grey Squirrel, all engaged in searching out the rich bounty of the wood. Red Squirrels, sadly, were already on their way out in Cheshire, unable to compete with the larger Greys, it was said. They would all be looking for and storing acorns, or hazel and beechnuts, or even berries and fungi, in the urgency of the coming winter. Yes, it was mild now, but by the length of the daylight hours they knew that cold and hard times were coming. Above, too, was very busy, as what seemed like endless birds hopped about and sang, emitting notes that seemed almost crystalline in their purity – although I knew the reality was that few birds sang at this time of year. But the high, thin winter song of the Robin, an early Song Thrush, and the constant contact calls of a large party of different tits, Goldcrests, Chaffinches and the like, added their strains to the whole glorious scene. And many faintly buzzing insects too, probably also getting their final nectar of the year from late flowering sources like ivy, and the odd Red Admiral butterfly in scarlet, black-and-white splendour, fanning about on any remaining blackberries.

Most of the woodland flowers were long gone, but here and there a late foxglove still displayed its spikes of fading purple bells, and I stooped to examine a lone Autumn Crocus in full bloom. Its pale mauve petals were wide open, exposing the saffron-red stamens to the life-giving sun. I mused over this strange plant, which does not flower until autumn, or leaf until the following spring – and which had certainly been planted in the high Victorian days of the estate, when these woods were an integral part of its garden. I admired the tenacity of this lovely little flower, which had survived so well over all those years, whilst the estate itself was gradually being broken up and destroyed.

Hobbling on, in a more open area, I disturbed a covey of Grey Partridges: mother, father and about ten full-grown young, which flew up on whirring wings from almost beneath my feet, almost unbalancing me. The sight of them pleased me tremendously, for although still a common enough English bird, they were susceptible to dampness, which in the winter months can kill them and so were declining thereabouts. Their presence cheered me no end, and added even more to the wood's magical effects upon my spirits.

I walked slowly on through this idyll, grief temporarily suspended, until coming in sight of the pool. Naturally, the first thing I looked at was the old fallen beech – I couldn't help it – but it was vacant, as I had feared. I sighed, and forced myself to concentrate on the pool itself, which was shimmering warmly in the sunlight, causing a heat haze to form, through which columns of dancing gnats were rising and falling in the dusty beams of light, piercing between the silvery trunks of tall beeches. Pigeons gently crooned, the sharp 'chik' of a woodpecker was softened by the tangle of trees, the mixed party of little birds moved steadily on, until the whole scene merged into a single, tangible 'note' of sight and sound, like a distant cathedral choir, soothing my damaged soul. This was exactly the sort of prospect I had been deliberately saving for last. Now, sitting quietly and gratefully down at the water's edge, tired and dazed by the sad beauty of it all, I allowed myself to sink into compete rest. Lazily, I watched a very late dragonfly, resplendent in iridescent yellow, green and blue armour, dashing to and fro over the glittering pool; then stared down, as I often did, into those wonderful clear waters, eyes in soft focus and thinking of nothing in particular. Today it would be called some sort of 'meditation', but back then it just seemed a natural way of dealing with the enormities of life, by 'turning off'. Only after I thought I had absorbed as much as possible of all this peace and tranquillity, did I allow my thoughts to return once more to the 'situation' – Lassie. With a huge sigh, I laid it all out again – she had been missing for over two months, now, and I tried once more to account for her actions and motives. How did she know I was in danger, and at the very instance of certain death, fly to my assistance? And why had she risked her life to save me? Had she been following us, perhaps even all the way to Black Wood and back, without me realising? Surely the dogs would have noticed her presence, with noses far keener than any humans? But then of course, she was expert at keeping out of sight, and downwind....

All these questions, and others, crowded in, but still I could not answer them. I felt there was some sort of finality about them – perhaps this was to be my last attempt to discover what the answers were? When, eventually, I admitted that I would never make sense out them, I decided to face – yet in a sort of detached, gloomy but clear state of mind the pool often gave me – the stark possibility that my beloved Lassie's absence was permanent. This is what I had come to Laurel Wood to face, I realised. But now I found myself clinging to the possibility that my parents had been right all along, that she was not dead but had returned fully to live in the wild. The wild she had never really left – and, well, wasn't it better for her that way? Wasn't it better that she was alive and well, living off her wits as my independent 'fox-dog' had proved so well she could do, even if I never saw her again, or only from a distance? Yet even as I thought this, a part of me still could not believe it. We had shared, I still thought, a rich and absolutely unique love – even if Lassie had a funny way of showing it – and had a bond so deep that it could bring her instantly, from God alone knew where, to save me from a murderous bull, a wild pig, or a flailing gander...?! How could it be?

Our life together flashed before me, and I realised that nearly three years, which had seemed to go by so slowly, had in fact passed so very quickly. Then, after having been relaxed about it, I suddenly became very upset that she hadn't left any puppies. There was no physical trace of her, whatsoever, left behind. As suddenly as my spirits had been raised by the wood, I fell into a state of morbid abjection. The spell woven by the talismanic place, and my gloomy thoughts, was so intense – but then with equal suddenness, with a great shock, at a far deeper level, I realised that I was no longer upset! There was something undefined trying to cut through my deeply emotional turmoil. I realised slowly that a strong, warm sort of force, had focussed itself on me – and it wasn't the sun. Jumping to full awareness, with clearing sight, no longer blurred, my eyes were drawn magnetically to the fallen beech – where lay Lassie, in her usual place, intently regarding me!

With her magnificent foxy pelt covered in what looked like little pearls of dew, or little glittering diamonds, she lay full-length, with languidly crossed paws, looking straight across the pool at me. Her familiar look was neither humorous, nor angry or sad but, as it so often was, devoid of any emotion I could recognise. She seemed like nothing less than pure intensity – so, little wonder she had pierced my rapt preoccupation. For a moment I actually believed she was there, so strong was the cruelly beautiful vision, produced by a combination of deep longing on my part and the hazy, shape-shifting, drug-like day, no doubt, and I turned away to bury my face in the grass, wracked with grief. And sure enough, when I next forced myself to look up, she was not there. Only the bare, beech trunk met my gaze.

How long I remained transfixed in that position I do not know. But all at once, for the second time, I had the strong feeling that I was being watched. Turning quickly to the side where the feeling was strongest – I was startled to see that Lassie really was there! This time she came quite close to my side, and there was little doubt that her presence was real. She was far too close for deception to have worked again. But I did close my eyes and open them again, several times, each time blinking aside the tears, to finally prove to myself that she was real. When her image persisted, I was still transfixed, incapable of voice or movement.

I finally croaked out the first words that came to mind: "Come Lassie, come on, girl!"

And she responded, cautiously inching forward until she was close enough to touch me, slowly stretching out her long, elegant nose and softly sniffing my lowered face and hair, sending shivers of ecstasy through my already shaking body. Impulsively, I threw my arms around her thick, furry neck and caressed her head, wetting it with grateful tears. The feeling of her warm, living and richly scented fur finally convinced me this was no fiction of the imagination, no phantom somehow dreamed up by intense longing, but real. My Lass! She had really returned. Overwhelmed with joy and elation, I continued stroking and petting her, mumbling endearments, and only gradually did my heartbeat and pulse descend to anything like normal levels. Not only was Lassie back, she was more affectionate than she had ever been, and also looked in splendid condition. My joy just grew and grew.

She was a very regal, full-grown collie, and her slender, red form seemed to glow with vitality and health as I continued to alternately hug her, and pull back slightly, but still holding on, to regard her. And she showed no inclination to move out of range! Instead, she was even leaning against me and gazing up with those intense amber eyes, staring deeply into mine. It appeared that Lassie, too, had doubted that she would ever see me again, as we drank-in each other's presence.

I soon fully recovered my wits, and now, wholly confident of her affection for me, I struggled to my feet, began awkwardly running through the trees, pain temporarily forgotten, crying, "C'mon Lass, c'mon girl!" For Lassie was back, and not only that, for the first time, was actually trotting at my side, and I was delirious at this sudden development.

By the time we reached the wood's edge, I had been forced to slow right down, but she seemed content to walk at my hobbling pace, and I couldn't help but keep stretching down and running my hand along her back, encouraging her to gaze up at me and swap loving looks. My beloved red 'fox-dog', from whom I had been parted for so long, had missed me as I had missed her, and was now showing that she wished to return, in full, the affection I had always heaped on her. In that moment, all the terrible weeks I had enjoyed seemed as nothing – in fact, as we joyfully made our way back over the sunset-drenched fields to the farm, they even appeared wholly necessary! Perhaps everything had led to this point, for she had at long last given me her heart, and nothing could be more gratifying than that.

From the moment of our reunion in 'our' special wood, Lassie really did seem to become the dog I had always dreamed she would be. She underwent very big changes. For a start, she abandoned her habit of slipping furtively away from the farm, hidden from sight, and in the days that followed she actually seemed to idolise me in every way! Instead of following, from a distance, she now walked by my side, staying with me the whole working day. I suddenly realised, since my earliest days, that I had been searching for a companion just like her – and now at last, here she was. It seemed that all my life I been grasping for something unknown, felt and needed at the deepest level, something that no ordinary dog could have given me. It was possibly a leftover from mankind's earliest days of domesticating the first 'wolf-dogs', when I imagined that we roamed free across a wild landscape unrestrained by barbed wire and other constraints. It was a thing I could not tell my parents, for they might have worried for my rationality, and so kept the feeling hidden. Yet, from the moment I had first seen Lassie in the back of James Cook's van I had known instinctively that she was the one who could fill that aching need. And so I had taken on this anti-social little 'fox-dog' which no-one else would have, who would otherwise have died, and now found all my desires fulfilled. My whole world felt renewed, and with the healing of my heart, the healing of my leg swiftly followed.

Lassie had apparently suffered no ill effects during her absence – on the contrary, it was obvious that she was now completely self-sufficient and bursting with health – and perhaps it was precisely because she had achieved independence by roaming again in the wilds, where she was born, that she now felt safe enough to properly befriend me? She continued to be hostile towards strangers, even, perhaps especially, my father, and continued to sleep in the hayloft, leaving to hunt each evening and returning at dawn. Yet now I felt no qualms. I had still never heard a bad word spoken about the well known 'fox-dog' from any local farmers, who would have been very quick to complain had she been worrying farm stock, especially sheep – or, simply just shoot her. As devastating as that would have been to me, they would have been quite within their rights.

Sometimes it seemed like Lassie had never been away at all, except that she now came when I called – if she wasn't already by my side – and let me stroke and fondle her virtually whenever I wanted. Yet my enigmatic dog still did not fuss and gush, or display any obvious pleasure, but would just stand there, regarding me with those big, pale-gold eyes, as usual waiting for events to take their course. Then, it seemed, she would act, decisively.

We became very close. Formerly, when Lassie had wanted me to see something, or assist in ratting, she would come for me. But now, it was slightly but crucially different: she would come and stand very close, then gaze up, intently but expressionlessly, and without making a noise, as though expecting me to read her thoughts. I would say, "What do you want, Lass?", and off she would set in the direction she wanted me to go, stopping regularly to check that I was following. I knew from this behaviour she had something to show me. She was never wrong, never led me away pointlessly, as some dogs are liable to do, when restless, certain they want to be let out, only to then want to come straight back in!

Still, Lassie did not wag her tail, jump about or play, or bark, like a 'normal' dog.* Her always refined, organised and very cool and calm demeanour had simply grown more intense, as had her loving communication with me. She was everything one might expect from a creature that had somehow retained the nobility of its wild status by a process of self-education afforded by a difficult life – yet also by sharing half of herself with the alien world of men. She was hybrid in more ways than one!

I stayed in plaster for several weeks more as my leg finally finished healing. As time went by, I found I could perform more and more of the old jobs, and father was very pleased to see that, too! Soon I was able to take the dogs for their normal evening walks – with Lassie. I was at the zenith of happiness. But if, in my heady, new-found contentment I made the reasonable error of imaging that Lassie was 'my dog', I was in for another awakening. She soon demonstrated that her friendship was given out of choice, and because she liked me, not out of doggy subservience and dependency – never that! Lassie would never have rolled over and begged for anything, like many dogs! I suppose in her own way, she regarded us as equals.

She enjoyed our evening walks with the other dogs enormously, but was never off duty, as it were, always alert and watchful. Regularly stopping to listen, or scent the air for some possible danger, was always her way. Lassie could scent another human from afar long before the person actually appeared, and when she detected someone, would become uneasy, and prepare to leave

*Much later on, after observing actual Red Foxes that my wife, Jean, had taken in as injured and sick cubs and raised back to health, and subsequently kept for some seventeen years, I discovered that they can learn to wag their tails and bark, in the manner of domestic dogs, and prove very affectionate in many other ways, and even lose their strong, fox smell.

me. She hated to be seen by other humans, and kept away from them as much as possible.

It was now winter, and one night, returning home, we were interrupted in our walk by the calls of a fox. The sounds were close by, only a few fields away. It called several times, and soon it was being answered by the shrill shrieks of an even closer vixen. The three dogs, Zena, Trixie and Rusty, heard the calls, pricking their ears at each new cry. They did nothing more than jump excitedly about. But Lassie was electrified by the sounds. Her whole being strained as she savoured sounds and smells on the air that were way beyond my perceptions. Unexpectedly, she threw back her head and pointed it at the moon, and before I had time to prepare myself, emitted her dreadful, spine-chilling, high-pitched howl. It was more accomplished than the noise she had made in the hayshed, a year before – it was an almost human sound, partway between a howl and a squeal. I was aghast once more!

"Stop that, stop that at once!" I cried angrily to her, unable to help myself. I was angry not at her, but at the horrible howl, as once more the gulf between us seemed to widen and the delicate balance of our lives together was threatened. It was that unnerving, I was also afraid that if anyone else heard then they might think that someone was being murdered! Almost immediately, I regretted my impulse. Hearing the tone of my voice she at once disappeared into the darkness. Though I called her repeatedly, urgently, lovingly, she did not return.

I suddenly found myself hurrying back home with the dogs as fast as possible, so that I could return on my own to find Lassie. Arriving at the farm, I quickly put them in for the night and then set out again, picking up a large power torch as I left. The fox cries were still on the air and, from the noise, I judged that there were at least three or four, very close at hand. I had been back only a little while when Lassie's weird howl once more rent the night air, somewhere to my right, and I shuddered. It was obviously an attempt to copy one of the vixens, which had just screamed again. It was a call frighteningly similar to that of a fox. I suddenly realised that I was deeply in the grip of my old fear – that Lassie's wild nature was to take her from me – which I rashly imagined had been so recently banished.

I moved as silently as I could across the dark pastureland, guided by the repeated calls (and yes, keeping a wary eye out for bulls!). Trying to keep upwind of the cries, I eventually found myself by a dense hedgerow. The shrill calls came from just behind the tangled mass of foliage. I moved cautiously along it until, finding a gap to peer through, there in the moonlight on the grass beyond, were the dim shapes of a large fox, and Lassie.

Snapping on the torch, I momentarily gazed onto the most unexpected scene. Sitting in a semi-circle were three foxes, facing inwards, whilst a fourth fox and Lassie were standing close by. The white light gave their red coats a bluish-grey cast, and lit up the five pairs of eyes turned briefly toward me, all glowing with identical, liquid amber light. I had time to wonder what on earth they could be doing, when the foxes, now thoroughly startled, sprang to their feet and raced silently away into the night. A moment later, Lassie, also briefly dazzled, got ready to do the same. But, collecting my wits together I called sternly to her, "Go home!", although not expecting her to obey. But, surprisingly, she did, and without a sound shot passed me. I was too confused – and relieved – to reason whether she felt guilt or shame, or had got out of her depth. I was again utterly thrown by her actions, and in a whirl again as to what would become of our fragile relationship.

Chapter Nine

FOR A while, I kept secret the eerie communion of Lassie and the foxes in the nearby field. Firstly, I doubted that I would be believed, and then wasn't sure if I should ever share the fact with Father. But the episode proved unshakably to me that Lassie was strongly interested in foxes, and classed herself among them. She had certainly never shown more than tolerant forbearance to any dog.

I continued a low profile where publicity was concerned, for Lassie's sake as well as mine. She would have resisted interference from outside. For my part, I was frightened of jeopardising her affections. No doubt, had I not been so particular, and gone through official channels, Lassie would have received the canine VC for her bravery in saving me from the bull. The Victoria Cross, awarded by the RSPCA, is extremely difficult to win, and I am certain Lassie deserved one. But I did not want to risk the attention it would draw.

She was so unusual, no reserve on my part could dampen the publicity altogether. More stories appeared in the Macclesfield Express, and in another local paper, The Courier – the results of reporters checking their files and coming to me to see what developments there had been. But I remained silent about the bull. A few close friends and neighbours had been told, and only they and my parents knew about it.

My father had now completely changed his position on Lassie, though neither of my parents had a relationship with her as such. He still retained some of his disapproval, which no doubt was partly personal, for she continued to avoid him. But his reaction had become rote. When Lassie behaved in a manner he viewed as wayward, he would say something like, "Well, I'm not surprised!", and then the very next day, "Oh, she's a grand dog!" My mother had more success, though Lassie would not allow herself to be touched by her. Both seemed genuinely pleased to have her back, pleased for the dog, not just for me, which made me happy. On one front at least, my battle had been won.

The year 1956 was now almost at an end, and the farms round about us were preparing for the spring and summer of the following year. The grain crops had long been cut and bound into bundles by the tractors and binders, and the 'corn stooks', left out in the fields to dry, had been brought into the Dutch barns. Completely dried out, they were now brought into the farmyards, and every farmer was busy thrashing the oat, wheat and barley, and storing the grain in bags, and binding the left-over straw into bales ready for the winter feed. Unable to afford hired labour, they did this themselves, together with the countless other jobs that could not be done in the summer: whitewashing the buildings, repairing broken machinery, re-slating roofs, concreting the yards, mending fences and trimming hedgerows, all accomplished at a steady, unhurried rate, in routines as true and timeless as the seasons.

The fields were now tilled, broken by black hedgerows and trees, and undulating in a frozen tapestry over the low hills. Pasture fields, studded with sheep or cattle, and woodlands great and small added greatly to the picture. Often colder in Cheshire than in other counties on account of most of the land being a flat plain and the rest being squashed up against the Cambrians and the Pennines, the weather this year, after the fine autumn was extremely cold. It was also dry, and fine working weather, and so with the work unhindered, there was time to attend to Christmas in every tiny detail. All looked forward to traditional occasions such as bonfire night, Easter-time and Christmas. It had been a very hard year, and we all felt we deserved some relaxation.

With so little other entertainment about, these holidays were vivid events, at which nearly everyone enjoyed themselves – even the drunken old gal, chuntering away to herself as she staggered past the house, managed a slurred greeting! A massive Christmas spread for about twenty relatives and friends was laid on by Mother. In times gone by it would have been Grandmother's task, who had seen to it that we spent many a happy Christmas at the old farm before it had been sold off. The days after the feast were spent going from farm to farm through a series of exchange invitations, lasting up to the New Year.

There were other bright spots amidst the work routine, and even my father, when he wanted to, could have his bit of fun. After the rigours of winter had passed, and spring had come round again, he discovered that a courting couple were trespassing onto our pig field and making use of an empty pig ark. He had caught them there several times, and shouted at them to clear off, to no avail. It took him some time to work out how they were gaining access. It was certainly not by the lane, for Zena, his Alsatian, would have boomed out a warning from her kennel, and Lassie rarely missed a trick. He eventually saw the young couple late one afternoon sneaking down from over the railway track, descending the steep embankment and climbing our boundary wall to spend their evening lovemaking in the ark. They did not really do much harm, but as the arks were kept full of dry straw, and cigarette ends and matches were always to be found the following morning, my father began to get annoyed. He tried once more to move them on, and when the pair persisted, decided to teach them a lesson they would not forget in a hurry.

A pig ark is a moveable wooden shelter shaped like a long, triangular box, resting on two skids. The skids enable it to be fastened to the tractor and moved when the grass underneath becomes bare, and these things were pulled around the field to different points and dropped off. The sows used them when they were pregnant, to sleep in at night, and they were big enough inside to house four or five pigs at a time. For two prostrate lovers, they were ideal, but there was no standing room except in the very centre where the sides rose sharply to form a narrow apex.

Our pigs were Large White breeding sows, except an old favourite of mine, Dusky, an enormous black female who had at some time before we bought her lost half an ear in an unknown accident. We could never fathom out what injury could have caused her cut ear, because it was sliced straight across and almost looked like a knife cut. She had been bought as an adult at a private sale, and to begin with had been very savage. But even pigs will respond to kindness, and she had grown to be one of the friendliest of all our sows, a very kindly sort of soul, and a very good mother. And pigs can be really friendly!

Having seen the couple go into the ark yet again, my father put his plan into action, and drove Dusky up the field. She seemed to know exactly what was required of her, and as the light was fading headed straight for the ark door. Very quietly my father crept up beside her, and opened the door. Then he gave the pig an almighty sharp slap on her bottom. Letting out a sudden squeal the old sow shot inside, and behind her my father immediately slammed the door and slid-to its bolt!

Inside the ark, all hell was let loose. Shouts and screams accompanied by frantic pounding and banging and the grunts of the enraged, madly-plunging pig, sounded instantly. Dusky must have been alarmed to find people in her bed in the hay. Equally perturbed, the couple must have jumped up for protection and all three thrashed wildly about in an area no greater than the inside of a small van!

After two minutes, when he felt they had learned their lesson, Father opened the door, and out rushed the girl, sobbing and screaming, with her hands covering her private parts, quickly followed by the boy. Both were completely naked, and due to the nature of their exit were covered in pig dirt and straw. They hopped about in front of us, dirty, wet and shaken-up – giving new meaning to the phrase 'tar and feathering'! – while Father gave them the ticking-off of their lives. He told them that if they ever came again on his land he would get the police. Then he ordered them to get dressed and leave his field, all the while watched by the furious pig,

149

grunting out its own warnings from the door of the ark. Afterward, Father, unable to keep a straight face for much longer, collapsed into a heap, laughing. He never forgot the incident.

Of lesser amusement value, yet still bringing stifled smiles, was the incident of the Lady and the Billy Goat. One pouring wet day in mid-summer, our five goats decided to push their way through the hedge that bordered our house, and stray onto the more tender grass on the other side. The hedge separated the house from a narrow public footpath that came down from the road past the yard gate to a pedestrian tunnel under the railway track, eventually leading to Hurdsfield, and the goats had congregated together along its verge to nibble. There were two white nannies, one with very young twin kids, and the other with a young Billy Goat. The young male, a year old, was frisky, and although quite tame, was in the habit of putting down his head in a threatening way if anyone came close to his mother.

Down the path at just that moment appeared a lady wearing a red mackintosh and holding an umbrella, who soon found herself confronted by the five goats. The young Billy at once stepped in front of her, blocking her way in a show of mock threat. She was not afraid of the goats, but instead of walking round the little fellow, which she could easily have done, the woman saw fit to roll up her umbrella and hit the goat over the head. This provoked him into butting her onto the hedge! Over she went, screaming and shouting. Attracted by all the noise, I ran over to see what had happened, and found her on her hands and knees in the hedge bottom. As I helped her to her feet, all the while apologising and trying to keep a straight face, she rounded on me. When Father came on the scene she harangued him as well. Apart from her mack, which was dirtied, and shaken nerves, there was fortunately nothing the matter with her, and we escaped with a dry cleaning bill!

1957 passed uneventfully, and in my contentment I experienced one of the best years of my life. The loss of Grandmother notwithstanding, this was a peace of mind that arose primarily as a result of the 'new' Lassie,

I was twenty-one years old. Lassie was now four, and both of us – judging by her vitality, looks and friendliness – were on top of the world. Intelligent to a high degree, she fell to working the sheep and a few cattle we had again acquired. Grandfather's old sheep dog, Floss, still worked our animals at the time. She was a smooth-haired, blue collie with a walleye – one eye blue, and the other brown – and an excellent, if ageing worker. At my insistence, Lassie would learn by watching her. The two dogs had never got on as friends, possessing the natural jealousy that bitches sometimes have. Lassie would have almost nothing to do with her, and if they came too close together a snapping match would ensue. Lassie saw how grateful I was to Floss for the work she did, and may have decided to learn from her in order to please me. Whatever the reason, in no time at all, she had picked up exactly what had to be done.

When she was learning, I would say to her, "Go on!", and she would follow the other dog. She watched carefully what Floss was doing. When rounding up sheep before driving them, the first thing a dog does is to close them up by running round the flock, compressing them into a tight ball. Cattle are easier to manage, because they do not run about like sheep do, and the dog can soon get round them, occasionally nipping a few heels to get them going. Once a cow starts, the rest of the herd follow, because all cows will walk the same way and will not try to run back (apart from some frisky young bullocks, that is!). Cows also know where they are going. With sheep, odd ones may try to leave the flock, and the dog will have to leave her place at the rear and run around to tighten them up again. Lassie watched all this once or twice only, and picked up the broad idea. Then it was left to me to help her with the smaller details. To begin with, she might drive the herd too fast, or too slow, and I would tell her to alter her pace. I would shout, "Yes" or "No" or "Get in there", or "Get up there", to encourage her, or discourage her, whichever it might be. Occasionally she lost her temper, and I would have to calm her down. But she was so naturally intelligent, I usually only had to tell her the once. Of course, her mother had once been a sheepdog of good breeding, whoever – or whatever – her father was.

Lassie's management of the farm animals increased to the extent that she soon had complete mastery over all, whether bird or beast. She could work any animal, was the best rat catcher and, as always, kept peace on the farm. I grew to have a high expectation of her. Yet she would manage to do something still cleverer, which would force me to revise my expectations even further upwards. She never ceased to amaze me – nor grudging Father – with what she could do.

One day, working in one of the chicken houses, a chicken I had picked up for killing, got away again. It lost itself instantly among hundreds of others crowded on the floor. Lassie, who had been watching, saw my problem and, without waiting to be told, jumped into the mass, picked one of them up, and brought it to me. It was the same one that had escaped. I was astounded, because I could not see how she could possibly have known which bird to choose. From that day on she helped me in the chicken houses. If I wanted a particular bird, I would point to it and she would see where I was pointing and immediately go and get it. My gestures would often be no more than fairly vague guidelines, indicating one of several possible birds, yet she still seemed to know which bird I wanted, and unerringly brought the right one to me. She carried the chickens carefully, without sinking her teeth into them, by gently taking hold of their shoulders, just like a gundog, but, of course, without their training.

The autumn 1958 arrived, and she was now nearly five years old. The relationship between us had become very close. It was still fragile, as I knew to my cost, but the new bond was tremendously intense – a mixture of love and trust and understanding, the like of which I had found in no other dog. She understood me without my having to speak to her first. The episode with the bull, when she mysteriously sensed my danger and came to my rescue, had made me wonder whether telepathy was at play between us. Her success with the chickens only bolstered a growing conviction I had. She would pick up on so many little things that I needed, and just do them. Whether she did this by reading my expression or by sensing small unconscious gestures, or a combination of these – and, in the case of the chickens, some inspired guesswork – I did not know.* She understood my mind and moods, without being told, by a process I found inexplicable.

I could not understand her as well as she could understand me. I could read her body signs – if her ears were down, and she was cowed, I knew she was frightened; if her eyes were flashing, I knew she was annoyed; if the slight curvature of her mouth, which was normally down, curved ever so slightly up, I could tell she was pleased; this was her smile, which gave her a pleasant, alert, interested appearance. These somewhat slight, but to me obvious signs, were easy to read, for they were common to most dogs. But I could not tell what my special little 'fox-dog' was thinking.

I had to accept that there were things about her that I might never be able to share. Her wildness, mainly. But I was now much more confident that our relationship would never break altogether. She was free to go, and could ably care for herself, yet she did not; she was always drawn back by something. Some magnet drew her to me.

After the time when I felt I had lost her for good, I began to long for her to have puppies. However

*Many dog owners' observations that their dogs are correctly 'reading' their 'expression', are born out by thorough scientific experiment. Dogs appear to be the only animal able to do this, by reading the correct 'side' of our faces. For we all have asymmetric faces with two subtly different sides, which anyone can see by slicing two full-on self-portrait photos in half, one reversed, then joining them up to make two different faces! By careful, repeated experiments, researchers showed how dogs immediately move their eyes to the left to read the most accurate mirror of our feelings – the right side of our faces. *The Secret Life of Dogs*, BBC 2, 1/2010, and on Wikipedia.

unwelcome and distant, the inevitable thought that Lassie might be the first and last of her unique line, distressed me. Earlier thoughts of, "Oh well, its all just part of her uniqueness", were probably more to do with our unsettled state at the time, than my real acceptance. Just look at the degree of satisfaction my mother got from breeding a single line. That impressed me. She could look back and say, "Well, I had the great grandma of this one", and it was true; her dogs had all been from one long line of Corgis for about thirty years. I wished to do the same. But no puppies came. The likelihood of her becoming a mother seemed increasingly remote. She mistrusted strange dogs, and snapped at them, greatly reducing any chances she might have had. I wondered whether she had ever even been 'on heat', for I had never seen any obvious signs, something that was very unusual for any dog her age. Once again, this time more gloomily, I concluded that, like most hybrids, such as mules born from inter-species mating, she was probably sterile.

When her fifth year went by, and there was still no sign of puppies, or even of her coming into season, as most bitches do every six months or so, I accepted the fact that she was probably barren.

Chapter Ten

1958/59 WAS a mild winter, with little snow. Our busy
farm life went on as usual, holidays were enjoyed, and
I even found time to attend a few parties. It was not all
'muck and braces'! Even the death of top rock'n'roller,
Buddy Holly, killed with two other stars in a plane
crash, did not go unnoticed, although I was never a
great fan myself, apart from of some of his ballads.
There was always a film to watch as well, in 'Mac', and
I especially enjoyed Disney's marvelous nature films, or
the occasional adventure or cowboy picture. Most of
the long, dark evenings, though, between routine work
and jobs that could be done under cover, were spent
indoors reading or watching television. As ever, the farm
and Lassie occupied most of my time, and she was still
usually out hunting for some part or even all of the
night, whatever the weather.

The days were lengthening, and the sun was gaining
strength, and even though only early February, the
weather was mild enough on some days to make one
think of the spring ahead. Grandmother used to tell
me as a small child that a good duck or goose would
begin to lay by the first week of February and, sure
enough, running true to form, our ancient black and
white Muscovy Duck began laying at that time. She

made her nest, as she did every year, right at the top of the hay bales, close to Lassie and the cats. They had long tolerated each other, and any 'aggression' on the duck's part was mostly ritual and habit. Many creatures naturally come to an accommodation with impressive threat displays such as ritual strutting, for injury due to physical conflict is costly and to be avoided wherever possible. Far beneath her, at ground level, our old grey goose guarded three enormous white eggs in a nesting sight between two bales. As the duck did, the goose would only give the odd hiss to Lassie when she had to pass close her by her.

I disliked these long, normally cold, dark winter hours. For me, it meant extra work, like the recurring task of priming and pumping the paraffin lamps. No fewer than six of these Tilley Lamps had to be prepared each evening. The outbuildings and poultry houses, being much further from the house, had no electricity, and so lamps were essential to provide the hours of 'daylight' necessary for winter egg production. They were in fact excellent illuminators, each casting as much light as an average light bulb, and the eggs they helped to produce were important to the smallholding's economy. Their main drawback, apart from their preparation time, was that they became very hot, and could be hazardous if knocked over or accidentally dropped.

Though Lassie lived completely outdoors, impervious to the colder weather, I found myself worrying for her on frosty nights, and was always sure to give her a warm milk drink before I went to bed. This job was usually done by 10 o'clock and, if Lassie was waiting on the hayloft, she had the milk at once, but if she had already left to hunt, as sometimes was the case, I left it for her return, hoping that the cats would leave her a little.

One freezing evening, untypical of this mild winter, I climbed the hayloft ladder with Lassie's milk, and suddenly smelled smoke. Not thinking much of it, I nevertheless decided to check, and on reaching the top of the ladder shone my torch around the lofty building. Lassie was waiting for me on her bed of hay, and her amber eyes lit up in the torchlight beam. Sitting close by, in attendance, was Sandra, the ginger-and-white cat, and the Muscovy, brooding her eggs against the chill night. The duck chided me crossly as my beam passed her nest. Shining the torch up to the roof beams I spotted our resident Barn Owl looking down at me with brilliant, unblinking eyes. The owl remained perfectly motionless, and I was pleased to see that already his mate had arrived to stake claim to their nesting site, and was standing motionlessly by his side. My father liked and encouraged the owls, because they hunted all kinds of rodent vermin around the farm, and there was nothing more beautiful than the sight of one wafting around the meadows at dusk, like a white spirit. After a few, still moments, both owls appeared suddenly restless, and simultaneously left their perches, flying out on noiseless wings. I wondered what could have alarmed them, for they were quite used to us. Lassie, too, appeared uneasy, and instead of taking her milk backed away from me and quickly descended the hayshed. What had spooked her? Even as I thought, the smell of smoke became more tangible, and suddenly was almost strong enough to burn my throat.

After a moment of panic, I decided that because I could see no sign of fire then the smoke must be entering the building from outside. Someone nearby, probably at the top of the slope behind our buildings, must be having a late bonfire, I thought, and the smoke was somehow being sucked down into our hollow. Leaving the bowl of milk I made my descent. But as I climbed lower, the smoke became stronger. It was thick enough now to see by the flashlight and, as I hastily descended the last few rungs, I realised with horror that the smoke was pouring out of the adjoining stable. Inside the stable was a store of straw bales – also Samson, our old retired cart horse. Samson was a loveable old white-coated shire bequeathed to us by my grandparents. Above the stable was a loft, full of my father's battery hens.

I realised that the straw was on fire, and at once knew how it had been caused. The stable was divided into two by a boskin – a low, wooden wall with a shelf on top, and strong metal bars which stretch up from the top of the wall to the roof. Before taking Lassie her milk I had left a paraffin lamp burning on the shelf-top, between the bars. Old Samson, rubbing against it, must have knocked the lamp over. The lamp had fallen into the adjacent section of the stable and set the straw alight!

Serious panic now gripped me. My parents had retired early, as they usually did in the winter, leaving me to lock up. I was on my own, and for several seconds I was frozen with fear, trying to think what to do. Samson's sudden scream of terror and the loud banging he made as he kicked the wooden stall walls, snatched me back to reality, and I raced out of the stable, across the yard and up the lane to the house to telephone the fire brigade. After phoning, I immediately started back out of the house again, forgetting to wake my parents in my hurry to help the animals. I had got as far as the yard gates when my mistake in not alerting them dawned on me, so I started yelling "Fire, fire!", back up in the general direction of the house – but now, seeing the huge gates, another thought struck me. They were closed and barred. How could the fire engine, when it arrived, be able to get past them? I flung down the heavy locking bar and began to slowly drag open each gate in turn. They were as tall as a small house, and built of tremendously strong, heavy wood. Normally, it took two people to open them, but now, with strength gained through my mad frenzy, I managed to open them on my own. All this took up more vital time and, when I had done it, I carried on yelling the alert, back over my shoulder, instead of returning to properly wake my father. I had decided that my priority must be to get back to the fire, and save Samson and as many animals as I could, before it spread to the hayloft.

The open stable door was now glowing from the blaze, and thick smoke was pouring out of it into the night air. From inside came the squawks of the poultry clamouring in alarm as the smoke reached up to the loft where they were trapped. Intermingled with them was Samson's screaming and banging. Not thinking about myself, I dashed inside the empty stall where the blazing bales were, to retrieve some sacks which I knew were on the floor. Picking one of them up I dashed outside again, soaked it in the yard spring, and immediately raced back in. I came to Samson's stall and flung it open. All was thick with smoke, and already flames were licking round the door casing. Behind their fumes I could just about make out the old horse plunging and lunging in utter terror with the effort to break free. Holding my breath I dashed inside and reached him, managing to tie the wet sack over his eyes. If he was ever to be got out, the sight of the flames had to be kept hidden from him.

Realising I had to get some fresh air into my tortured lungs, I burst out into the yard, where the fire engine had just arrived, it seemed almost preternaturally quickly. Whilst distractedly thanking them for their response, I began to run back inside the blazing stable, still determined to rescue Samson, when strong arms took hold of me from behind and attempted to restrain me. Fighting with the furious strength of a maniac, I hit one of the firemen and struggled free, and pelted back into the stall. By now the flames were burning high up the doorframe, but I didn't care what happened to me such was my state of mind.

Blinkered, Samson was much calmer, but in the heat from the flames he was still panicking and in the confusion as I tried to get him out, he trod on my foot and nearly broke it. As heedless of pain as I was of the flames, I continued groping around in the smoke for his halter, managed to find it, and by pushing and pulling somehow manoeuvred him outside.

This time, when I emerged, I was grabbed firmly and rushed safely away, despite my protests. The firemen had now managed to connect their hoses to a water supply and were preparing to play them on the flames. All the time I had been shouting for Father, and now, finally aroused by the clanging bells of the fire engine, he was standing with the men in the yard in his pyjamas and Wellingtons, looking on grimly. Gallons of river water soon began gushing in thick jets from the hose nozzles and, as the fire had been caught in time, was quickly quelled.

As soon as the fire was out, acting as one, my father and I ran into the now soaking interior of the blackened stable to rescue what we could of the hens. Behind the stalls, on the wall at the back was a plank ladder – a plank with foot-holes cut into it – fixed vertically to the wall, and this took us up through the ceiling into the loft above. Fortunately, the upper storey was ventilated by open windows covered with chicken wire, but even so the smoke was still heavy, and at one stage must have been choking and deadly.

At any given time, we carried a stock of two hundred or so birds, and fifty of these were kept up here in batteries. The others were kept in deep litter in the poultry house on the opposite side of the yard. Unlike the deep litter hens, which had the freedom to scratch about, these in the loft were confined to their individual boxes. Subdued, and half-suffocated, the birds were sitting at the bottom of their cages, crouching down as low as they could to get away from the smoke. I had never liked the idea of caging the birds, and now felt doubly sorry for them in their plight.

By the light of the loft's own lamp, which ironically was still burning, we hurriedly began ripping the cage doors off their hinges and snatching out the birds. One by one we threw those that were still able to fly sufficiently, out of the windows, where they fluttered safely down to the ground. Coughing and spluttering in the smoke, which was still thick enough to obliterate most of the light from the single lamp, we finally brought out the last bird and climbed thankfully downstairs.

Of the fifty hens, only six had perished. We were exhausted by our ordeal, and after giving our thanks to the firemen and seeing them off, returned to the house to clean ourselves up. The whole episode taught me the lesson of a lifetime regarding oil lamps. In future I would treat them with even greater caution than I already did. We lost the straw, and suffered some structural damage to the stable. Samson was frightened, but otherwise unhurt. I had damaged my big toe, and we had lost six birds. Father kept repeating over and over again how amazed he was that the damage had not been far worse, that all the livestock had not perished. He blamed me, of course, but because there was so little damage the incident was soon forgotten.

It was a 'marvelous' way to start the spring, and acted as a kind of omen for the next 'big event'. The whole farm seemed to look forward to springtime. During the winter, the animals lived quietly, moving slowly, as if purposely saving energy. Then, all of a sudden, the farmyard exploded into noise and bustle – boastful parades of plumage that would cause jealousy and squabbles, and happy squadrons of young, needing food, entertainment and living space. In the fields, the corn and root crops were planted in earth that had been ploughed up during the winter, and was now freshly tilled to provide a fine, friable topsoil, or tilth.

In Cheshire, at this time of the year, it was still the hunting season. Hunting had started in the autumn, and carried on right through the winter into spring. Local to us was the famous Cheshire Hunt, enjoyed by riders from all over the county, a regular feature of our lives for as long as I could remember. Farmers, doctors, solicitors, and other professional people mainly took part. The hunt had a series of set routes, depending on conditions and events. Before the start, any farmers not already in the chase and likely to be affected by it, were advised to move animals that might be frightened. This particular meet, the hunt was to run from Prestbury to Tytherington, and the route took it past our farm by a distance of one field. I had known about it well in advance, and to avoid possible mishaps, on the morning of the hunt, moved our in-lamb ewes from the far boundary field, closer to the house, in case they panicked at sight of the hounds.

Lassie helped me to round up the twenty ewes and drive them through three fields into a small croft, where they would be safe. I was so proud of the way she handled the sheep without any guidance from me other than an encouraging, "Go on Lass, bring them in." With a few kindly words, and a little pat, I praised her as I always did when I was pleased with her, and she accepted this indifferently, without any show of emotion. I was so used to this lack of doggy gush that it no longer troubled me. As soon as we had finished, I hurried back to the yard to catch up with the rest of my work.

About midday, I suddenly missed Lassie. She had been with me all morning, as usual following me about, and helping. I called and looked everywhere for her. She was not around the farmyard, or up on her hay bed. For some strange reason, she had left the farm in broad daylight. I began to feel uneasy, for she never normally roamed abroad during the day. I had recently seen the

Jennifer Jones film, *Gone to Earth*, about a girl who had reared a fox. The fox had got caught up in a hunt. Watching the hunt pass her farm she realised that it was her fox being chased, ran out and rescued it in the nick of time from the snapping jaws of the beagles. To protect it she held it high up above her head, while the hounds surrounded her and jumped up to try to reach the fox. Forced backwards by the pressure of the dogs she tripped over the low wall of a well, and both girl and fox plunged to their deaths. The images of the film were still hot in my mind, and I suddenly had the wild notion that by a fateful coincidence this melodramatic scenario was about to recur!

Far in the distance I heard the horn of the advancing huntsmen, and all at once fear gripped me. Lassie, my little Lassie, was somewhere out there alone, and because of her shape and colouring might be mistaken for the fox. What on earth had possessed her to go out on this of all days? A cold sweat broke out ever me. I had to find her, and quickly, and reassure myself that she was out of harm's way. Forgetting both lunch and work, I rushed from the farm, up the railway embankment, quickly crossed the track and ran as fast as I could over the next two fields. All the while I called out her name, but could see no sign of her.

The climb up the third field, which was steeper than the others, slowed me down. The hill was ribbed with countless sheep paths and, although not very far from the farm, it seemed to take me forever to reach its brow. But at length I reached the highest point, and breathlessly gazed down into the valley fields on the far side to see if I could glimpse her.

"LASSIE!" I shouted. "LASSIE!" But up here a terrific wind was blowing, and the words were flung back in my face. For a long, anxious moment I could see nothing except the valley terrain below – the low, sloping fields leading toward the river, and more fields rising gently on the far side to a scrubby, gorse-filled field belonging to a farm called Paradise Farm. Beyond that, far in the distance, were the Kerridge Hills, backed by the blue outlines of the Pennines.

From far away to my right came the sounds of the baying hounds, a loathsome sound which had always depressed me – and I knew that the hunt was drawing close. Still before I could see anything, the baying sound changed to full cry, and I knew the quarry had been sighted.

Out of the corner of my eye, far to my right, I suddenly spied movement, and as I turned to gaze toward it I was gripped with horror. Over what was called the North Ride ran Lassie, her fiery-red coat gleaming in the blustery afternoon sunshine. Not thirty lengths behind her came the first of twenty or so hounds, all bent on a kill.

"LASSIE, GET HOME! LASSIE, GET HOME!" I yelled hoarsely at her, but to no avail, my voice drowned by the wind. I ran down the bank toward her, and even broke a huge, dead gorse branch out of the ground intending to intercept dog and hounds before realising the futility of my actions, and returning to the brow. By the time I had descended to them, they would have passed.

The first of the foxhounds, a large brown-and-white fellow, determined to have blood, was rapidly gaining on Lassie, and appeared to be only a matter of yards behind her when the absolutely unexpected happened. Stopping dead in her tracks the little collie crouched and turned to face the approaching hound! I could not look, and closed my eyes. She was no match for a pack. To fight its leader would allow them to gain on her, and seemed suicidal folly to me!

An ear-splitting yowl, carried on the wind toward me, caused me to open my eyes and look again, just in time to see Lassie with ears flattened back and her whole being ablaze with fury, attack the foxhound full in the face. Those powerful, razor-like teeth found their mark faster than the hound could strike. She momentarily clung on, then released her hold, only to whirl away again in the deadly chase of life and death. She had not been as stupid as I thought!

Still not knowing what to do, but realising I must try to do something, I helplessly began plunging down the slope once more. If Lassie continued diverging my way, as I now realised she was doing – possibly I might be able to catch them before they crossed my path. It was possible I could divert them, or speak to the riders and make them understand that what they thought was their quarry was my little wild dog. Before I got far, though, the scene in the valley changed again. Just as the pack, in full cry, seemed to be gaining on her, Lassie now put on extra speed and drew away from the leading hound. She was running as I had never seen her run before, and I realised that up until that moment she had been playing with them. The extra burst of speed quickly widened the gap between her pursuers, and now she was effortlessly leaving them behind. Still not a rider in sight.

I was now more hopeful, but still pessimistic. Stories

of huntsmen shooting down foxes out of trees, which the fox had unnaturally scaled in an attempt to evade death, or of the hunt sending in terriers, or digging out any foxes who had been 'run to earth', flashed through my mind, as I recommenced my headlong run. The hounds were still to my right, so there was just a chance that, once Lassie came within range of hearing, I might be able to attract her to me. But now Lassie abruptly veered to her right, and began taking a huge loop, coming back on her tracks, and I stopped again, this time in puzzlement. It took me some moments before I worked out what she was doing. She was heading toward Laurel Wood! Of course, I should have known that she would make for her own territory. The wood was much nearer to me than it was to her, and I set out, running harder than ever, certain now that I could reach her first. Blindly, I climbed through hedges and over fences and ditches, heedless of cuts and scratches, my mind blank and my body anaesthetised by fear.

Now the riders were in view, and approaching fast. I heard the horns sounding triumphantly, loud voices shouting encouragement to the hounds. The baying was so intense that it almost deafened me. At last the wood came into sight, and I raced toward it. I had almost reached it before Lassie, but then she put on an extra burst of speed and effortlessly entered the dense foliage ahead of me, as I struggled through the fencing. Three of the leading hounds tore in after her, the rest of the pack not far behind.

The fencing surrounding the woodland would act as a barrier against the huntsmen, I knew. The outer fence was stout, made of three-stranded barbed wire about four feet high, to prevent cattle and other animals from eating the poisonous laurel leaves. The inner fence was small, but rigid and made of wood, and lay about a yard beyond. I knew the riders would not risk a double jump with such dense foliage on the far side, and so would have to dismount and enter the wood on foot.

By the time I gave an exhausted glance back through the trees, the rest of the hounds had slipped through, and a group of about fifteen riders suddenly arrived at the wood's edge. Despite the rigours and fury of the hunt, the men were quite resplendent in their 'pink' hunting jackets and white trousers, the ladies dressed in all-black habits, and not for the first time I contrasted their elegance with their deadly aim. Every one of them was keenly intent on having fox blood that day. Some were already dismounting, cursing shouting to the hounds, and testing the fence which, fortunately, was far too strong to be pulled down easily.

Disregarding them and still unseen, I tore on into the wood, after the lead hounds, hoping I was not too late. Pressing through the tangled undergrowth. I came to the stream that fed the pool, and then spied Lassie at its far end, belly deep in water, moving cautiously downstream toward the pool – and cleverly letting her scent wash away. At the point where the stream entered the pool she began to swim, and made swiftly for its furthermost bank. Once across the pool she climbed out of the water, briefly shook herself, and vanished from sight. I had not dared to call out to her in case I attracted the attention of the hounds, who now seemed completely baffled.

They converged on the pool a few seconds later, having lost the scent at the stream, and were milling around its near edge, yelping wildly. Five of the huntsmen had entered the wood, still shouting, urging the hounds on, but their cries had no effect save to confuse the hounds further. Lassie had been too smart for them.

Though my mind was still reeling, and chest still heaving, I was extremely relieved. But I was still far from happy. I had intended to rage at the huntsmen, but I suddenly thought that my protest would not be taken seriously. Who among them would believe that a collie could look like a fox, which their hounds had then put up? I recognised no local farmers in the hunt that day, for they would certainly have known about the famous little 'fox-dog' and possibly put two and two together, and decided that, as Lassie was now safely out of the way, I would say nothing.

In the chaos of it all I had somehow remained out of sight to most, and so now crept away from my hiding place in the trees, disgusted with the riders and their dogs and the entire hunt.

As I walked back across the fields, one of the riders overtook me to ask whether I had seen their fox. Of course I replied that I had not, adding that there were very few foxes here nowadays. He rode away – if not before giving my tattered and ripped appearance a suspicious and puzzled look! – and, from far behind me, I heard the Chief Whip calling in his hounds. They were pulling out of the wood. I allowed myself a sarcastic smile.

The confused mêlée in the wood behind me ceased, and the sound of barking hounds and thundering hooves approached once more. In the next instant the whole pack had overtaken me, and were racing across the fields towards the farm! This was something I had not foreseen, and once again I was seized by blind panic. I broke into a fast run in their wake, exhaustion forgotten.

The pack charged on until they came to the River Bollin that lay between them and the farm, and I arrived in time to witness the whole company dismounting yet again, this time on the river bank. Some of the hounds ran along the bank, attempting to cross. But I remembered thankfully that the river was in spate, and far too deep and fast for them. This time the hunt was finally beaten. I watched with relief as the hounds were called in a second time, and the disappointed huntsmen admitted defeat.

My ordeal was not yet over, for I had no proof that Lassie had managed to reach home. Had she been forced to cross the river? Had she really been cunning and brave enough to face its deadly currents? Could she have been swept away as, on occasion, our ducks had been, when they had tried to cross it? Still fearful, I hurried along the bank of the meandering river, on the circuitous route to the road that led back home.

I arrived, breathlessly, at the top of the hayloft, and called for her through parched lips. From the gloom of the bales came a sound of rustling and, as my eyes became accustomed to the dim light they were rewarded by her familiar shape, lying on her bed, waiting to greet me. She seemed to give me a very knowing look, as if to say, "You need not have worried, I can take good care of myself. I am perfectly capable of outsmarting slow-witted foxhounds!" I smiled joyfully and, kneeling down, gently caressed her noble head.

Lassie appeared to be quite unperturbed by her most recent adventure, and lay quietly, unconcernedly washing her forepaws, as was her way. Thank goodness, I thought, for such a clever animal! But, as I thought that, I also realised that the drama provided even more proof of her wildness, for the hounds would not have picked up, and followed so blindly, the scent of a collie. They were not that dim-witted, I thought. They had chased Lassie because her scent must have smelled similar, or identical, to that of a fox. This, I reasoned, would also help to explain why she avoided dogs other than our own, which were well used to her. In retrospect, as I have mentioned earlier, foxes in captivity do lose their strong, distinctive fox smell – but Lassie must have retained enough for the extremely keen senses of the hounds to pick up.

At supper that evening I told my parents the whole story, and even they found it hard to believe, though my badly scratched and bruised body, and tattered clothes, were pieces of evidence difficult to ignore.

"I always said that wildling was no ordinary dog," my father commented at last. "She is of fox blood, and this just proves me right."

In truth, he had often said that Lassie's 'fox blood' was bound to make her kill poultry or livestock, but I did not remind him of that! Next day, we all had a broad smile on our faces when we heard the tale of how a fox had been chased 'to earth' near our farm, and lost!

My 'fox', not deterred by that day's happenings, went out again the same night, and hunted over ground on which, earlier in the day, she had been hunted herself!

I loved this super-intelligent collie more than ever. She may have had the advantage over most other dogs, on account of her wild, natural-born instincts, but she still had been lucky to find me, who could understand her, and had given her the necessary space, and love, to grow.

Only those owners who really love their dogs can expect to achieve such a close bond with them. All too often, they are unable to recognise their dog's intelligence. The dog cannot mature, and remains a 'non-creature'. There are dogs that are positively unintelligent, through no fault of their owners (often due to over-, or in-breeding), but usually, when someone obtains a young puppy, they have the chance to mould its mind and decide its future. When you see people with dogs that seem just plain silly, or owners breaking their necks running to keep up with dogs on the lead, nine times out of ten it is the dog that should draw your sympathy and not the owner. The poor dog has not had an owner with sufficient real empathy and dedication. And aggressive dogs often belong to aggressive owners!

Of course, Lassie had been the very reverse of this 'ideal' dog. Yet now, after long years of patience and genuine understanding, she was more than ideal to me. She was far more than I could ever have wished for.

Rainow from Kerridge Ridge

Chapter Eleven

FOLLOWING THE hunt, the first summer of a new decade was mainly one long, hot drought. The dry weather started in March, when the crocuses came out, and went on until the end of October. The weather started out being very nice, a welcome change to the many wet years, but then gradually the heat became unbearable. Macclesfield stopped short of turning into the Wild West – there were no scenes of withered cattle lying around dried-up water holes – but large areas of land were burned and cracked by the sun. Trees died, crops were ruined and there was a great shortage of grass. No one could wash cars or other vehicles, or swill down yards due to a government ban on hosepipes. Some farms ran out of water entirely, and those not close to rivers or lakes suffered worse. Living close by the River Bollin we were among the more fortunate. When the spring in our yard dried up we pumped water from the river to water the greenhouses, and with a great deal of extra work managed to suffer no real loss.

More permanent, subtle changes in the character of the rural world about us began taking place. These were not at all to do with the weather, but with the pressure and affluence of human life. Here and there, a field had turned into a small housing estate; a wood, which only a year previously had delighted the eye, was razed, and replaced with ugly stacks of bricks, the land dug out and marked with taut white builder's string; a country lane which had seen only tractors and carts and occasional cars, now hummed with a more urgent activity. Shops were being built in Tytherington for the first time. There were more people about, yet less sense of community. Much of the land I had known as a child and as a teenager, was becoming a memory. As much as I realised that the post-war generation had to live somewhere, I couldn't help but think: if this was progress, it needed better planning.

Even I had eventually succumbed and bought a car, replacing the bicycle I had used for years to get me backward and forward between the farm and my outside day job. My part-time job as a poultry worker had changed, and I now had to travel further afield, as a poultry manager at another farm in Gawsworth, which made the bike somewhat impractical. The job was at the 'Pigeon House', the very place that Father had landscaped so beautifully a few years before and, like my previous job had, involved looking after a wide range of wildfowl from all over the world.

The changes affected Lassie. To our mutual dismay, part of the fields at the back of Laurel Wood were built on. She had been using the wood again, but now was seen there less frequently, forced to hunt further afield, making her nightly outings longer. Lassie was now in her seventh year, and although still a most strikingly beautiful dog, showing little of her advancing years, I realised only too well that she was middle-aged. All those wonderful, semi-wild years of self-rule seemed to have denied Lassie her motherhood, a topic on which I still brooded. Inevitably, the old claim that hybrids are usually barren came up again. Or, perhaps, it was because she was caught between two worlds, and hadn't settled completely with either foxes or dogs. But that too was only a guess...

Motherhood was a dream, of course, but I could not help thinking how beautiful it would have been for her. I knew how other bitches changed when they littered, becoming more mature, just as humans often do after they have raised their families, becoming more at peace with themselves and the world. In dogs, the body shape is usually improved. Bitches without young are normally not as happy as they can be. Some become habitually bad-tempered. Lassie, of course, had always been a bit on that side, but rather than getting worse with age, she was actually the opposite with me, reserving her occasional bad temper for unwelcome strangers. But sweet as the thought of her having puppies was, I had to put it out of mind. Life, as it was for Lassie and I, was better than it had ever been. Both of us were truly happy, and despite the ups and downs, were mostly contented.

There seemed to be no set pattern to Lassie's more intimate sojourns in the wild. Since her communion with the foxes, there had been no similar incidents that I had witnessed, but periodically she would disappear, and I would not know where to, or why. I would become aware that our relationship had hit a smooth patch; we were together and getting along splendidly. Quite as suddenly, I would realise that we were not; the wild would call her again. I had taken her for granted again, and lagging behind her moods and moves. Oh well, came the old thought, with a sigh, this was the price paid for her supreme uniqueness.

Towards the end of the year she began to go missing for prolonged periods. At first, she disappeared for an hour or two each day during daylight hours. Having so many other animals to occupy my attention, and thinking that she was entitled to go off occasionally, I did not worry, but as the habit persisted, I became concerned. One minute she would be loyally following me about the farm whilst I did my chores, the very next she would be missing. At first frustrating, it soon became very annoying and perplexing, for she appeared to be slowly returning to the wild, raising once more my old fears. Yet, on the other hand, she always returned home to be my protector, as a new incident demonstrated.

My father had decided to introduce a breed of Danish pig onto the farm. The much-heralded Landrace had become popular with breeders on account of their fast growing rate and their long backs, which provided excellent lean bacon. That, with the EEC and our newly diet-conscious times, meant that Danish bacon was fast becoming a symbol of excellence. The traditional Large White pigs – actually coloured pink, or black – were theoretically not so lucrative. The Landrace ultimately proved to be not such a good buy, for a variety of reasons, but just then the market was agog, as every farmer tried to buy the pigs at auction, and prices soared.

My father returned one afternoon from the lunchtime sales at Chelford bearing in his trailer a large, pure-bred sow, close to farrowing. I was surprised, because it was not like him to spend so much money. But it was not entirely out of character, for when he could afford to, he occasionally speculated. In this instance there was the added incentive of the pig as status symbol; by keeping up with trends, it would make him look up to date.

Most of our breeding sows were rung with special copper rings to enable them to live outside the sties and enjoy the grass without ploughing up the field, but when they were in farrow they were brought back into the farm and put into sties to have their litters. Some of our pigsties were the old-fashioned types, comprising of a little walled, stone-paved yard, and a cote. The cote, entirely enclosed, had a low 'pop-hole', through which a pig could walk with ease, whilst a man had to enter bent down, head-first. My father had unloaded the new Landrace into one of these, and it was my job to feed her and put down fresh straw for her bedding.

I prepared her some boiled potatoes and a swill of corn and water, which I put in the trough in the yard of her cote, then crawled through the pop-hole into the dark interior with an armful of straw. Just as I had laid the straw and was turning to leave through the small hole, I received a nasty shock. For some reason the huge, six-foot long sow had taken it into her head that I meant her harm, and had walked up the yard. She was now blocking my exit and growling, and trying to snap at me. Before they bite, pigs make a kind of threatening growl. Then they make little sideways runs. They cannot bite forward because of the length of their snout, and therefore have to bite from the side. This Landrace kept walking sideways towards me on the far side of the hole, and taking lunges as I tried to get out. Those who are familiar with pigs will know that although normally the friendliest of animals, an angry one can be the most dangerous of all farm livestock.

The cote I was in had at one time been part of a stable, and had been modified by my father into a sty. Inside, it was quite large, with enough room to stand, and on the back wall there was still affixed the old horse cratch, a slatted wooden rack containing straw. When the pig decided that, come what may, she was going to have me she began forcing her way through the hole toward me. Shaking with fear, I grabbed the yard brush which I brought inside with me, and tried to prevent her entering by pushing the bristle end into her face and heaving onto her with all my strength, at the same time yelling at the top of my voice for assistance. For a while, my tactic worked, and the enraged sow tore at the brush, savaging it with her teeth, while I pushed for dear life. It gave me time to think what to do next. No one had heard my cries, and realising that the sow's superior weight and strength would soon enable her to break in, I ran to the back wall and jumped up it onto the cratch and hung on.

The sow rushed inside and immediately began a fresh onslaught. I had managed to climb all the way up the cratch, but my flailing feet were within her reach, and to keep her away I began beating at her with the brush. Shouting brought no response, for the stone cote must have deadened my cries for help. It seemed that all was lost, because the brush – and the soles of my boots – were practically chewed away! I hung for what seemed like hours, my thoughts reduced to hoping that the pig would eventually tire and lie down. My arm was aching unbearably, and I was preparing to think the worst, when all at once the sow gave a loud squeal of rage and turned on something behind her. The light was so dim I could not see what was happening. After a moment she charged out of the hole, leaving me alone, and outside she was apparently attacked again, for she gave another loud squeal. Cramped and aching, I climbed down and crept to the hole to see what was happening. Bending down and peeping out I saw that Lassie was now standing in front of the doorway with her back to me. Her hackles were raised, head down and white fangs obviously exposed toward the sow, guarding me, all the while growling very menacingly. At the opposite end of her yard, growling noisily as only a savage pig can, stood the trembling sow. Her little red eyes were rolling in rage, but it was obvious she had met her match. She was not about to take another bite from the tense and angry collie standing there! Not in a million years had I expected to see Lassie, for I had got used to her being absent. When I saw her, it was like something from another world arriving.

Seizing the opportunity, I quickly ducked out of the hole and vaulted over the wall to safety, with Lassie hot on my heels. The bond, whatever it was that connected Lassie and I, had worked again, and unless she had been coincidentally returning home just then, and had heard my shouts, I could no longer rule out the notion of telepathy. She was not at all scared, and while the feelings of relief and gratitude I felt at having been rescued yet again in the nick of time washed over me, I hugged and stroked her. She stood silently, almost impassively, whilst I did this, a slight smile of contentment playing about her mouth.

My father had been busy elsewhere, and had heard nothing of the commotion. Later, at tea-time, when

I told him what had happened, he registered surprise, especially on seeing my ruined boots! But he was even more surprised the following morning when he visited the Landrace to feed her, and found that she was ready to attack anyone who went near her. We realised, with disappointment, that she would have to farrow alone, without help from us, for it would be quite impossible to go in and sit with her as we normally did with our other pigs. Under normal circumstances we attended to the mothers all night as they gave birth, cut the umbilical chords for them, dried off the young piglets and left them warm under an infrared lamp until their mother had finished littering. With this pig, we could do none of that, and were worried for the safety of her coming young.

For the next day or two, we fed and mucked her out together. One of us would drive the sow into the cote and stand there with a pitch-fork at the door to keep her inside, while the other quickly brushed out the yard. We planned to look after her until her piglets were reared, and then sell her on to some other unfortunate farmer – in the same way that she had been sold to us, for my father now realised that he had been hood-winked into purchasing an obviously useless animal.

She began to farrow two nights later. Father arrived at her sty to find her in a kind of frenzy. She had smashed up her wooden bed, and bitten great chunks out of the cote door, and was in such a berserk mood that no one dared go near her. In order to provide for the coming birth we hung a paraffin lamp inside the cote, but now even that minimal requirement had to be removed. It became increasingly apparent to my father that the pig was quite worthless, and he was filled with gloom at the amount of money he had lost.

"If she kills the lot she'll just have to kill 'em, there's nowt we can do," he said resignedly as we watched her snorting with fury at our presence. "But then she goes for slaughter hersel'!"

She began to tear up the wooden floor of the cote, but against expectations, as the inevitable birth processes that were going on inside her took control, quite suddenly lay peacefully down to have her piglets. She had them in the dark, and as we could not see what was going on, we decided to leave her to it and return in the morning.

To everyone's dismay she produced only three piglets. She had not killed any though, and ironically turned out to be quite a good mother. But my father was so disgusted by the amount of money he had outlay for her – he had paid something like £50, a sizeable sum back in 1960 – that as soon as the young ones were weaned he impulsively sent her for slaughter. While leaving, she tried to attack the driver we hired to take her, escaped, and had to be brought back, and reloaded into the wagon. I must admit, we were extremely glad to see her go!

The sow's brief stay at the farm brought some good. Of her three offspring, two were males, and were reared for bacon. The third, a female, I reared on a bottle and, just as a home-reared lamb will follow its owner, so this little pig followed me. I was allowed to keep her! At this, I was thrilled to bits, for she was an adorable companion and behaved just like a dog. When told to sit, she would obligingly seat herself on her large pink posterior. She was friendly to everyone, and followed me everywhere – even when she had grown to the same enormous size that her mother had been. Because of the haphazard way she had been brought into the world, I christened her 'Lucky'. She did not like the sty, and so was often permitted to roam about quite freely and, had I let her, would have happily accompanied me on my walks with the dogs. There could not have been a daughter more opposite in character to that of her mother!

Like all young animals, Lucky liked to play, and often engaged in chasing games with the dogs. Lassie was loathe to join in, as usual preferring her own company, but in any case was still regularly absconding. But Zena, and the Corgis, loved to play tag with her, playing the game just as humans would do. One ran away, the others gave chase, until the pursued was nipped, and then the whole procedure was reversed.

Lucky could not be kept solely as a pet, though, and had to be mated if she was to earn her keep. We made several failed attempts to introduce her to a boar on a neighbouring farm, while all the time she grew bigger and fatter and ate more. A year passed, and she became a fine gilt of her breed, but looks were secondary characteristics to my father. He eventually declared that unless she became pregnant, she would have to be sold. And so she continued to live with us for a while under the cloud of an ultimatum. Still she did not mate successfully. The idea of such a big softie going for slaughter seemed horrible to me, as used as I was to the regular comings and goings of many farm creatures, but there was nothing to be done. We made one last attempt with her. Secretly, I hoped this time she would live up to her name.

Before final pronouncements were made, Lucky decided to take herself for a walk. Pigs are every bit as intelligent as dogs, and she was clever enough to be able to unlatch the door of her sty at will. While we were all out for Sunday lunch, she let herself out, ran up the lane from the yard and turned left into Beech Lane, the main road leading past the house into Macclesfield. Lassie would no doubt have stopped her escape had she been at home supervising. In her absence, Lucky had no deterrent and made good her getaway. Fortunately, she had good road sense, and must have kept well to the footpath, and walked a hundred yards up the road, stopping outside the Ship Inn, a small pub with revolving doors, which on this day of rest was packed with drinkers. The noise and activity of all these people obviously appealed to Lucky, who loved human company, and when the next customer arrived she followed him inside through the revolving doors.

By now, we had arrived back at the farm and been alerted by her escapade, and set out looking for her. She had been spotted walking along the road by a neighbour, and so we followed, and soon arrived at The Ship. By the time we arrived, the pavement outside was packed with a large crowd of milling, excited people, shouting and gesticulating, and it immediately dawned on us what had happened.

Lucky had entered the pub, and caused a riot. Everybody had jumped up from their tables, not knowing what to think but not taking any chances. But she had not entered to bite them, only to be friendly.

Dad and I dashed inside, and found her sitting by the bar, grunting happily. She had emptied the whole public house! The bar and tables were covered with drinks, the ash trays filled with smoking cigarettes, only the odd overturned chair was witness to what had happened. Very fortunately, she had not caused any accidental damage, and whilst the landlord and his customers returned, laughing, to their drinks and fags, Lucky squeezed her enormous body back through the revolving doors and happily followed us home.

Following that little escapade, she never wandered again. We made sure of that by securing her door on the outside as well as on the inside. Even more pleasing, in due course, was the timely arrival of ten fine piglets, which truly saved her bacon!

Chapter Twelve

ALL THIS time, Lassie had continued to go missing for several hours each day, and on occasion had ignored my calls when I had seen her slip away. I had not been able to come up with an even remotely sensible idea why she should behave in this strange manner, unless it was that she had decided simply, and more openly than usual, to share more of her time with the other side of her two big loves – the wildwood and me.

I often wondered whether the gradual despoliation of the farming country, causing her to hunt further afield, was also causing her to desert me. Though middle-aged, in behaviour and mind she was still young, and loved the free open spaces where humans rarely trod. I made many more attempts to follow her, but pressure of work prevented me from making a thorough search. I speculated that perhaps my own heavier responsibilities were combining with the effect of limited hunting ground to make her bored, and I grew more than usually irritated by both. But the longer the situation lasted, the more my determination grew to find out what was going on. I had to discover soon, for my peace of mind.

Lassie's closest friends among the animals on the farm continued to be the two cats, Beauty and Sandra – the once-orphaned kittens, who grew up alongside the wild puppy, and who remained closely bonded to her. Beauty, the white one, was an albino and had probably been born deaf, and Sandra, her sister, who was ginger-coloured, enjoyed the privilege of being at the top of the farm's cat pecking order. They were disliked by the other cats, and probably would not have had much friendship to speak of if it had not been for Lassie. Although she did not play with them, she continued to allow them full favour. They were still permitted to eat off her dish. She would even save their share for them if they were away. The two cats knew this, and would fawn around her, making a great fuss of her whenever she was home. The lordly wilding still let them lie against her and snuggle up close on her hay bed when it was cold, and often still hunted rats with them.

Each morning and night, when our goats and our then one house cow were milked, the seven farm cats gathered round to await their share of the rich, warm harvest. This had become a ritual treat, which the cats always looked forward to, and nothing would keep them away from it. One morning, only six cats turned up, and I quickly noticed that Beauty was missing. I thought that perhaps she had gone further afield than usual, and had mistimed her drink. When the evening session came round and her place was still empty, I decided to look for her.

It happened to be one of the evenings when Lassie was around, so I took her out for what used to be her usual evening walk, and kept a special vigil for the little snow-white cat who I knew would be easy to see against the greenery in the low, autumn light. We reached the top of the steep railway embankment, and were about to cross it to reach the pasture fields on the far side, when Lassie put her nose to the ground and began following a scent trail. She often picked up these trails, which might prove to be the scent of a rabbit, and I carefully strolled along the railway track behind her, scanning left and right along the sides of the embankment as I went, all the while alert for trains and aware of being exposed on top of the high banking. Lassie moved on ahead of me, and about a hundred yards distant I saw her halt beside something white between the railway lines. I knew it was an animal body of some kind and, because I did not want her to continue nosing it and, also fearing the worst, hurried over. As I drew close, I saw that it was indeed poor Beauty lying there. She was quite dead, and had been for some hours, probably at least a day. Quite deaf, she had neither seen nor heard the train coming toward her, and had obviously been struck.

Lassie knew that something was wrong, and spent more time than usual sniffing round the still form. Carefully, I picked up the sad little corpse, its fur still soft but its body stiff and cold, and carried it back to the farm to bury it.

Animals have a short memory for death, and Lassie seemed to forget Beauty after a day or so. But Beauty's sister, Sandra, missed her terribly. The two of them had been inseparable for almost all their lives, and throughout that first night she sat on the hayloft waiting for her to return, looking out into the darkness. All the next day she was agitated. But then, on the third day of Beauty's absence, mercifully she too appeared to forget. With Beauty finally gone from her mind, she now directed all her attention and affections on to Lassie.

Lassie grew ever more tolerant of her. One day, climbing the hayloft, I found them both together performing an amazing ritual. Cats normally groom one another, but it is a rare sight to see a cat groom a dog – it is a sign of very deep affection indeed. But there was Lassie, sitting very still, while Sandra washed her, licking her round her face and mouth. After that, Sandra often cleaned her. Apart from Lassie, she now had no other friend, and the two of them, when Lassie was home, became virtually inseparable. They could often be seen curled up together on the bed of hay they shared, and where no other cat dared to tread.

A few days later, working in the field while Lassie, as usual, lay quietly nearby, I noticed her rise and begin to slink away stealthily. I did not let her know I had seen her, and decided to follow her. Chance that day had mostly left me free from work. Keeping well out of her sight, I trailed her as she unhurriedly climbed the embankment, crossed the railway lines and walked over the next field – just as in the days of old. I was lucky, I realised, in having the dry autumn breeze blowing against me, preventing Lassie from scenting me too easily. With her above average sense of smell, stronger by far in her than in any other dog I had known, I had to be extremely careful, for a slight shift of wind could give me away.

She repeatedly paused to look over her shoulder, checking to see whether or not I had seen her and was following, but each time I managed to dodge down out of sight behind a hedge or a bush. She continued at the same casual pace across the fields, curving round in a wide arc. On at least one occasion I felt sure that she must have seen me, as she always seemed to do, but apparently not, for she continued on her course at the same leisurely pace. To my surprise, I realised she was heading toward Laurel Wood.

For some reason, today, I was not as concerned as I had been on earlier occasions about her being drawn back to the wild. In any case, Laurel Wood was scarcely the place to go to if she were. I could not think why she would want to come here now. After the erection of the housing state behind the wood, she had left it more or less alone, so it crossed my mind that she may have once again changed her resting-up place. She was still capable of being rather coy toward me. Irrationally, I thought, she might simply be playing a rather long and protracted game with my feelings. She knew I fretted after her, and I sometimes thought she went off like this deliberately to tease me. She was such an unpredictable, and bright dog, she could have been doing almost anything. Mona Lisa's enigmatic guise had nothing on this dog!

As Lassie moved to the wood, the vitality of her movement and the exceptional beauty of her coat, contrasted against the deep, dark green of the laurels, making her look quite exceptional. She walked with a very proud, high step, with head held high and her tail low. Her coat, which had long reached full maturity, was a slightly wavy, deep russet-red, and her full tail still looked like a fox brush. Her little ears were all the while pricked, scanning around for any suspicious sounds.

On reaching the wood, she halted. Repeatedly, she turned to face where I was hiding, standing motionlessly for a few moments, holding her head very high while moving it from side to side to test the air. Finally satisfied that she was undetected – or was she just playing with me again, knowing full well I was there?! – she wheeled round and slipped between the fencing into the tangle of green leaves and branches beyond. I gave her a moment, and then followed.

I passed slowly through the dark outer edge of evergreens, including yews and the odd holly tree as well as the laurels, and entered a bewildering world of colour. Amidst the inner decay were the deciduous trees and the tall bracken and bramble thickets, all aflame with copper, brown and gold. With all this foxy-coloured richness around I realised she would be even harder to see – then twigged that virtually every one of her great adventures had happened at this time of the year. Lassie was truly a child of the autumn. I could not see her at all. Helplessly, I began to search, realising as I did so that the sounds of breaking sticks and rustling leaves that I was making would notify her of my presence. There was no bird song to mask my progress this time. I made my way first to the pool, but she obviously had not been there. The pool's surface was calm, scattered with fallen leaves. Her beech trunk was deserted. Knowing that it was pointless to pretend secrecy, I began calling her name, "Lassssieeee, Lasssiiieeeee!", affectionately, in the hope that she would come out from wherever she had hidden herself. For half an hour or so, I searched what remained of the still quite substantial woodland. But Lassie did not respond.

In a somewhat piqued mood – for I knew she was in the wood, and had decided to ignore me – I was forced to leave her. This time she did not return home. Perhaps she had become cross with me for distrusting her, and had stubbornly decided to teach me a lesson; perhaps, now she knew she 'had' me she was taking her weird 'game' a stage further. The thought of losing her forever was driving me to distraction, and all sorts of crazy thoughts raced through my head!

This time, unusually, she stayed away for several days. She once more succeeded in filling my days (and by extension, my parent's and the farm's) with doubts and fears. If it was a Gawsworth day, I would race home from work at furious speed to check if she had returned. I felt sure that she was still in Laurel Wood, or its vicinity. I just had to find her, and so one afternoon made the time and set out again.

This time I was luckier. I had instinctively set out at the right moment, and hardly had I stepped into the wood than I caught sight of her returning from the field carrying a rabbit in her mouth. I moved quickly behind a tall beech tree, so she did not see me as I watched her pass closely by. She was moving very slowly and cautiously through the undergrowth, twice putting down the dead rabbit to test the air before continuing. Lassie was no foolish dog, but a true creature of the wild, with all the instincts necessary for survival. As I remained immobile behind my tree I felt sure that she was fully aware of my presence – yet she showed no signs that she knew. The 'game' continued, yet I felt little joy in it. Following her as silently as I could, I watched her veer to the left and press quickly through a large patch of shoulder-high bracken, out of sight.

In all, I had caught no more than a few moments' glimpse of her. That I had done so had been sheer fluke, and I congratulated myself on my good fortune. At least she was alive and well – so far, so good. I think I was also now beginning to sense the emergence of an answer to her behaviour, though it remained dimly unformed inside me, and I did not put two and two together. The main part of me was still as mystified as ever, yet thrilled with excitement that I was on the verge of a discovery so incredible that I dared not think, let alone voice it.

After waiting for some minutes, and hearing or seeing no further sign of her, I decided to venture into the bracken, and began pushing my way through the tall stems. Scarcely had I entered, than a magpie, perched in the branches above, began to chide me. They are always the first creature to sound the alert if intruders are near. Its loud, shrill, mocking sounds burst forth with every new movement I made, and reverberated throughout the wood. Probably this patch of bracken happened to be in her territory. My mood, suddenly darkening, with all my heart I cursed the fact. Damn the bird! Lassie would now know for certain that I was near. Fuming, I pushed my way further into the bracken, realising any further stealth was useless.

The ground in Laurel Wood is not completely flat. In parts it undulates, and here, beneath the briars and bracken, were many small hillocks and sandy banks. I moved as cautiously as I could over the uneven terrain, searching it for signs of Lassie's presence, while the bird above continued scolding me out of its domain. Almost immediately, I came across a giant ash tree lying on its side, almost completely enclosed by the bracken. By the state of the ferns, it looked as if it had fallen in the gales the winter before last. Walking along its length amidst the waving fronds, and examining both of its sides, I eventually came to its enormous roots, splayed wildly in the air. The tree had grown on one of the sandy banks, next to a tall companion – a beech – that was still standing. And here I stopped dead in my tracks, for beneath the roots of the ash I made out the unmistakable entrance to a fox earth. It was almost completely hidden from the outside world by the bracken. Around its mouth was an outpouring of freshly-dug soil. I was amazed, because I had never seen a fox earth in Laurel Wood before. I went nearer, to investigate, thinking it may be the badger's sett, whilst recalling that they could sometimes share with foxes. It only slowly dawned on me that perhaps Lassie might be down there – my earlier chaotic, barely-formed thoughts once more rushing to the surface!

Mesmerised, I got down on my hands and knees and crawled closer to the hole. At either side of me, the roots of the ash snaked frozenly out into the air, some of them still skinned white from the day when they had been ripped from the ground by the huge force of the toppling tree. The soil round about was a pale, sandy, reddish-coloured loam. It had been worked possibly only that day. My thoughts were confused and anxious.

Without thinking, I called down into the darkness of the lair, "Lassie, come on Lassie!" Instantly, something furry and furious shot up from the earth and snapped at my face, grazing my cheek. Jumping back, I saw Lassie's face glowering from the earth opening. Had I not been so used to dogs, and animals generally, I would not have reacted so swiftly, and would have been badly bitten. I felt an awful, paralysing shock grip me at the thought she – Lassie, my Lassie – would have bitten me!

She was in a terrible rage, snarling defiantly with curled lips and gleaming teeth, whilst her pale eyes blazed a deadly amber-green. I watched as though through a kind of unreal haze. I had never seen her so violently angry before, and on my account, of all people! Finding my senses, I reluctantly moved back from the scene. As I did so, her growling stopped, and she disappeared back into the blackness.

And still I did not put two and two together. Instead, my old fears, kept at bay by the churning hopes of that fine day, perhaps, suddenly rose up inside me. Here was the proof I most dreaded that Lassie had returned to the wild. She had approached such rage only with other humans, never so ferociously with me before. She had never even so much as growled at me since those early years. She had forgotten what I had meant to her. What hurt me so, was that she could forget me so easily, after eight years of friendship – me, who had given her so much of my life, and love. And these were my uppermost feelings as I turned away, sick at heart.

Certain that further intrusion would only result in a more severe attack, I withdrew from the bracken patch. But I could not bring myself to leave the wood, and hoped forlornly that she would reappear and realise her mistake. As the minutes went by, filled with a sense of black futility, I became convinced that our friendship was at an end.

I returned to the farm feeling frightened, bitter and perplexed. Our 'magic' wood had not cast its spell, as so often in the past; in fact the very opposite. Lassie had lived probably three-quarters of her life. Whatever had possessed her to behave again as a puppy? These thoughts, and darker ones, clouded my mind during the day and through the night. Would she ever return? If she did, would that mean that for the rest of her life, in spite of all that I had done for her, I could never be certain of her feelings for me?

Lassie, though a wayward will, had been my one close friend and companion. Now she had finally deserted me, I thought, as I fancied all the long years of patience and hard work crumbling away at my feet, to mean nothing.

Chapter Thirteen

THE NEXT morning, Lassie was home again. I became more confused than ever! She had obviously returned to the hayshed during the night. When I awoke, automatically the first thing I did was to rush down to see if she was there. Her behaviour towards me was indifferent – but that was not unusual, either, apart from in the circumstances. She appeared to have forgotten completely about last night's attack. But I couldn't stay to investigate further, or attend to her in my usual way, as I had to leave for work, simply contenting myself with the thought that she was back. So it was on my return at lunchtime that I climbed up to her bed with the usual bowl of milk. Normally, she would have enjoyed this, but instead of greeting me she growled menacingly. She did not move at all, but simply looked slightly cowed, with her ears flattened back, as she always did in a bad temper. I still could not believe what was happening, and extended the milk to her, crying out, "Why, whatever is the matter with you Lass?!"

She disdained the milk, and growled again. This time her hackles rose and she began to back away from me. I left the milk and began climbing down. I was almost as deeply wounded as I had been the day before, and as I had been when she had first been given to me and she had made her home beneath the turkey verandah. I found myself trying to put forward some reason for her behaviour, still clinging to the idea that she had become wild again. Now, she could not even simply share it with me, as she had being doing, but had to repel me instead. I thought something must have happened in Laurel Wood to force her to return to the farm, and she was here against her will. Nothing else I could think of made any sense. To imagine that the farm, the scene of so much that had passed between us, as alien to her was just too much to bear.

When I looked in her eyes, I could see nothing familiar, and had the uneasy feeling that, all along, I had simply put my own interpretation on a creature that was essentially living but which had no soul. It was as though a door had closed. There was no sparkle left in her. Being unable to understand, I decided that the best thing to do was to leave her alone. As I reached the bottom of the hayloft, another chilling thought occurred to me. She might now, in her head, not only have returned to the wild but also be mad. The conflict between my pull on her, and the draw of nature, might have been too much for her to withstand. Or was it the dreaded rabies, known to be spread by creatures like foxes?! My hand went involuntary to my scratched face. But no, she was not frothing at the mouth, the classic symptom of that awful disease. Still, I could not reason properly about her, or her behaviour in Laurel Wood, and even as the this latest fear sprang inside me Lassie leapt down from the hayshed and, ignoring me, quickly left the farm again for the open countryside.

A whole week went by, and she did not return. I did not try to interfere by going to the wood to coax her from her retreat. I decided that if she wanted to come home, she would do so of her own accord and, if not, she must remain there – forever, if that was what she wanted. I could not stand the pain of rejection, and did not wish to risk it happening to me again. At the same time, I was disillusioned that I had become reduced to this kind of self-protective and selfish person. But I was helplessly caught up in my emotions, and could find no way out of them.

When dusk succeeded dusk, and there was still no sign of her returning, when I started to think the wonderful friendship I had found with her was over for good, I was shaken from my despondency by the sight of a shape I thought was Lassie slipping through the farmyard, carrying something like a rabbit in its mouth. It was evening, and all was quiet and, because there was no sign of her on the hayshed, I decided that I must have been mistaken. I had just finished closing the poultry houses, and was about to retire for the night. Just as I was about to leave for the house, I heard a weak squeaking sound coming from high above in the hay bales. Listening intently through the still air, I again heard the cries, repeated quite clearly. I walked hurriedly back to the barn door, and took the ladder from its place by the hay bay. Positioning it by flashlight, I climbed up into the darkness.

The squeaking sounds had stopped as soon as I made my approach, and I reached the top of the hay bales in total silence. I waited in the darkness, and was about to return down the ladder when the noises started up again. They were coming from the direction of Lassie's bed. I shone my torch in that direction, and was astonished by what its white rays picked out. A tiny, black, squirming animal, the like of which I had not seen before, lay illuminated in the electric light. At first glance it looked like a newborn kitten, but its size, and the loudness of its cries, belied that. Could it be a puppy? Crawling toward the little mite, I saw that it was indeed a puppy, only a few days old. Its eyes were still unopened, and it was obviously feeling very alone and sorry for itself.

The shape I had seen slinking through the gloom must have been Lassie, but still I could not work out what was happening, for the emotions that were necessary for insight were still blocked, too deeply, inside me. Instead, I thought what on earth was it she was up to? Where had she got the puppy from, and what was she planning to do with it? Scarcely had these thoughts crossed my mind than Sandra, the old cat, appeared on the scene. Also attracted by the cries, she hurried by me to see what had happened. Immediately, she plumped herself down next to the little dog and started to mother and wash it. Knowing that it was no longer alone, and soothed by her attention, the puppy snuggled close to the old cat's warm fur, and its whimpering stopped. I was becoming more amazed by the moment – and suddenly, the feelings that I had blocked for so long, deep inside, me began to rush up. If Sandra, who distrusted the smell of strange dogs, was prepared instantly, without qualms, to mother this pup, then…?!

My thoughts abruptly returned to Lassie. Could this tiny creature really be hers? It seemed too incredible to be true yet, as true thought and feeling finally connected, a faintness gripped me and would not go away. My head swam. Could this puppy be the reason for Lassie's unfriendliness toward me? Could she have given birth there, in the wild, just as her own mother had done all those years before? The sight of her carrying the rabbit to the foxhole, of putting the rabbit down to sniff the air to make sure she was alone and safe, her maternal aggression toward me at the foxhole itself – all these images rushed vividly back as the correct interpretation was made. Climbing down the ladder, clutching the flash-lamp, I suddenly began to feel like a prize clot for not having read the signs sooner. I had barely reached the ground, still with the torch in my hand and dizzy with the revelation, when Lassie reappeared and swept passed me with yet another tiny puppy dangling by its scruff from her mouth. Before I could say anything to her she had leapt up the hayshed and disappeared.

It became clear to me now why Lassie had been so secretive these last few months, and so angry when her chosen earth had been discovered. She had found what she thought was a secure place, not too far from home to bring her firstborn into the world – and where more convenient in this respect than Laurel Wood? Even with the encroachment of the housing, the wood was still kept tightly enclosed by the farmer, and it fulfilled the qualification of being close at hand. It was also, in my newly kindled romantic mind, very special to us both, and bridged our worlds.

The tension of the week fell off me as I stood at the bottom of the ladder and I laughed outright in joy – though I still could not fully accept this miraculous occurrence, happening in her approaching old age and after all her years of apparent infertility. Why, I had never even noticed her being in season! I had wanted her so much to have children. In a fit of selfish pique, jealous of her wildwood and fearful it would reclaim her, when puppies did not come I had punished myself, and buried my feelings, and refused even to look at the evidence when it was pushed right in front of my nose.

The night, so gloomy and oppressive a few moments before, no longer pressed in on me. As it must always have seemed to Lassie on her night runs, when she was released from the human pressures of the daylight hours, my own life now once again felt immensely open to possibility and adventure, and I ran and danced excitedly about in the yard, caught up in the spirit of the wild. Oh, Lassie darling, you've done it again! Taken me from the depths of despair to the heights of joy! Eventually, I ran off the boundless energy that filled me, that tied me with the night, and with nature, and when I had calmed I returned to the hay barn and waited at the bottom for Lassie to reappear with the rest of her litter – for I felt certain that there must be others. While I stood waiting, I relived in my mind the physical changes that had happened to Lassie that could possibly shed light on the happy event. But I searched in vain for a clue to her condition that I might have missed. Never for one moment had Lassie seemed pregnant, except in the telltale signs of her behaviour that I had so wrongly interpreted, yet here the fact was – a mother, for the very first time, and at nearly eight years old! Incredible!

The scene I encountered in the night fields, five years earlier, when Lassie had been amongst that ring of foxes, sprang vividly to my mind. Since the moment I had seen Sandra mothering the first puppy, I had been thinking about who the father might be. To my knowledge, Lassie had never once allowed a strange dog near her – she had certainly not cultivated any friendships among the dogs on the farm. They were merely tolerated, possibly for my sake, and kept at a distance. I could not imagine that my mother's aging Corgi, Rusty – the only male dog we in fact possessed at the time – could have been responsible! That only left the foxes, in whom she had been interested, and had always secretly encouraged. Then, there was the puppies' very dark colouration, which would only gradually change to red – if they were from a Red Fox ...

As I waited at the foot of the hay barn, and the time dragged on, I grew concerned about the fate of the other puppies, still feeling sure there must be more than two. I expected their mother to appear once more in the darkness. I was in a dilemma. I could not go up to the hayloft again because I sensed my presence was not yet wanted. On the other hand, if I went to bed I would miss the chance of coaxing Lassie into finishing her duty and retrieving the rest of her litter, which might otherwise perish.

Hard as it was, I did not disturb Lassie or the puppies further, but went to bed. I slept soundly, content in the knowledge that Lassie had not only returned but had returned with her children. She had decided to give up her wild lair, where her instincts had led her, and return with her family into my trust. For the first time in what seemed like ages I drifted off into sleep. I was up at the crack of dawn, to see if the small family was still there. Fortunately, my work that day was on the farm, and so I could afford more time. At the top of the hayloft I was reassured by the heart-warming sight of

Lassie, her coat a resplendent blaze of red, lying on her side in the hay and suckling the nearly-black puppies. There were still only two of them, both females from what little I could make out at the distance, after much careful peering and head craning. Their coats were very sleek-looking, their eyes tightly closed, and I realised that Lassie must have waited only to give birth before returning immediately to me.

Hearing me climb up the bales made Lassie raise her head, and growl a warning in my direction. This was nothing like her infuriated snarl of a week ago, and in a soothing voice I spoke slowly and regularly to her. The growls subsided. Accepting my presence, Lassie protectively curled her head round and over the little mites by her side who, now having drank their fill, were on the verge of falling asleep. Lassie looked peaceful and placid, but watched me warily the whole time. She seemed to accept the fact that I would not harm her puppies, but left me in no doubt that she would defend them if necessary. Once more her two natures were on show, and once more, I was happy to let that be – for now.

Sandra had stayed with them all night, in a perfectly amazing extension of her role in her relationship with Lassie. For a bitch to allow a cat such complete involvement with her litter, must be almost unheard of. She sat next to them like a nursemaid, while every so often Lassie raised her head and washed them. Feeling that I could do nothing to help, and that it was just a question of time before Lassie's protective maternal aggression receded, I climbed down the bales and happily left them to it.

I breakfasted like a king, after informing my amazed parents of the good news, and immediately afterward set out to the foxhole in the bracken patch in Laurel Wood, armed with a spade. I trusted Lassie's good sense implicitly, and did not expect to find further puppies, but it was unusual for there to be only two. Normally, a collie will have four or five, and sometimes up to eight. A fox usually has four, and so a litter of two would more closely approximate that. On the other hand, Lassie's age could have accounted for the small number. But I had to make certain that there had not been others who had somehow perished, or been otherwise forgotten.

Boldly this time, for there was no reason for me to be otherwise – even out-whistling the scolding magpie with the latest pop hits – I pushed my way through the bracken, and soon arrived at the lair's entrance. It looked quite ordinary now, in the cold light of new knowledge. When I thought about how, inside it and perhaps alone, she had undergone her labour, possibly in fear of the consequences of what was happening to her, it seemed a sad little spot.

The lair was now obviously uninhabited, but I could not decide whether it was a real foxhole, or whether she had built it herself, although I was certain that it was she who had newly enlarged it. The prints around it were muddled and indecisive, as Lassie's slender foot could possibly have been mistaken for a fox's, but it was not the sort of soil for retaining a clear print. I put my ear to the entrance, and then pressed it to the bank above it, but could hear no sound at all. Methodically, I began digging out the earth. After a great deal of strenuous activity I reached the earth's nesting chamber, which was completely empty. I was now confident that there had only been two puppies born to Lassie. Yes, I should just have trusted her...

All that day Lassie remained with her puppies, never once leaving them alone. Whenever I could leave my work, I checked on them. Knowing that the puppies were the only two, I felt safe in regarding them with great pride and joy. Sandra and Lassie continued to take the greatest care of them. Whatever fears Lassie might have had, here in the hayloft she had taken naturally to motherhood. She did not know what I knew – that almost exactly eight years previously her own mother had done exactly the same thing. She had given birth in the wild, in what she had considered to be a safe place. And many times it went through my mind that perhaps Lassie had done this for the same reason, to see them born safely, away from men, away from everything human. And, perhaps – because the father was also a Red Fox.

Teddy & Llyn

Chapter Fourteen

THE PUPPIES grew rapidly and, most surprisingly, seemed to be twins. My parents were as astonished as I was by this rare fact, coming as it did after the unusualness of their mother's late pregnancy, and both were more than normally interested in them. After ten days, the puppies' eyes began to open. Although they would not have been able to see much at first, they saw enough to make them feel like walking, and by two weeks were on their shaky little legs and stumbling into one another in the hay. They were about six inches in length, much bigger and fatter than they had been at birth. Their dark, almost black colouration was now revealed to be a very dark red. As all very young puppies do, even foxes, they had blue eyes.

As soon as they began walking, they started to need a supplement to their mother's milk. In the wild, this would have been provided by the father, who would have hunted for solid food while the mother suckled and rested at home, and it occurred to me that perhaps this was the reason Lassie had brought the pups to me. She had not paired-off in that sense, and no father – whoever, and whatever he was – was available. In the circumstances, I helped out. At three weeks I was providing three bowls of milk a day – extra to Lassie's mother's milk – which I gave to them in the morning, at lunchtime and in the evening.

Apart from these regular visits with milk, and periodic checks to see that all was well, the family of puppies with its odd combination of parents, had to be left much to its own devices. Lassie preferred it this way, and it suited my work schedules. The only worry I had was that, whilst playing, one of the puppies might accidentally fall the twenty or so feet to the ground. During the next week, as they grew bigger, this anxiety of mine increased. At four weeks they were scampering and tumbling about quite dangerously, though they always seemed to know how far they could go without coming to harm.

For the first time ever, I managed to get Lassie to eat cooked meat regularly. She was at a disadvantage, having the pups to look after. With the puppies' milk, I brought an extra bowl in the mornings and evenings for Lassie. In the evenings I just brought her the meat. The food was sometimes received rather disdainfully. She never gushed over it, and would not gobble it, as other dogs would have done. Instead she looked at it, smelled it over, and finally picked out little bits – as though to say to me, "What is this substandard food you insist on giving to me? You've got to be kidding!"

As soon as she was able to leave her family for short periods, she was off hunting again. She also returned to doing farm work, coming back to the nest only at feeding times. She was not able to leave all that often at first, but it soon became obvious she was getting bored with the endless lying about and the demands made on her by the tussling youngsters, and yearned to get back to her usual life.

On her farm rounds she helped me in all the old things, and showed keen interest in my work. It was hard to imagine that she had puppies waiting for her up in the hayloft! There were two beneficiaries of this 'new' Lassie. One was myself, for I was as pleased as Punch with her return to the farm and the birth of her daughters. I continued to feel quite ridiculous about the way I had misread her, and the near-hysterics I had undergone. No amount of embarrassment and depression could put me off the collie I loved, and now all the recent past was swept aside, just as though it had been a bad dream. I was now doubly assured of her loyalty to me. With every change in her life it seemed that a new threat to our relationship was posed, but I was beginning to realise that the threats were in my imagination alone. I swore to myself that I would not be caught out again the next time, and fall victim to the awful doubts that had plagued me.

The other beneficiary was little Sandra. When Lassie departed the hayloft during the day she was left entirely to her own devices, and loved nothing more than to take over the responsibility of mothering the pups. She immediately moved into the nest, and covered the puppies, who now had the best of both worlds – a fond mother and a doting nursemaid! They could be quite naughty with her, and at wash-times went mad trying to escape, but she would hold them down firmly with her paws, whilst licking them all over.

Waiting until Lassie had gone one day, I crept up to the hayloft, and was greeted by the two friendly little creatures. They were pleased to be seen and handled – quite the reverse of their mother in her puppyhood, who had been virtually abandoned in early puppyhood, and had grown up rightly afraid. They behaved like ordinary puppies. They wagged their tails, especially when I brought them up to me, as I had done regularly since not long after their removal to the farm, and talked and played with them. At first, Lassie was clearly ambivalent about me doing this, but I had decided, after long and careful thought, that they had to become used to me handling and controlling them, for the thought of three wild dogs eventually roaming free was just too much to contemplate! I did not do it too often at first, allowing Lassie to slowly grow used to the idea. To my delight, she now let me do what I wished, and eventually even allowed my parents to handle them. My intention now was a slightly more daring one, though. They were six weeks old, and their size was quite enormous by comparison with what they had been. I had seen them waddling about the edge of the hayloft, peering down from their dangerously high elevation, and I decided I had to get them down.

Carefully I carried first one, and then the other, down the ladder and onto the hay at the bottom. I immediately offered them some warm milk, which they greedily gulped-down. Sandra came down with them, to see that they were alright. I waited to see what would happen. When Lassie came home, and saw her family on the ground I expected her to snatch them up and replace them on the hayshed. Instead, she did nothing of the kind, but simply lay down beside them and fed and tended them as normal, joining in the frequent feeds which I brought them. All I had to provide was a low barrier of hay bales to prevent them wandering about the farmyard for the time being, but not deny Lassie access.

Whether Lassie, with her cunning, wild ways and her undeniable attraction to foxes, was a fox-dog hybrid, might have been debatable, but probably, if their behaviour was any guide, her puppies were not. Both were friendly, normal little pups who, so far, fingers crossed, lacked their mother's waywardness. The fact did not bother me. On the contrary, I welcomed it, and I made up my mind to keep them both.

The puppies loved human company – everyone's, not just mine – and would rush forward at the slightest sound of my voice. My parents took to them straight away, and were soon playing regularly with them. Unfortunately, Lassie resented such openness on her offspring's part. She had protected them from my parents during their weeks in the hayloft, growling at my father when he had tried to see them. Now they had been brought down she had less control over them, and soon realised that threatening tactics to thwart this tenderness in her pups, wouldn't work. Instead, she devised a more subtle ploy, demonstrating just how inventive and clever she was. She would 'spook' them. There had been moments through her life when she would respond to some invisible presence, or signal, rise suddenly, and walk up and down, uneasily, listening and looking, or stop what she was doing and pay intense attention to some sound or impression undetectable to humans. At such moments there was no reasoning with her. She did it so often that I grew used to it happening.

"Lassie is spooked tonight," I would I say to my parents.

When the pups came along, and she found she could not get her own way with them, she did this more often. It occurred so regularly in their presence that I began to suspect that craft was involved, and it was her way of keeping control. It seemed that she was deliberately trying to draw the attention of her puppies to her own wild world, beyond the confines of the farm and away from human influence. The puppies would watch her, but it was plainly evident that they could not hear or feel whatever it was. It meant nothing to them, at least at this early stage, and they soon resumed their playing.

Animals compromise about how they want their children to be, just like human parents have to do. Their children are pulled by a different world to the one their parents grew up in, and reluctantly a compromise is made. Lassie instinctively knew this, as she instinctively knew her wildwood, and though their lack of respect for her ways bothered her a great deal, she did let this affect her duties to them. She knew they needed regular feeds, and what the best way to provide them was – by eating lots of wild rabbits herself, despite my provision of extras.

The puppies followed their mother everywhere, and although they could not do certain things themselves, they would watch her and learn from her example. They would watch her ratting, and even made one or two cautious attempts themselves. During the days when I was present, the whole family would follow me about the farm, doing and learning. If they got into difficulties, Lassie would come to their aid – she was always very aware of their presence and needs – but apart from this, and her spooking attempts, she remained more or less as she had always done, except she drew the line at playing with them. When they tried to clamber on her, or run at her, she sidestepped, and left them playing together. She was far too quick for them, and eventually their attempts to get her to join-in became less frequent, until they stopped altogether. They mostly played with each other, jumping on one another, rolling and rushing about, and biting, just like ordinary puppies. One minute they would be friendly, but then one or other of them would nip a bit too hard, and they would have a little fight, which would usually peter out within a few minutes. Tempers wore down quickly. They grew tired and went to sleep together and, when they awoke, incidents would be forgotten.

Whenever I had the time, I got down on my hands and knees and romped about with them myself. By this time they had grown too old for Sandra. Cats normally dislike being jumped on, and when the puppies tried to show their rough affection to her, she would now turn on them and scuff them. She would show them the power of her paw! Sadly, her little duties were largely over.

The puppy's fun and frolics knew no bounds. They had to be constantly watched. If we let them, they would play with the chickens, chasing them about the farm unmercifully. And they were not shy of larger animals. They would get up to all sorts of naughty things. As time passed, they became increasingly physically alike.

They were now very gangly. Their legs were longer, and faces and noses had become more elongated. Their coats, still fluffy, had become lighter, though they had not yet reached their mother's beautiful chestnut colour.

They yapped instead of squeaked. At eight weeks they had increased their strength tremendously, and were growing even as I looked at them, and were becoming increasingly difficult to tell apart. They were becoming independent of Lassie too, and though in most respects Lassie had been the perfect mother to them, she now spent less time with them. She became angry if they made the mistake of trying to jump on her. She had, of course, intended to teach them her wild ways, but they were too normal to take notice. Although this 'normality' actually pleased me, as I now had the best of both worlds, I still found myself wondering whether they were as normal as they looked – did it mean their father couldn't have been a fox, despite Lassies antipathy to dogs? Their cautious attempts at ratting proved nothing, for 'normal' dogs will all naturally hunt from a very early age, as will cats. Once again, Lassie had me sitting on a very sharp fence!

Their markings, and even their behaviour, were confusingly similar. It occurred to me, for the first time, that not only were they twins, two sisters, but they might also be identical twins. If true, this was a greater rarity still. The birth of only two puppies is unusual enough for a collie-type dog, but the birth of true twins is extremely uncommon, and has only rarely been recorded.

About this time, David Hopkins, my latest vet (James Cooke having retired), examined the pups and was amazed to find himself agreeing that they were identical twins. Much later, in their old age, he was even more emphatic about this, and wrote an article about an identical operation carried out on the dogs, just twenty-four hours apart, for a leading British veterinary journal.

Like James Cook, and others before him, he had been inspired by Lassie, and followed her developments with keenness. He was not the farm vet – my father still had Drs Wright and Monroe, who specialised in farm animals. David, like his predecessor, dealt with small domestic animals and pets, and helped me care for my small 'zoo' – the various strays and lame creatures I still harboured, and the exotic poultry I kept, or looked after, at Gawsworth. He was a young married man, who had qualified and then come north, and this was his first practice. He had run it for ten years, building up a big reputation for himself. I had recently changed to him, and never regretted the change. He showed concern for his animals, and was kind to them, and had a fund of common sense. He kept an open mind about Lassie's heritage, his attitude being that the chances of her being a hybrid were "probably improbable"(!). The birth of puppies, whose behaviour was normal, strengthened his opinion, though it did not disincline him to believe that Lassie and her puppies were unique.

One of the reasons David was astonished, was because of the rarity of twins, let alone identical twins, in collies, or any dogs, that usually all have large litters. It had been two hundred years since a documented case had occurred. The Macclesfield Express, who had always kept an eye on Lassie's progress, took up the case. They published an updated story of Lassie, covering the birth of the now officially recognised identical twins. Once again, she was a celebrity, and the publicity brought a flood of fan mail from animal lovers and well-wishers.

The puppies' behaviour grew to be almost totally empathetic, and convinced me that they were identical.

They always followed suit – what one did, the other did – and they could not be parted without a great deal of upset. They were inseparable, and soon, only I, by close observation of small differences in their bone structure, could tell them apart.

I had not yet named them because, although I had decided to keep them, I wanted to be absolutely sure I was. When further delays in naming them added to the confusion, I decided to call them Lynn and Teddy, after previous dogs belonging to my parents, although breaking our tradition of never reusing names. I think I was also holding out an olive branch to my parents, after all the upsets Lassie had caused, directly or not!

Both puppies were now assuming Lassie's unique flaming-red coat, and were obviously destined to be very like her in looks – though they did not have their mother's bushy fox-tail 'brush'; theirs were straight, with short fur. I began to settle down very nicely with the thought of keeping this happy, unusual little family exactly as it was when, once again, my father dropped one of his bombshells. One of the dogs would have to go. We had seven dogs in total, including my mother's Corgis, and he declared the farm was unable to support all of them. I argued, of course, that the two identical puppies could not be separated, but there was no avoiding the fact that, chronologically speaking, they had least right to remain.

Chapter Fifteen

I RELUCTANTLY decided that Teddy would have to be the one to go. In spite of the similarity in behaviour between her and Lynn, there were quite marked differences in temperament. Teddy was the most boisterous and the most self-assertive, whereas Lynn was more inward. She was more demure and quiet, and nervous. I decided that the strain of separation would be felt most strongly by her, and wanted to make sure that she got the extra care she needed.

Nevertheless, it was a terrible decision to have to make, bearing in mind their obvious closeness, and one that brought me a great deal of misery. Perhaps, I felt, my father was taking his revenge for all the years he had to put up with Lassie.... Then there was the ongoing friction between my parents, possibly adding grist to one of Father's 'hard' periods. He was currently in one of his farm reductionist moods, and also had his landscaping work to consider. Once more, we had too many of this animal, too many of that bird – even though, like the Landrace he bought, it was he who was responsible for the numbers and expense of the major animals!

I did not sell Teddy, but gave her to friends of the family, who lived in Carn, in Wiltshire. When the day arrived for her departure I grew extremely mournful.

To avoid unnecessary pain between the pups – and myself – I abruptly gathered Teddy up and took her to my van, popped her in a box, and drove off. Lassie and Lynn stayed behind.

The new owners, a young couple who we had known for many years, were friends of mine rather than of my parents. Like us, they were livestock owners, and so I felt that I was leaving Teddy in good hands. When I arrived I found that they had gone to the trouble of erecting wire netting around the garden to prevent the new puppy from wandering into danger. They seemed to be responsible people, and my troubled mind was somewhat calmed – but my thoughts kept racing ahead to the awful moment when I must leave Teddy to her fate, and then to the moment when I returned home, there to find a grieving mother and sister.

After seeing to Teddy's welfare as best as I could, I departed, too depressed to tell my friends the story of Lassie. They would never know, in Teddy, what a special dog they had got.

I missed poor Teddy, as did Lassie, but neither of us felt the loss as much as Lynn. From the moment of separation, her introverted nature worsened. She developed a nervous streak, and became shy and more withdrawn, a complete reversal of her happy, self-assured days of puppyhood when she had played in such innocence with her sister. She was of training age, and I thought she would learn quickly from Lassie, but her cautious first attempts, taken earlier with Teddy, were not developed. Disappointingly, she even refused to try to help work the livestock, despite every encouragement. I tried to coax her with kindness, but she was just not interested. She became the kind of dog who, if she was told to do something and she made a mistake, would interpret it as a sign of defeat. If I then raised my voice to her, not to shout at her but to urge her to try again, she would mistake this for a reprimand, and would put her head down and leave. She liked the hay barn and, like Lassie before her when she wanted to escape, would retreat to its safety.

She would not go up to the hayloft, which was still Lassie's domain, but to the stable next door – Samson's stall. After she and Teddy had been brought down from their first home in the loft, I had arranged the spare stall into a sleeping quarter. I had laid down plenty of straw to make the puppies comfortable. Mindful of my experience with the fire, I always left the door open so that they were free to run in and out. She now slept in the house kitchen at nights, but had grown to think of the stable as a daytime retreat.

After a few days of searching, Lassie resigned herself to the fact Teddy had gone, as most animals will. She wore a rather slack, blank look, as she searched around the hay bay and all about the farm. She always wore this look when worried. It was not so much an expression, as a lack of her usual intenseness. She looked down, slightly battered. When she eventually gave up her search, she turned her attention back to her normal interests – and to Lynn.

She had long ago proved that she was the farm's best ratter, and now looked to her daughter to be her partner. Whenever her mother was about, Lynn would always stay with her, and should have learned to catch rats, but had no inclination. When Lassie tried to get her to, she remained seated, and allowed both rats and mice to escape unharmed. Lassie grew very frustrated with this, her mood made the worse because often there would be a wire net fence between them – Lassie would be on one side, Lynn on the other – and the rodents would run through the wire to Lynn's side and get clean away. Lassie would be left on the wrong side of the netting, unable to intervene. For this, she often scorned her daughter.

This went on for some time until, early one morning, just after breakfast, Lynn was finally forced to act. Knowing that a rat was hiding beneath a chicken coop where she could not reach it without help, Lassie came running to attract my attention. I walked to the spot, lifted up one end of the heavy coop, and discovered two large rats nestling there. Lassie immediately shot beneath and killed one of them. The second rat, however, escaped, and ran straight into the path of Lynn, who was standing by watching. The rat jumped up at her and bit her between the eyes, and for a second – but for what to me seemed to be an age of time – it hung on to the puppy's face. She must have been badly bitten, for she yelped loudly at the unexpected shock of the pain. But then, in a sudden fury her temper rose. She rolled her head on the grass between her paws, dislodged the rodent, and sank her teeth into its body. Though she had not been injured badly, from that day on, Lynn, like Lassie, would kill any rat on sight. In the same way as her mother before her, she had been forced to make her first kill, and had learned the lesson the hard way. I was secretly pleased, though knew there was still a long way to go with training her.

Ironically, within six months of Teddy leaving, our Corgi, Rusty, and the Alsatian, Zena, died of old age. Rusty became thin and weak, and could scarcely walk. At fifteen years of age, we had to put him to sleep. Zena hung on a few weeks longer, but died younger, at ten years old – the average age for Alsatians, often weakened by inbreeding. Like Rusty, Zena first lost weight, but with her, the fatal problem was heart trouble. She became quite poorly, and my father, whose favourite she was, spent lavishly on her in a vain attempt to put her right. She too had to be put down. My father grieved over her more than any other animal but, practical man that he was, quickly got over her death.

Sad as it was for all of us, both dogs had lived good long lives by way of compensation. But now I wished that we had never let Teddy go. I began to think how stupid I had been to give in without more of a fight. I had let her go, and now our old dogs were dying off. I could have kept her so very easily, had I but reasoned it out more objectively, and presented the hard facts of the dog's ages to Father – as he so often presented such hard facts to us.

During the weeks that followed, I found that my heart went out to Teddy more frequently. I had made the decision not to see her, in order to protect everyone's feelings, but now I found myself aching to reverse this decision. Usually going on holiday with Mother, this year I decided to holiday alone, in Bournemouth, although I did take Lynn, who always needed reassurance, whilst Lassie, firmly back in her old hunting pattern, was far more capable of handling separation. I don't think that it was any coincidence that on my way back

I decided to call at my friends', in Carn, to see how Teddy was progressing.

Almost as though fate intended, I arrived in time to save Teddy. Far from being well looked after, she was dirty and uncombed, and thin, quite unlike the pretty, well-fed puppy I had so trustingly let go. The couple had had a baby, and after the baby was born had neglected the dog. They were due to move to a flat where dogs were not welcome, and told me they had been about to let her go again. They were unaware of her condition. I was terribly shocked, and there and then I put her in the van and took her back with me to the farm. Lynn and Teddy were reunited straight away, in Wiltshire, and spent the journey totally absorbed in each other, and most of the way home the back of the van rocked with relieved delight!

Fortunately, Teddy's condition soon repaired; I had caught her in time. But I was shocked to realise that she had been treated so indifferently, and by friends whom I had trusted. I was overjoyed to have her back, and so was Lassie. I expected some hostility at re-introducing her, for animals quickly forget their own offspring, and often resent them. Not so with this happy little family, who seemed to recognise her immediately. Teddy was fully accepted by both Lynn and Lassie, as though she had never been away, and I am absolutely certain they all remembered each other. I could not have brought just any dog home without Lassie attacking it, so I was certain, by the friendly acceptance Teddy received, she recognised her.

Within a few days, Teddy looked a different dog, and was ever ready to learn from me and to please me. Lynn quickly changed her ways again, and her shyness and withdrawal receded. The two sisters were devoted to each other once again, and I marveled at this wonderful change.

Identical twins often need each other's company, and in this case the shock of splitting up had accounted for Lynn's strange behaviour. Together again, with Lassie to guide them, they quickly learned how to drive both cattle and sheep. Proof, as if I needed it, that Lynn's aversion to work had been both temporary and psychological.

Teddy slept with Lynn in the kitchen in two large wicker dog baskets, whilst Lassie, as before, remained alone up in the quiet of the hayloft. Her habits of a lifetime, and her preference for the wild, would not be broken, and try as I often did to coax her inside the house she was quite unresponsive, even though the pull of her more domesticated daughters must have been strong. She would stand at the open door to wait for tidbits of food, but would go no further, quite unlike the twins, who depended wholly upon human welfare. Lassie was to remain to the end an aloof law unto herself, with a preference for independence, and an alert ear to the call of the fields and woods.

At nine months, Lynn and Teddy were the same size as their mother, and looked very attractive. Their coats had turned almost the same lovely hot red. Their eyes, at first blue, had changed, and were now a warm brown – in marked contrast to Lassie's. All three, when they stood together in a row, made a marvelous portrait for the camera.

On walks, they were a lively and energetic trio. To vary my routine, I would occasionally take the twins on walks further afield, in a new van I had bought. Before going on holiday, I had sold my old car and bought a more practical Mini van. When the Minis came out in 1960 they came in two colours, either bright orange or bright green. I couldn't get a green one, and so had to settle for orange. For three days a week I continued to drive back and forth to the poultry farm in Gawsworth, and from time to time needed transport to get away and carry various things, as well as dogs. The twins took to the idea of being conveyed right from the start. But not so Lassie, who still disliked traffic of any kind.

It was now summer, 1962, and Lassie was in her ninth year. The farm was doing well. The decade which began in the mid-Fifties and ended around the mid-Sixties was the best there had been since before the war, and most of these years were good for us. As in the world outside, we had "never had it so good", to quote a well-known politician of the times. My father, in one of his rare, expansive moods, decided that the time was right to erect a new poultry house, and increase our production of eggs.

The house, a large wooden structure, was erected by hands hired from a larger farm nearby, and took two days to complete. During their tea break on the second day, one of the labourers decided for a reason of his own to inspect the farm buildings, and on his way passed the hayshed. There, he came face to face with Lassie. Mistrusting him, just as she did most people, she growled, laying flat her ears and showing the whites of her eyes, as she always did when angered. Before I could shout out a warning to the man, he had picked up a length of wood and aimed a blow at her. The blow, of course, never landed for, as he raised his arm to strike it, as quick as an arrow, Lassie flew forward and sank her teeth into his wrist. The man did not know what had hit him, and took several moments to come to his senses. By this time I had got Lassie off him, and undoubtedly she would have savaged him badly, or even tried to kill him, for she was in a blazing temper. When the incident was over, a heated argument took place between the men and my father, but it was eventually decided that the man had been in the wrong by trespassing where he had not been meant to go. He was sent home and the matter taken no further. But it proved to us two things. Despite her age, if unduly provoked Lassie could still attack effectively, and belatedly proved to my father her prowess as a farm guard dog. From that day forward she officially took over the treasured position once adopted by faithful old Zena.

Once more, autumn rolled around, and for once it was a quiet one. I badly needed a break from the roller-coaster ride that Lassie so often put me through! The twins were now fully one year old, identical in mind and body. I remained the only one to consistently tell them apart. They could be distinguished from their mother by their brown eyes and slightly smaller bodies, for although the same height as Lassie, they were slightly slimmer, not having reached the same body weight. Lassie was distinguished further by her bushy foxtail, and by a small line of silver round her mouth – one of the few signs of her age. Because she no longer wished to expend the same amount of energy as she had done when she was younger, her more sedate and calmer behaviour was another distinguishing point.

Their intelligence and excellent manners made them a joy to behold, making me so very proud of them. They would do anything I told them to, and were quick to learn, and rarely needed to be shown twice. The youthful boisterousness of the twins had more or less gone, and they would no longer steal food from the cats or knock them out of the way whilst feeding.

I would not let them hunt with Lassie, because of the risk of their causing damage. One dog on its own, self-trained to avoid the dangers, was acceptable, but three roaming around together, as in human groups, might have caused them to behave irresponsibly, and would have quite rightly raised concern in the farming community. The mere sight of three dogs in a field, running or not, would have spooked the sheep. The dogs might have egged one another on to do the unexpected, and chase them, and even running harmlessly amongst sheep could have got the dogs shot. Although Lassie still very occasionally tried to get them to accompany her, to train them in the ways of the wild, I continued to sternly forbid it. They accepted my ruling. The twins themselves showed little inclination, although occasionally, on walks, all three would hunt rabbit together. For this they had a set routine worked out – or at least Lassie did! While the twins raced straight after the rabbit, barking madly, Lassie would run wide of them and catch the rabbit as it turned. Only she would eat the flesh. For the other two, reared largely on cooked meat, the taste was too strong. It was another of the marked differences between mother and offspring, and another I welcomed – I didn't want them getting the taste for wild game, and wandering off to hunt, with or without her!

In spite of the fact that they were an exceptionally close family unit, Lassie reserved, and strictly maintained, her right of dominance. She was territorially inclined, even to her Lynn and Teddy. Neither of the twins would dare to go up to her on the hayshed, or go near her whilst she ate her own meal. If they did so by accident, she would go for them straight away, with no growling or warning. On the other hand, it was considered to be quite alright for her to walk up to them and to push her way into their meal if she so desired!

Her sense of territory was far more acute than that of other dogs I had known. She regarded the whole of the farm as hers, and defended it up to its last square inch. And she knew every inch, although she never contested the ground outside it. She would allow no other animals entry. If other dogs strayed onto it, they were attacked. On the farm itself, there was still no fighting. She was the undisputed boss. There was a strong pecking order – with her at the top. The twins, naturally, respected their mother, and made way for her to lead.

Chapter Sixteen

LIFE CONTINUED in this largely peaceful and uneventful fashion for a further year. With the domestic bliss resulting from Lassie's unexpected entry into motherhood, I scarcely registered the social changes in the outside world: 'Ban the Bomb', the death of favourite film star Marilyn Monroe and, biggest of all, the explosive arrival of the Beatles. The protest movements and expressions of individuality seemed to be happening in another world, whereas I was in a bubble, insulated from the changes that were going on. Lassie continued to be a wayward individual herself, still hunting as she chose, and devoting her life between me and the wild world she had always known. As always, it was mainly on her terms, but we both wanted to keep things as they were, and resist any change.

Alas, all too soon this was to change dramatically, leaving big scars on us all. Several of the animals I had grown up with had already died, and now Trixie, our faithful old Corgi died suddenly, leaving us with just the three collies. She had lived in the house all her life, and was the last of my mother's Corgis. She passed away at the comparatively old age of twelve, from a heart attack brought on by her age. The attack happened in the morning and, after it, she was unable to get up. In the afternoon, when it became evident that she would never walk again, she was put to sleep.

Almost as suddenly, my father became ill and died. He was at first suspected of having a stomach ulcer. This eventually proved to be a malignant cancer. He was operated on and, three days later, died in hospital. He and Mother had not particularly got on together, though like many couples they had presented a respectable face to the world. Mother was therefore saddened, but not too deeply shaken. I myself, unexpectedly, was shattered. Despite his bullying and inapproachability, I realised, Father had been close to me, and I to him. Now, there was no way of saying this to him.

His death was all the more shocking because his surgeons, after his operation, had told us that he had a life expectancy of about a year. Even worse was to follow, however. After his demise we discovered that, by an unexpected and cruel twist of fate arising from his will, the smallholding would have to be liquidated and the property and livestock sold. The livelihood and way of life, which had been ours for so many years, was to come to an end. Mother's reaction was one of fury. She railed at his memory for the stupidity that he – self-declaredly such a cautious, correct and methodical man – had in the end shown. My reaction was different. It was not anger that I found, coming so soon after his death. It was intense shock. Father had told me many times that after his death that the farm would fall into my hands, and I had planned my future life on that understanding. For as long as I could remember, I had thought the house and land would one day be mine. Many occasions sprang to mind when

Father had promised that it would be so. We would be walking round the perimeter fences, inspecting them for damage, and he would suddenly stop, look back over his land and gesture with his arms, and say to me, "All this frontage will one day be built on and be worth a lot of money. By then it will be in your hands." I could not at first take in the fact that the farm would not be mine after all – even less that I had to leave it completely, and so soon! The complex and foolish investments of his outside interests, mainly hidden until now, were revealed to us, and although Father had hinted to me, whilst lying in his hospital bed that we would be well catered for should he die – he obviously hadn't expected to die so soon. His mumbled remarks, of "don't worry, I'll see you alright in the will", now came back to me. Was he trying to tell me that he had made 'mistakes' and changed his old will, which he had always intended to make out to us, but now intended to change it back? With his sudden death, whatever he had intended to do, it was not done. Oh Father, what have you done?

Before his death, I had reached twenty-eight years of age and, ironically, part of that future I had idly imagined for myself had become close to possibility. Through my work, I had fallen in love with a young lady called Jean Hodgson. After a whirlwind romance of only a few months, I was shortly to get married. Jean had two young children, and I expected that we would live out our lives on the farm, and that it would provide for us. Our children would grow up in a healthy environment, learning to love nature. Lassie and the twins would work with me, and everything would be wonderful. It was a dream I had only just dared to imagine, a splendid vision of my special world and the best parts of the world 'out there', coming together. Now, the sudden uncertainty about where we would all live came as a terrible blow. Not to say that I would soon be relying only on a part-time job for income, as well. I was stunned.

For many days I could not think what to do. Despite the fact Jean was still ready to marry me, my inner turmoil did no go away. My mother was kept busy at her hairdressing shop, having to run that as well as coping with all the extra work that now, for a short period, fell on her. Responsibility for the farm work, whilst the business was being sold off, fell to me. These duties helped to keep me preoccupied, pulling me away from darker thoughts, and I tried to find solace by taking the dogs on walks to our old haunts. But now the magic did not work, and all too soon, Mother and I began the paperwork, winding-up the business, selling the animals, and salvaging what furniture and other effects we could.

Father had begun to ail in the July of 1963, three months before he eventually died. He grew weaker and had less energy, and all the while we blamed this on the suspected ulcer. Whilst he was, as we thought, recovering, he had left off doing the more strenuous chores, and my mother and I had been doing the extra work. We had managed to keep the market stalls going, although, of course, these now had to be closed. Even so, it was almost impossible for two people to cope.

I was given every help by my Gawsworth employers, who initially allowed me a week off, then let me work flexi-hours. With my van and a petrol allowance I was able to manage, in a half-satisfactory fashion, but eventually had to let the job go, making our position more perilous still.

After a month, financial necessity caused Mother to sack three of her assistants at the hairdresser's. For years she had suffered from a rare form of sugar diabetes, and finding the extra work at the farm too much, she retreated to living accommodation behind her shop, where she could look after her interests better. The furniture that had been bequeathed to her by her parents from the Old Farm and which was threatened under the liquidation order, was secretly taken out and moved there.

The final stages of work at the smallholding were left entirely to me. Disposing of the animals gave me the greatest heartache. If it had not been for our legal difficulties I would have found them individual homes, but the deadline given to us by the liquidators was so short that I was forced to get rid of them at auctions as though they were pieces of furniture. Not only were they sold off haphazardly like this, but they were sold at well below their real asking price. The poultry and our goats, the remaining sheep and cattle were easily sold. Lucky, our beautiful pig and dear pet, went also. Samson, the old shire, had been retired to a horse rest home earlier in the year, so was fortunately being spared. The cats, including Sandra, all in good health, if aged, were put to sleep. I made the bitter decision to kill them painlessly rather than allow them to go to an uncertain future, to owners who may mistreat them or be unable to offer them the supreme freedom they had always known – and, for Sandra, the special companionship of Lassie, her only friend. David Hopkins, my vet, helped me in this thankless task, and spared many moments of his valuable time to assist me through this very difficult period. The only animals to come off the farm with me were Lassie, and her family of twins.

Soon, all the livestock and appliances had been sold, including the farm itself, and the day for legal completion was approaching, bringing with it the awful final wrench that we had to endure. Outwardly, Mother showed little emotion, though inwardly was still deeply hurt, not for herself, she claimed, but for her son, who had lost everything, including his rightful heritage.

Jean, although having little knowledge of my former life or Lassie, was nevertheless interested in the countryside and wildlife, having lived for the first twenty-three years of her life in the Lake District villages of Sawrey and Hawkshead. She would rescue anything in distress, from a beetle to a badger. Her familiarity with animals generally was a huge help at the time, and I don't think I would have been able to cope without her. As before in my life, this new support from elsewhere helped me to soldier on and make the most of a bad job. Because of financial considerations, our marriage went ahead at a local registry office, quietly and without fanfare. By a piece of good fortune, we were offered a council house. At least the problem of where to live was solved. I had always assumed that because I would take over the farm, I would not qualify for one. But I was approaching thirty, and employment continued to worry me. I had neglected my education, and few firms were prepared to train me. Through the haze and confusion of events I managed to pull myself together and force myself to make the various job applications, although often feeling that there was nothing in the whole of life worth considering.

Uppermost among my fears was the thought of moving to a suburban, three-bedroomed house with a tiny garden. It distressed me badly enough – but how on earth, I wondered, would the dogs react? And what was to become of Lassie now?! Even though she was ten-years old, she was seemingly ageless. If she wanted, she could still easily outrun her daughters. I thought that the move might kill her, and I am certain that it shortened her life.

Saddened as I was to know that the mission had to be embarked on before long, for her part Lassie had started to sense much earlier that something was wrong. When the bailiffs and other officials and would-be buyers began to arrive, she became very subdued. She had to be fastened up while all this activity was going on, and so she often became intensely annoyed as well. Neither Lynne nor Teddy liked the strangers walking around the farm taking measurements and inspecting the items for sale, and became almost as moody. Forlornly, until the last moment, I continued to hope for a reprieve, but none came. I was too distressed to make a last tour with the dogs.

The day to quit at last arrived. The feeling of inevitability in all of us had turned to a terrible gloom. When I woke up that day I felt crushed and lost, but knew that there was nothing that could be done. I found myself wanting to run away, to have done with everything I loved. Mother, who spared time whenever she could to be with me, arrived. Bleakly, we waited for the van I had hired.

Together, we gazed round for the last time at our old home. It was deathly quiet, with no sign of life. The bustling, hectic, but often happy times had passed, now memories only, left behind in the misty, waterlogged hollow that years and years earlier I had cursed for its cold and dampness. Today, as it always seemed to be, the sky was overcast, and it was raining. It was also autumn, that fateful time of year when so many things seemed to happen to Lassie and I. But today there was no golden glow on the horizon. My mind flashed back to that early morning after the little blue collie had been killed, and I had struggled back from James Cook's surgery carrying the tiny, hostile ball of red fur.

With a heavy sigh, and a last glance at the desolate farm, I turned and opened the van door. Both Teddy and Lynn jumped in, without needing to be urged. I turned to Lassie, intending to pick her up and carry her bodily into the back of the car if need be. But somehow she knew that she just had to leave. Like me, she had no other option. As on many occasions before when it appeared that she had read my mind, without even being told to do so, she entered the van. My weary, hopeless and helpless look must have spoken volumes to her. For the first time in her life she entered and settled herself inside a vehicle, and lay calmly on the van seat.

Mother climbed in next, her feelings, finally shocked into outraged acceptance by this final leave taking, turned suddenly to anger and bitterness once more at the way Father had left us out of his will. Hurriedly, I followed her inside, closing the door. With a heavy heart, I drove quickly away from all that I had known and loved.

As I drove through the pouring rain I looked neither to left nor right, but went directly to the housing estate where I was to begin my new life. Apart from the few meagre house possessions, which had gone ahead of us, I had only the clothes I stood up in. From being comparatively well off, I had sunk almost to nothing.

The council house was situated at Broken Cross housing estate, about five miles from the smallholding, in the heart of suburban Macclesfield. The area was not very salubrious. By my standards, it was rough. Brick-ends and glass shards littered the streets. Saplings that had been planted by the council in an attempt to brighten the arid parts, had been snapped in two, or ripped up by their roots. The house next door to ours had fourteen kids. The neighbours on the other side, I later discovered, were horrible people. We were situated in the centre of the worst patch on the estate, and it was the direct opposite of the kind of area I had been used to. Because of my poverty, there was nothing at all that I could do to change it.

The council house was semi-detached, with a small mud patch in the back, no more than about twenty square feet, which passed for a garden. Before we moved in I had fenced off this squalid piece of land the best I could and so, at least, when we arrived, we were able to let the dogs off the leash while we began unloading my few last bits and pieces, sorting out my personal belongings and arranging my few sticks of furniture. Fortunately, we had enough of the basics from the large farm, and Mother's town place was already furnished, in fact now positively overstuffed, what with her precious heirlooms from Grandmother.

Inside, the house was in a terrible state. The air smelled from the mounds of debris and dirt left behind by the previous tenants, although I had already cleared out the worst. It would need completely redecorating, to rid the walls of graffiti and unsightly blemishes. Because of her own family commitments, Jean could not yet move in, but her mother was a valuable help with the decorating. Together with my mother we began the enormous task of making this hovel into somewhere decent we could live. The days went by, and Jean eventually moved in. She carried on her day job, but we both pitched into the work at night. A grim Christmas was spent there, jollied along by Jean and Mother, the 'other' ladies in my life apart from Lassie, Lynn and Teddy.

Very slowly, I became inured to the depressing surroundings, but to my huge surprise, the dogs seemed to adapt wonderfully well, and settled down almost at once. I was wary of making assumptions about Lassie, however, as it was difficult to read her true feelings, especially when she was stressed. As a matter of fact, many animals often appear able to cope with change far better than humans can, as they can deal with pain and injury with astonishing fortitude. For the first time they all slept together, and inside the kitchen. In the daytime, they had the 'freedom' of the 'garden'. I had expected the twins eventually to settle, but not Lassie. She seemed content, but occasionally it broke my heart to see her sniffing around the base of the fencing and stunted hedge that confined her to her small territory. How much she missed the open country, it was really impossible to say. Often, I thought that her very compliance with the ways of this new world might be a sign of her distress, for it was totally alien to her. I did not dare let her wander free at night – and that must surely have been the biggest blow of all to her. We had our regular, daily walks, but even she now had to be on a lead until we reached open ground. Again, I could only marvel at how she seemed to be accepting. Lassie would now come into both house and van with equal ease, and at times it was hard for me to believe how wild she had once been such a short time before. I was astonished to find that not only did she appear to enjoy the car, but once inside it was ready to guard it protectively. When all was said and done, it seemed that the main casualty of the move was I.

To kill the monotony, I got away as often as I could, and that Easter accompanied my mother on a day trip to one of my aunt's, at Colwyn Bay in North Wales. But in one way it proved not to be so welcome an interlude.

Mother was still in the habit of visiting her favourite sister once or twice a year, who had moved from Birkenhead to Wales. Aunty Lillian was a colourful woman who, since her retirement as a secretary to a top Sixties' pop vocal group, spent much of her time touring abroad. This was one of her brief stays back home.

We set out in the van, taking the dogs with us, and travelled uneventfully until we reached the tail end of an enormous traffic jam just beyond Chester. Waiting for what seemed an eternity for the blockage to clear, we slowly inched our way forward while the dogs grew restless on the back seat, and the heat and fumes built up. At length we were able to notice what was holding up the traffic. The vehicles had formed into two lanes, and at the front of each was a roadblock. Two uniformed police officers stood on either side of the lanes, questioning the drivers. I was in the left-hand lane, and it eventually became our turn. I pulled up on the left, next to the constable concerned. To speak to him I had to talk across my mother through the passenger window, and so all my attention was directed that way. There had been a gaol-break, we discovered. The roadblock had been set in an attempt to capture the prisoners. With the unexpected heat of the day, I had been driving with my right-hand side window rolled down and, as I answered the policeman's questions, the policeman from the other lane, without me noticing, came to my right-hand window and put his hand on my shoulder. I was never able to find out what he wanted, for in the next instant Lassie sprang from the back seat where she had been lying and sank her teeth into his hand!

The officer let out a cry, and pulled his hand clear of the enraged collie while I, confused, but gradually realising the consequences of what had happened, turned and held on to Lassie, pushing her back onto her seat. I knew that it had not been her fault. On the contrary, it was the policeman's for intruding unexpectedly into our territory. But, as I expected, the policeman would have none of that. After nursing his injured hand for a few moments, and holding it up for inspection by his colleague, and I kept a secure hand on Lassie's collar, he told me that I would be charged. Glumly, I got out of the car, making sure that all the windows were sufficiently closed, and waited, while he bandaged his hand in a handkerchief, and then importantly pulled out his notebook to take down my particulars. The subject of the gaol-break was forgotten as I pulled away to continue our journey. The whole episode had quite spoiled the little trip, and I discovered later that I was to be formally charged with having no control over a dangerous dog. I was summoned to appear in court.

I reflected bitterly on the thought that, had Lassie been back on the farm, she would never have been forced into a position where she would have bitten anyone, let alone a policeman. Quite simply, she would have chosen not to come with us in the car, but stayed and roamed her beloved woods and fields instead.

The hearing was held at the Magistrates Court in the country town of Mold, then in Clwyd, now Flintshire. Fortunately for Lassie, the magistrate sympathised with my defence. I did not bring Lassie to the court because I did not wish to risk a repeat of the incident by subjecting her to a very stressful experience. Almost certainly, she would have cowered and snarled at almost anyone who came anywhere near her! Instead I brought along a photograph of her, and showed this to the magistrate. I did not mention Lassie's background, either, for I thought that might prejudice the outcome. Nor did I want it publicised that she was regarded as a menace, if the case went against her.

I explained that what had happened had occurred very quickly. I told the court that if I had known the policeman was going to put his hand through the window, I would have stopped him. After hearing me out, the magistrate dismissed the case. He declared that it was a foolish thing for the policeman to have done, but added that, even so, I should see to it that Lassie was kept under even tighter control. The policeman had charged me in the heat of the moment, and then allowed the charge to stand, wasting everyone's time. I was too relieved to think more about the matter, and drove thankfully away.

But Lassie did have a growing aggression problem. I had been correct in suspecting that her seeming adaptation in her new surroundings was not all it seemed, and I became sure that she was instinctively hiding her feelings. The confines of her new home were having their effect. In the past, she had always been able to get away from people. Now, with this denied her, she snapped out more readily than she had ever done. She would strike out at anyone who persisted in trying to touch her. In a way, the incident with the policeman was a warning that I had to be more alert, and from then on I and was careful to see that no one ever did get close to her again. To keep her as free as possible, each evening when I came home from work I made a point of taking her and the twins by car into the country, where we could have a good long walk.

One of my many job applications turned out to be successful, and I was now employed in animal welfare. In a way I was extremely lucky, for my lack of formal qualifications, as well as my age, was against me, but fortunately for me a sympathetic recruitment officer had realised my potential. He responded to a long, impassioned explanation of my current predicament and past experience with working with animals of many different kinds, and granted me a temporary position on the understanding that I would catch up with the academic requirements at night school. This job, which involved becoming a technician in charge of looking after many small animals, would become permanent if I proved to be satisfactory. So, at least one pressing lack in our new life together was now eased. Jean continued in work, and was eventually to get a job looking after computers at the world famous radio telescope at Jodrell Bank.

My favourite walk with the dogs was at Gawsworth, only a three-mile drive in the car, where the farming countryside was still unspoiled. We would set out from Gawsworth New Hall, a magnificent old Georgian building, cross over the road to St James's Church and from there make our way to the black and white half-timbered Old Hall, built by Lord Fytton in the early 17th Century, a site that dated back to Norman times, and where are still to be found the remains of the tilting-grounds used by armoured knights in their tournaments. It also had a series of lovely lakes and pools in the grounds, near one of which I had at worked, caring for poultry and ornamental wildfowl at The Pigeon House.

Along the route of this walk was a rather unpleasant conifer wood, which I did not take to. It reminded me of Black Wood. But Lassie always liked to go there, and so I kept it in our walk. It was dank and bleak, and had very little life in it. There were no foxes, but its similarity to Black Wood might have led Lassie to think so, or the lingering scent of their presence in the recent past. Chased by the twins she would race happily about among the trees, searching amongst the occasional bracken-covered sandy banks. Simply, she got comfort from being among the shapes and smells that reminded her of her youth.

The wood did harbour a sett of badgers, and very often at night I would watch out for them. One evening we were fortunate enough to come across one of the badgers hunting at the edge of the wood. By the moonlight we could see his ghostly silver, black and white form quite clearly, but on spotting him the dogs were unable to keep quiet or still, and away he shot at top speed into the darkness and the shelter of his sett.

Further along the walk was another, much more pleasant, mixed wood. Though not ringed with laurel, this one reminded me of Laurel Wood and, strangely enough, it also had a pool at its centre, around which we would sometimes spend time drinking-in the quiet beauty of the scene.

These daily walks were an absolute necessity. However, on occasion, I was unable to drive out, and we were then forced to take our daily excursions about the neighbourhood of the estate, which were a complete contrast. Many of the estate's residents had tried to make the best of their situation, and had brought their houses and gardens up to the highest standards. But every so often, as we went through the featureless groves of brickwork, we would come across areas of appalling damage... to trees, hedgerows and grass verges alike. Birds' nests had been ripped out and destroyed, and left in the gutters, and any piece of green living thing that could be uprooted or chopped down was either vandalised or constantly at risk. The culprits were both youngsters and their parents, who allowed them to roam about in destructive gangs. It was not as if they could have been unaware of what their kids were up to on their own doorsteps! In short, everything that Lassie and I stood for, was here directly under attack by a mindless and hateful element of society.

I had never encountered 'trouble' before, having always kept myself well away from it but, one evening, walking through the estate with the three dogs firmly leashed, I encountered a gang of these kids. They had just forced an old man off the footpath and now, laughing at their success, were walking toward me. As they approached, it became clear that they were out for trouble, and as there were five of them and only one of me it was also equally clear that there was no match. They were all older teenage lads and, as I expected, when we drew closer, they blocked my way. One of them stepped forward and asked me roughly whether I had a match. I told him that I had not, and prepared to walk on. At this, he menacingly pulled a lead pipe from his pocket and took a further step toward me, swearing foully.

"I want a match!" he shouted.

The dogs had sensed the threat as soon as I, and by now the twins were barking and straining at their leash. Lassie, on the other hand, was standing quietly, waiting to be unleashed. I knew she was carefully assessing the situation, taut and quivering with anger, totally prepared to combat this threat to me. But the youths seemed not to notice. Collies can look soft and inoffensive dogs, unlike Alsatians or Dobermans, which are generally recognised to be hard dogs, and obviously this gang thought that the dogs would not come to my rescue.

"Stay out of my way, or it'll be the worse for you with the dogs!" I warned them. When there was no response, and the lout with the pipe refused to put his weapon away, I hurriedly unclipped Lassie from her leash. At once she sprang forward and shot around the leader's legs so quickly that he almost overbalanced with surprise. Once again, as in the days of old, working the sheep or cattle, or ratting, we were in mental accord, linked-in with each other. She knew exactly what was required of her, and that I did not want her to bite them, but, at this stage, only to threaten them. After she had given them this display of her intentions and agility, she then rapidly crouched between us, her ears flattened and teeth bared toward the gang, growling quietly in a menacing undertone. She waited for the first one to make his move, but none did. They could pick up the waves of menace coming from her perfectly clearly. Realising their mistake, to a man they backed off, and hurriedly left me alone. I clipped Lassie back on her leash, and we continued with our walk. How I would have fared if she had not been with me, I hate to think. Even in her advanced years, she had once again come to my rescue. Bulls, geese, turkeys, hares, rats, policemen, gangs – nothing seemed too much for her! On one of our favourite Gawsworth walks, she even saw off another huge bull that was about to attack some friends of mine – so, although she mistrusted all human beings other than me, Lassie included them in her circle of care on that occasion.

This 'telepathy' we experienced had not disappeared. Since leaving the farm, we had less cause to use it, but I found it was still strong. What's more, the twins were now 'linked-in' too. If I felt something – if I was happy, or sad, or wanted them to do something – they could sense it. Furthermore, all three of them could relate in this way one to the other. Lassie felt it the strongest, of course, and I therefore had more influence over her than the twins. But Lassie could act as a transmitter. If I thought of something, she would pick it up first, and then the other two would get it off her. I could influence the twins without the intermediacy of Lassie, but to a lesser degree.

I could not say how the mechanism of this 'extra/ fourth' sense worked, whether in fact it differed from rapid cognitive deduction. Due to the closeness of our relationships, were we unconsciously reading small, normally unnoticeable signs and signals? This 'Super Nature' explanation, though, did not take account of the many occasions when the dogs seemed to sense thoughts without visible contact between each other or me. It could not explain the times Lassie had sprung from nowhere to save me from harm, or the effortless way she moved sheep at my silent mental commands. I only knew, whatever it was, that it worked, and was content to leave the explanation open.

Out on the streets, the dogs never needed a cross word. I would see other owners being pulled along by unruly dogs, or helplessly standing by during dogfights. Many were the estate residents who came up to me to exclaim their astonishment at the good behaviour of my three. They wanted to know why their one dog was uncontrollable, while mine was perfect. It found it hard to convey to them that my dogs were the way they were because of the empathy we had, that we acted as a unit. I did not have to tell my dogs anything, because they already knew! This contrast, between the behaviour of town dogs and their masters, and my own dogs, put into sharp relief one of the many things that in the country I had taken for granted. It was only really in the town that I came to see what a unique family we were. Sadly, the walks were the only way of properly experiencing this, and the only feature of interest left in Lassie's life.

Like the encounter with the youths, drama was sometimes never far away, mingling with the many fun times we had on our walks. During the deep freeze of the winter of 1963, driving home once evening we were caught in a very heavy snowstorm. The winter was one of the worst in living memory, with the snow starting before Christmas and continuing well into the spring. The ground had become so hard that by January a drought had set in. Many houses were without water. Council water carts were employed on the estate, bringing water rations to the residents. The cold weather was countrywide, with many areas hit by water shortages, and millions of pounds worth of livestock and crops either killed or damaged. Many water birds, especially, were to die during those freezing times, and it would take the likes of herons and kingfishers many years to recover. In this weather, it was difficult exercising the dogs. Sensibly, I usually confined walks to the immediate estate. But on this occasion, I had risked the car, and I had rashly driven further than usual. Night had fallen, and on a B-road, still about six miles from home, we had become stuck in a huge drift.

Cursing myself for being so stupid, I let the three dogs out, and together we headed for a main road, where I hoped we might still find buses running. They were, but, of course, they were running late. After waiting about half an hour in the freezing cold, in clothing that was less than adequate, my heart was gladdened to see a bus on its way, radiating its warm yellow glow onto the snow. When it arrived, I persuaded the conductor to allow me to take all three dogs on board. Thinking I was making good progress, I waved at the twins, who promptly bounded on board. But then it came to Lassie's turn, and she flatly refused. I had grown used to her being 'domesticated', and I did not expect this. Try as I might, she refused to comply, and after several attempts she slipped her collar and ran away into the darkness. It was the first time since her youth that she had disobeyed me so adamantly.

The passengers were waiting for the bus to start, and the guard, who had not extended his initial generosity much, simply stood by, watching, and moaning about the time I was taking. Eventually, he said that he bus would have to get on its way, and even I could see his point. Realising there was nothing to be done but to walk home the whole six miles, I called to the twins to get off the bus, and set out to retrieve Lassie. The dogs, of course, with their thick coats, felt not a thing as we marched along through the frozen mounds of snow – not so I, who had only a thin wind-proof jacket. Nonetheless, I marched on with them undaunted!

Lassie's parents?!

Chapter Seventeen

FOUR YEARS of comparatively uneventful, suburban living, went by, during which time our two lovely daughters grew up – Judith, a quiet placid-natured girl, and Caroline, like her mother of a fiery temperament. Judith had straight, dark brown hair. Caroline's was curly but mousy-coloured. Both girls were sensible and home-loving, and loved animals. The ageing Lassie's reaction to them was predictably indifferent, whereas Lynn enjoyed their lively, young company. Teddy was standoffish, and inclined to be bad tempered like her mother. Caroline persevered with Teddy, and got lots of little nips for her trouble. Judith, somehow different, was able to charm her – and many other creatures – although I did not dare let her near Lassie. If that relationship was ever to be, it must come very slowly and steadily.

I was often to contrast Lassie's – and my – early 'wild-lives' with the situation in which we now found ourselves, and continued to be amazed at how she had adjusted to virtual confinement, her temper problem excepted. Whereas work and family left me far too busy to brood much, I could only guess what must have been going through her mysterious mind as she spent day after day in that tiny garden, or in the even smaller kitchen, waiting only for evening to be 'set free' on our regular walks, which were almost as important for me as for her. Yet the controversy that surrounded her was never far from the limelight, and Lassie's story was once again resurrected by the Macclesfield Express. The main points of her life were updated, and the twins given star treatment. As before, the unique collie and her family brought in a flood of mail.

As well as notable zoologists like Gerald Isles and Brian Fitzgerald, there were others who now came forward to acquaint themselves with Lassie. One was Douglas Reay, the Yorkshire animal lover and writer, who wrote a regular nature column for the Manchester Evening News and had seen Lassie's story on their files. From the outset, on being introduced to Lassie and the twins, he was convinced that Lassie was a hybrid, and that her twins were also unique, and suggested I write the story of Lassie's life.

Another naturalist, George Cansdale, who presented his own pioneering television nature series, *Looking at Animals* for BBC TV, after seeing Lassie also decided that she was probably a hybrid 'fox-dog'. Cansdale, known as the 'Zoo Man', had a lot of experience with many kinds of creatures, and was the author of the Ladybird Pet books, and later head of Chessington Zoo.

Lassie's unusualness had now attracted a mixture of opinions from the experts, which ranged, in roughly equal proportions, from 'Impossible' and 'Improbable', to 'Probable' and 'Certain'. I received more requests for blood tests, and again I refused, on the grounds of the stress they would cause Lassie, even though she was now mature and more used to the world. She was still not used to human handling, other than by me.

I was still the only one she would let get near her, and in allowing the tests I would have risked being seen by her as complicit, which seemed to me like a betrayal. She tolerated my family only as long as they didn't try to touch her. She was perfectly happy to share the house with them, and often relied on them to let her in and out of the garden when I was absent. Her little corner in the now rather cramped house was hers alone, and always respected. That had been one of the very first things the girls had to be taught!

Her ripe old age was now a talking point. Physically, at fourteen, she had inevitably slowed-up, but otherwise showed little of her advancing years other than the silvering of her muzzle. And when she wanted she could still give the twins a good run for their money.

The country walks continued to be the main focus of daily life. From Gawsworth, we had several favourite walks to choose from, and now regularly took a route to the peat fields of Dane Moss, a typical Cheshire 'raised bog'. These natural deposits of thousands-of-year-old decayed vegetable matter on the halfway stage to becoming coal, were still in use. The peat was cut from the ground in the spring, and dried throughout the summer in lines of neat, aerated stacks. In the autumn, it was sold as fuel for burning. It did not burn as hot as coal, but was cheaper and, together with wood, was at one time used extensively as a domestic and even light industrial fuel. From the roadside fields at Gawsworth, the moss was easy to get to, and a delight to walk on.

It was probably about four acres in extent, hewn into hundreds of long, regular, symmetrical cuttings, bordered on the east side by the Macclesfield Canal.

This picturesque waterway was then in use to transport some of the peat, and many other items, the barges still sometimes pulled by huge shire horses. It was a favourite place for me, to stroll and to watch attentively, while the dogs were otherwise engaged in their own activities. Of equal interest were the little embankments of the old railway line, once used to carry the peat to the canal and tracks. The most recent workings covered a small area on the far side of the peat fields, with the older and more overgrown parts occupying most of the remaining space. Then there was the wild life. Protected by laws that prohibited the use of guns, this peaty haven was home to many kinds, especially ducks. A variety of waterfowl were to be found on those cuttings that had flooded and formed permanent waterways, especially in winter when many ducks and geese flew in from the cold north. Sometimes they contained mysterious and very rare Arctic strangers, like Snow Geese, or Asian Red-breasted Geese, although they could well have been escapees from the sort of collections I used to look after at Gawsworth Pools, and not truly wild vagrants. Sometimes I would find a partly white one – the result of a wild goose like a Canada or Greylag, mating with an escaped farmyard goose. Apart from dogs, I think wildfowl are my favourite creatures, and this was one of the main reasons I so loved coming there. The dogs, of course, loved anywhere with wild scents where they could run free.

In other cuttings, as well as on the strips of land in between, there was a plentiful supply of creatures like rabbits and hares, or lizards and snakes. Stoats and weasels also abounded, thriving off the duck eggs and the smaller animal life. The plant life, too, was varied and lush, living as it did on the rich 'acid' ground. As the ground varied from drier to damper depending upon the age of the cuttings, heathers and mosses were typical and put on glorious shows of colour in their seasons. Because some of the cuttings invariably flooded, Grass Snakes, frogs, toads, newts and other water life flourished. Dragonflies and damselflies abounded in the summer, and certain rare butterflies also ensured the moss's protected status.

A public footpath crossed the fields, which I would use while the dogs ran off to play and hunt. The cuttings were about two feet deep and about three feet across on average, but every so often there were deeper and more perilous ones. The dogs would leap over all with great ease and tremendous enjoyment, and because the older fields were so overgrown and therefore uninviting to man, we all three enjoyed virtual isolation.

One wintry day the dogs were enjoying their favourite pastime of putting up a hare and then racing after it in hot pursuit, when there was a tragic accident. The hare came to the first deep cutting, leaped and cleared it easily. The twins followed, without difficulty. Then came Lassie but, sadly, she did meet with difficulty. The jump was a long one, and because of her age she landed just short, with only her front paws on safe ground. She clung to the lip of the cutting momentarily, before crashing down to the bottom, shoulder deep in the slimy-green, ice-cold water some seven feet below.

Frantically, I ran to the cutting's edge and peered down at her. I realised straight away that I would have a terrible job getting her out on my own. She made a few half-hearted attempts to claw her way up the slippery peat sides, but each time she slid back down again into the water. Then she began swimming sluggishly up and down the cutting, looking vainly for a way out. The walls of the deep, dark trench were as steep and high at each end as they were at the sides, and the low winter sunlight was completely cut out. I looked around for someone to help, but our isolation was complete. We were a good distance from the road, and I was stranded with her. Helplessly, I stared down at her soaking wet form whilst thinking frantically what on earth I could do. I knew that at all costs I had to quickly get her out of that freezing prison, and without thinking further jumped down and joined her – and the immediate shock to my own body reinforced the urgency of it all. It was so cold, it was painful!

She had almost ceased to struggle, overcome by the shock of the cold water, and looked terrified. Like most animals when they get into a predicament they cannot control, she seemed as though she wanted to give up, and because I had never seen her accept defeat before I was seized with a sudden dread. The dark sides seemed to tower above us like the sides of a grave.

At first I tried lifting her above my head, to see if it was possible to heave her up to the top, but with her water-drenched coat she was so heavy and slippery I could get her no further than my shoulders. I began to tear at the sides with my hands, to make footholds in the friable peat, so that I could carry her out. Hampered by my jacket and, now, soaking wet and freezing cold myself, I tore it off and flung it up onto the ground above, and continued making step holds.

When at last I thought I had made sufficient of them, I lifted Lassie with great difficulty with one arm, and attempted to scale the wall with the other. But with her dead weight holding me back and the peat crumbling beneath my flailing feet I just could not manage the climb. I made several attempts, and each time we both fell back into the brackish water, now both thoroughly soaked and frozen – and on my part, plunged into ever deepening despair. Lassie's coat was completely sodden and blackened with the water, and she was becoming weaker by the second with the extreme cold. The water covered her back but not her head and neck, which still stretched desperately upwards out of the water, shaking with the cold and effort, but it would not be long before she was unable to support herself. Her movements were becoming weaker and weaker, her once magnetic yellow eyes slowly dimming and closing.

Teddy and Lynn were still standing above us at the cutting edge, or running ineffectually back and to, barking all the while and looking anxiously down at the plight of their mother. They knew something was terribly wrong, and could not help. But could they? I thought wildly for any other way out. Then, remembering, I scrambled quickly out of the cutting and reached into my pocket for a handy piece of thick twine that, by a chance, I happened to be carrying. I looked quickly at the twins again, their gazes mute, pleading, then down to their fast-failing mother. Would they be strong enough to haul her out?! With no time to think, I fastened their leads together, attached Lassie's lead to them, and the twine to her lead, to give the extra length needed. Jumping down once more, I plunged my jacket under Lassie's belly and folded the arms of it over her back. I attached the twine firmly to the arms. Heaving Lassie once more out of the water as high as I could, I yelled up to Lynn and Teddy, "GET BACK GIRLS, GET BACK!"

As though by a miracle – or their remarkable intelligence – the twins understood what I wanted of them, and I felt the twine go taught. Soon, as the dogs strained, I felt Lassie's weight being taken off my arms. With my arms temporarily free I found a foothold and pushed upwards with all my might. Somehow, with our united efforts, we managed to get Lassie clear of her trap and up onto safe ground. Relief filled me as I rapidly scrambled out after her. But now I had the problem of getting her back to the car.

It was possible that the twine, pulled tautly about her, had injured her. But on a brief examination I could see no sign of any damage or raw, rubbed marks. She was just completely exhausted, torpid with cold and shock, and lay heaving on the ground, unable to rise. Squeezing out the now ruined jacket as best I could, I rubbed her briskly, hoping she would revive. When she did not, there was nothing I could do but carry her and so, wrapping the jacket about her, I hoisted her bodily over my shoulders, held her forepaws with one hand and hind legs with the other, and set off to the van. I was mindless of the cold water streaming down me from her shaking body, and staggered the whole painful mile to where I had parked, with the twins following quietly close behind.

To this day I do not know how I completed that journey, or from where I gained the extra strength required to carry her. Sheer determination to save her, and mind over matter, won out. The task lasted for an age. At length, it was done, and thankfully I lifted her into the dry and relative warmth of the van and raced home, with its little heater blasting out. Once back home I rushed our dripping, filthy forms upstairs, past the astonished gazes of the family, and Lassie immediately received a warm bath, which she took without complaint, even though she had never been washed before let alone put into a bath, and within a couple of hours she appeared to be perfectly recovered. Yes, this Lassie was a strong old dog indeed, although really it was Lynn and Teddy who deserved the praise, for without their strength and intelligence I could not have saved her.

I felt now that the debt of life owed to this great dog had been paid – although, of course, I would have saved her a thousand times, had it been required of me – but then, remembering, I realised that she might never have had a life at all if I hadn't stepped in to save her in the first place! Whatever the anguish she may have accidentally caused me, Lassie truly deserved her life, and I would never stop being grateful to her for our time together.

Years roll on all too quickly. Now 1968, Lassie was fifteen years old, and, looking at her, this was hard to believe, for she continued to age so gracefully that one hardly noticed. Her muzzle took on a pearly-white appearance, though her eyes and lovely fiery coat glowed as youthfully as ever.

I decided one day, in the spring of her fifteenth year, to revisit our old Laurel Wood. Five years had elapsed since I left the farm, and though I originally looked on the house at Broken Cross as a temporary measure while I found something better, I was still on the estate. In truth, we could not afford to move anywhere else, what with a growing family and all. No matter how ugly or horrible the estate, I had grown immune to its unkempt shabbiness, though not used to it, and had found a tolerable routine. Work with animals was, as always, interesting enough to keep me occupied during the day, and when home, the combination of walks and family life was compensation enough. I was less angry with my father's actions than I had been. Like Mother, contentedly ensconced in her town flat, busy social life and business, we had no option but to let it all go, as hard as that was, though we would always feel it as a kind of betrayal of our earlier years. I at least still had the dogs from those increasingly distant times of youth and innocence. Impulsively, I had made an emotional decision never to return to it. The thought was still a loathsome idea, for I had heard that the farm had been resold, and that the expected building programme around and on my former home had commenced. Yet for Lassie' sake, while she was still alive, I decided to have one last look.

I arrived with the dogs, expecting to see changes. What I actually saw appalled me. The area was almost unrecognisable! Tytherington fields, where once cows had grazed contentedly, had been invaded by rows of town houses, each with neatly kept gardens and service roads. Worst of all, our old farmhouse had been converted into a well-heeled dwelling, whilst below, the busy old livestock acres had become a featureless playing field – all dominated by a huge, humming electricity pylon which hung ominously across the entire shallholding! The rest of the farm had been dug up in readiness for more house-building. My grandparent's farm, partly built-on when I had last seen it, was now fully covered, and the swathe of development reaching down from it almost met that rising up the hill from the village below. Tens of thousands, probably hundreds of thousands, of pounds had been made by the owners of both properties. Ironically, one of the few remaining and greenest bits was the flat playing field, our misty old farming hollow, now almost totally enclosed.

In the direction of Laurel Wood, most of the familiar landscape had also gone. Many trees had been felled, hedgerows uprooted. A nearby farm had entirely disappeared. In its place was sheer devastation. The muddy ground was convulsed with a tremendous upheaval, with pipes for sewage, gas and water running in the open trenches. The broken land, tormented with the mass of people that would soon come to live on it, seemed to stretch all the way up to where the remains of the wood still lay. Could this possibly have been my home, I wondered, closing my eyes, in an attempt to recall how it had once looked? I brought myself back to reality, and turned away, sick at heart. With Lassie, Lynn and Teddy trotting along besides me, gently reminding me that all was not lost, I hastened to see if our old haven had not also been destroyed.

The sun shone strongly on our backs as we reached the edge of the destruction and stepped thankfully onto pastureland. Only two fields now separated this side of the wood from the encroaching urban sprawl, and if I closed my mind to what I had just seen, I could still imagine that all was as it used to be. Reinforcing this illusion, as though heralding our return, a bank of white albino bluebells came into sight along the last hedgerow leading up to the wood. Reaching the laurel trees, I climbed through the wire fencing as I had done so many times before – but this time, uniquely, I had all three of my beloved 'Laurel Wood Fox-Dogs' by my side in perfect harmony – and pushed my way inside. I was soon brought-up short by the unexpected beauty of the still scene lying within. Here, at least, in the still timeless wood, everything seemed unchanged. A great feeling of happiness rose up inside me. The elfin wood could still enthrall, just as much as it had when I was a boy.

I walked thankfully through the trees towards the pool, savouring each moment, bathed in the healing energies which sprang right onto me from the foliage, and pushed instantly upward through the ground, so starved was I of Mother Nature's embrace. The deciduous leaves were all in bud, their shiny embryonic leaves catching the bright sunlight and making the air dazzle and jump with reflected light. The rays flashed off the bright green of the gently swaying beech buds, the red of the oak and Horse Chestnut, the purple of the birch and the pale green and fox-red of the pines. I felt as though I had been transported back into another, more innocent age. The song of blackbirds and thrushes floated through the invisible velvet textures of the unchanging spaces around me. It seemed as though they had always sung there, and would always do. Further on, the old dead ash beneath which Lassie had brought her first-born secretively into the world, still lay with its roots wildly exposed to the sky. It looked smaller now, and less consequential than it had at the time, when I had so anxiously peered into the depths of the foxhole at its roots. Nevertheless, the tree was still there, and it seemed as though time had stood still for me.

Gazing around, I was filled once more with pangs of sadness that we were all growing much older and that, all to soon, this wood, as well as ourselves, would one day have to go. As I looked about me, enchanted by this magical sadness, it registered dimly that Lassie had gone missing. I called for her, though unconcernedly, as we walked on through the trees, admiring fresh beauties of nature at every step. Above everything the usual cooing of pigeons and doves, muted cries of pheasants and woodpeckers, magpies and chattering jackdaws, all merged into the single golden 'note' of sight and sound. All of a sudden, a weasel darted across our path, causing us, especially Lynn and Teddy to start. The dogs made to go for it, but automatically, I forbade them. As scavengers, these little creatures clear up dead or ill creatures as well as unflinchingly tackle much larger prey – and, besides, had very sharp teeth! Scarcer than they used to be, I liked to see their lithe and sinuous forms going about their business, even if they were, like their larger cousins the stoats, quite deadly killers, well able to kill and drag away rabbits over three times their size.

Before we came to the clearing where the pool lay, I was forced to stop again, this time by the small stream which still danced and sparkled merrily on its way. I lazily dangled my hand in its crystal-cool waters, while I relived past memories. Setting off again, we soon came across the large pool, and my breath was stopped by the magnificent sight of the great yellow water lilies which flowered as profusely as ever on its motionless surface. Around the edges of the pool were the golden king-cups, or Marsh Marigolds, all opened and lifted upwards to the light which streaked down through the swaying golden-green buds of the beeches. The water was exceptionally clear, and about a foot beneath it, lying across the whole of the bottom, was a carpet of Canadian Pondweed shining up at me with a brilliant emerald-green light. I could plainly see little fish and diving beetles going about their business, whilst above, pond-skaters rowed about the invisible surface, and dragonflies darted above it in iridescent splendour.

Beyond the pool, on its far bank, was the bank of white bluebells I had seen many times as a child. There was a whole mass of them, perhaps turned white by a chemical in the ground, or simply because they had been planted that way by the owners of the old Tytherington Hall. The bank stretched upward, away into the trees on the far side.

Whilst I looked up, a slight movement caught my eye, and directed my gaze to where the fallen beech trunk still lay out over the water. There, was the most wondrous sight of all. Reclined on its trunk, in exactly the same position that she had so often adopted in bygone days, was Lassie. Looking quite radiant, she began washing her forepaws, as was her custom, while the dappled effect of the sunlight from the surrounding trees fell onto her fox-red coat. She was like a living jewel in an exquisite setting. As I watched her, enchanted, I was once again transported back in time, vividly reliving whole scenes. I recalled how, on the occasions when I first saw Lassie reclining there, not long past puppyhood,

I would sit for hours gazing at her mute form, quite enraptured by her beauty. The time came to mind when I had returned from holiday, to find her gone, and had searched frantically, only to find her resting-up like this, on this log, in this wood, over this pool, stunned by her wild good looks. I thought of the time I hobbled to the wood on a crutch after she had saved me from the bull, to again discover that this was where she had retreated to; of the day she had cleverly outwitted the hounds by swimming down-stream and across the pool, and the time I had dug-out the fox earth to look for her children. A hundred different occasions, of Lassie in all her stages, and of a young boy whose dreams had reached into adulthood to protect and preserve her way of life, passed through my mind.

Lassie looked quite ageless, and for some long moments more I continued to watch her contentedly cleaning herself, savouring the sight, and even trying to imagine what she herself might be thinking of the scene. Beyond doubt, this domain was truly hers. But she who could no longer survive alone, was soon to make the final return from the wild.

Chapter Eighteen

A YOUNG news reporter looking through some old files came across the Lassie story and calculated that, if still alive, she must surely be a very old dog by now. He telephoned me, stating his desire to reopen the story yet again. I agreed and, together with Lassie, Lynn and Teddy, posed for a whole battery of photographs. Almost before I realised it, we were in the local and national papers. I received more fan letters than ever. Simply hundreds of letters from dog lovers and well wishers poured in. Many were from dog owners claiming to have dogs exactly like Lassie. Needless to say, their dogs were not in the least like her. I received many visits from owners who showed their dogs to me, absolutely convinced they were, like Lassie, possibly hybrids. Yet the behaviour of these dogs, and their markings, were patently dog-like, not even remotely ambiguous, and I was sometimes embarrassed to have to point out to them these obvious facts. Lassie was unique amongst collies in being all red, her whitening face notwithstanding, and the current revival of popularity of the Welsh Collie only serves to emphasise that. They are all a much darker reddy-brown and white – only the very different Red Setter has Lassie's all fox-red coat, and they are fairly distant 'cousins'.

Shortly after her sixteenth birthday, 1969, in the late autumn – that fateful time again – Lassie fell ill for the first time in her life, and would not eat. Sickness shows in the eyes. They develop a dull look, and I could see this now in Lassie's.

Anxiously, I called David Hopkins, to examine her, but he could find nothing wrong. He told me that it was just old age. Dogs do not just suffer from old age – there is always something else they suffer from, usually resulting from it – but I knew what he meant. Lassie was simply worn out. She had been alive for sixteen years, and that was very good indeed when one considers that the average lifespan for a dog is only eight years. Perhaps it was that old 'hybrid vigour', perhaps not.

I realised Lassie was approaching her end. Heartbrokenly, I knew there was very little that could be done for her. It is so difficult beginning to lose something that you have loved, and have loved all your life. The prospect of losing her was like losing a large part of myself. She was a part of my boyhood, of the happy days spent on the farm. Let alone the fact that she was no ordinary dog.

Despairingly, I tried my best to hand-feed her, tempting her with every tasty morsel imaginable, just as I had tried to do when she was a puppy hidden beneath the recesses of the turkey verandah. She did not really want food, but accepted it from my hand, piece by piece, to please me – only to bring it back up, moments later.

She had been spending most of her time in the kitchen, sleeping all night there, right by her two daughters. Now she slept there for most of the day as well, waking only for odd moments to lie weakly in her basket, staring at me with that still impassive gaze she had, or trying to rise shakily to her feet. She arose only when it was absolutely necessary, either to go out to relieve herself, or to stretch. But when she moved, it was sluggishly and with great deliberation – it was terrible to see how her athleticism had left her so abruptly. She looked the picture of abjection. Her once flaming fox-red coat had become as dull as her eyes, and for the first time she looked her true age, very old and worn out. Only her vision and hearing were unimpaired, together with a thinking faculty that was able to understand what was happening to her. In the midst of the greatest drama of her life, facing her mightiest foe, she accepted that she could do no more than be carried along to her inevitable fate.

She continued to decline, and grew thinner and more fragile with each successive day. The twins grew quieter, realising that something was amiss. We went about on our usual walks, but without Lassie, it wasn't the same.

One fine morning before I was due to go to work, about a fortnight after she had first fallen ill, she was clearly much worse. When I greeted her she struggled to her feet, and tried to cross the floor to the back door, but was unable to make it. I lifted her in my arms and carried her outside and laid her gently on the grass, where I sensed she wanted to be. The garden was by now grassed-over, and a hedge of quick-thorn grew at the bottom, overshadowing my old fence. The hedge had always been there, but had originally been very scrubby and stunted. After we moved in, I cut it back and encouraged it to grow properly, and it was now a fine thick hedge still with its late summer foliage. Lassie lay on a rug, in its shade, perhaps thinking or sleeping – I could not tell. She wanted to be left alone, and so I left her. The twins could only stand around looking puzzled – and dejected. They even seemed to subdue their usual vim and vigour, in sympathy.

I could not afford to take the day off work and, as Jean worked as well, Lassie had to be left there beneath the hedge until lunchtime. When I came home to see how she was, she had barely changed her position at all. It had started to rain, just as I was arriving. Choking back the tears, I gently lifted her emaciated frame and brought her back inside the house for her own safety, though she persisted in trying to get out again, feebly crawling across the floor. Once more I gently replaced her in her basket, sickened inside at having to leave her again. The twins lay quietly in their own baskets, watching her. It had dawned on me that her attempts to get out of the house were not made for exercise or to get air, but for somewhere to die – as so many animals prefer to do – alone. That thought alone near broke my heart. Perhaps, somewhere near the farm, or a wood – of course, probably it was her dear old Laurel Wood itself that she had in mind. I was just too upset to do much work, and returned home as soon as I could get away.

Jean, and the children, who were well briefed on the enormity of the situation facing me, mercifully left me alone with Lassie in the back kitchen. They had also taken Lyn and Teddy out for their usual walk for me. I watched over Lassie's still-breathing form for many more hours, and then, at ten o'clock in the evening, she came suddenly to full awareness. With more energy than I had seen her muster for several weeks she arose again from her basket, and walked feebly out into the garden. Slowly, she cruised its perimeter, from time to time trying ineffectually to push her way through the fence – the barrier that had imprisoned her since she had left the farm.

Once again, I carried Lassie back inside the house, for her own comfort as I thought. But she would not return to her basket. I locked-out the twins, so that we could have more privacy, and knelt next to her on the floor, crying softly. I tried to comfort her as best I could as she leaned against the wall with her head drooping down to the floor, but there was nothing I could do.

"Oh, Lass, my poor girl," I wept. "What can I do for you?"

Raising her old head the sick dog looked up, and our eyes met. Gently, I caressed her. For the very first time, there was a slight movement of pleasure in her bushy tail as she acknowledged me. At least she knows I am here with her, I thought, as I slipped my arms about her and hugged her gently, rubbing my face against her soft, warm neck. Her head dropped again. Without further warning, she uttered a low moan, and gently slipped through my arms the short distance to the floor. With a little shudder, the dramatic life of the great Lassie was over.

For one long moment, I knelt there with my arms about her, with my face resting on hers, refusing to believe that this moment had arrived. Without being able to help myself, I burst out into loud racking tears, and cried long and deeply.

At length, rising to my feet, I stood over her peaceful form for a long while, once again silently reliving our lives together. Sixteen adventure-packed years sprang fleetingly to mind. Her habits, her moods, the way she walked or ran, the way she shook water from herself – all the little personal things about her came unbidden, and I was helpless to stop them. Strongest and most persistent of all was the episode with the bull, when she had saved my life.

Truly, she had been a dog in a million. I told myself I would carry out her last wish, and take her back to the wildwood, and there make a final resting place for her. With this thought, my grief abated slightly, and I was able to pass the night in some sort of peace, though waking regularly, only to cry myself to sleep again.

Early the following morning I buried Lassie in Laurel Wood, close to the pool where I felt she would have liked to be. I was only able to get the van so far, and had to carry her poor body the rest of the way across the fields. The large difference in weight since the last time I had carried her, soaking and shaking across the peat moss to the van, brought back yet more memories, and I could barely see where I was going for tears. I would have given anything to swap that living burden for this tragic one.

How is it possible to carry such a thing over two fields without attracting attention? I had wrapped her in a sack, and carried her like a haversack, with a spade held surreptitiously upright against my side. To walk in this way, trying to appear 'normal' when every part of me wanted to scream out my grief, was a deeply traumatic experience. But looking so, I entered the familiar old wood and pushed my way through the foliage.

I chose a small bank at the foot of a huge old elm tree, and dug deeply into the sandy ground. All the while

I remembered the fresh smells of the earth of long ago. When the little grave was complete, I gently lowered in her body, wrapped in a blanket. Then I covered her over, and packed down the sandy loam. To mark the spot where she lay, I partly buried a large log, with its upper part protruded from the earth, signposting for me her position.

For a long while afterward I stood by her grave, paying silent homage, tears streaming down my cheeks as the memories, still arising in an endless flood, refused to lessen. Finally I prepared myself to leave her.

"Goodbye, my Lass. Goodbye my sweet, sweet girl. I shall never forget you." I spoke aloud, then turned away, walking back through the wood in which, only a few scant months earlier, four of us had strolled and played in the best of health.

As I meandered slowly, deep in my grief, along the wood's familiar pathways, through its faerie glades, I tried to celebrate her life in my thoughts, but the enormity of what I had lost weighed heavily on me, and would not leave.

But by the time I reached the fields, some of the wood's healing magic had affected me, at least. Lassie had not died in pain, I reasoned, but at peace with her world, after a full life, and in the presence of someone she trusted and who loved her deeply. That was far more than many domesticated animals ever manage. Be grateful for small mercies, I chided myself as, freshly, more tears began to fall. There were still Lynn and Teddy to think of, who were less independent than Lassie had been, and who needed my love now. Not only had she not died in pain, she had not died in vain. The twins were Lassie's great and unexpected legacy, her special gift to me, trusting and knowing that I would cherish and love them. She had left them not to their mysterious father to bring up – but to me.

But I could not keep the other thoughts at bay, and by turns felt bitter at the world for not having been more accommodating of Lassie. The world with its sham ways had not really wanted either of us. Lassie's early life had been a harrowing ordeal. Had it not been for my intervention, she would probably not have survived. And the world had seen to it that the last third of her life had been cruelly restricted. The only positive thought I was able to take from all this – and I clung to it blindly – was that she was now safe. She was beyond any hurt.

For months I suffered her loss. For all my apparent worldliness – job, house, wife, two young children – I was still at heart the loner I had been as a schoolboy, when I had first been given Lassie. The world of nature, not human beings and their artificial world, was still my natural realm, just as it is now and always will be. For me, Lassie meant everything. It was as though, in her loss, I had suffered a severe human bereavement.

The more positive thoughts that had come into my turbulent mind in the wood, slowly came to the fore again, and stayed, and though I felt that nothing could ever replace Lassie's physical presence, I came to see that, in spirit at least, she lived on.

Jean supported me throughout the whole of this time. Although she had never really understood my relationship with Lassie, she tried hard to, and helped me to keep from tipping over the edge into deep depression. But it was to my mother, who still lived at the back of her hairdressing business in Macclesfield, and who knew well how deep my relationship with Lassie had run, that I turned to for solace. From the beginning, she had favoured this little wild collie with its foxy manner, and had genuinely been fond of her. She was deeply upset by her death, and comforted me, and told me the things I had struggled to tell myself: that Lassie had lived to a very good age, had not died in pain, and that Teddy, Lynn and my own family now needed my love and care. I reminded myself, as I listened to her, that I was not the only one to suffer the great loss of the farm – or of a beloved dog. Coming from her, the words had more impact, and slowly I began to feel them in my heart.

Lassie lived on in the twins. I sensed this almost from the point of her death, after which her spirit seemed to take them over. The twins sensed my loss, and attempted to fill in, which to begin with I found unnerving. For the first time I noticed little actions and mannerisms in them, which were Lassie's. In life, very often, Lassie would stand at my side and lean on me. Lynn suddenly began to do the same thing, although she had never done so before. Before Lassie's death, on our walks, the three dogs adopted strict positions, to which they always adhered. Lassie would walk on my left, the twins on my right. Now Teddy moved over to my left, leaving Lynn on the right. If, thoroughly spooked, I tried to put a stop to this and position them both on my right, when my attention was elsewhere they would fall behind me and cross their leads, and Teddy would end up on the left hand side again.

Teddy began the habit of resting her muzzle on my knee in exactly the same way that Lassie used to do. She and Lynn were similar in so many ways, and I could not tell whether they were empathising with me intelligently, using telepathy bequeathed by their mother, which I still thought was possible, or whether they were merely copying their memory of Lassie now that they were in their new role.

Always the most extrovert of the two, Teddy replaced her mother and became dominant over Lynn, whose humble and softer nature made her content to remain in her twin's shadow. Whereas before, they had eaten out of the same food bowl, now they required separate ones. That is not to say that Teddy was over-aggressive, or over-assertive. She was just taking her natural role, as nature intended. Like Lynn, she was normally quiet and well mannered, at least to me, and so the roles were accepted quite naturally and amicably. They showed no jealousy toward each other, although very occasionally had their differences, which they would resolve by growling, never fighting.

Their physical looks and actions were so like their mother's that in unthinking moments I often mistook one or the other of them for her, and even called them by her name. But what had at first startled me, I soon accepted. Fortunately their brown, not yellow eyes, also reminded me of the difference. Very gradually, I made good progress on the road to recovery. For this, I depended in great part on those two remarkable creatures who filled the raw gap left by Lassie in my heart.

Chapter Nineteen

WITH BOTH Jean and I working in full-time employment, we had finally saved up enough money to buy our own house, and my long-cherished dream of escaping Broken Cross was realised. The children were well taken care of in school all day, allowing us the time we needed to make a search, and we eventually found a nice family bungalow with its own land on Gawsworth Road, Macclesfield. The prospect of moving there filled me with fresh hope. Although only a brisk fifteen-minute walk from the estate, the area was a marked improvement, ideal for dogs and children, and the land that came with the house – a third of an acre – immediately lead me to think that here was the opportunity of capturing something of the spirit of the old smallholding, if not in scale.

Fortune smiled on us. After the preparations and negotiations were done, we moved into this comparative haven in the spring of 1970, five months after Lassie's death. The change was instantly apparent in the dogs, who now found they had much more freedom to run about. As well as having more private ground, at the back of the bungalow lay school playing fields where exercise was much easier and far more enjoyable.

I gladly lost myself in all that the move entailed, and began, as I promised myself I would, to build up a new collection of animals. I started off with a few pigeons and doves, and built an aviary for them. These were followed by smaller aviary birds like budgerigars, and then by bantams and other fowl. In no time at all the garden was converted into something approaching a fairly large pets' corner, filled with aviaries and wire runs. Sensibly, I curtailed my grander aims of opening a commercial centre. Lack of time and space, and the cost of investment, restricted my natural urges to hobby only! However, I was more content than I had been for years, and began to feel that I was at last entering a new and happier phase of life, with Broken Cross and Lassie's death put behind me.

Over the next few years my family grew up, and the children, Caroline and Judith, who had both missed out on the experience of farm life, were able to share more fully in the pleasures and lessons to be had from all these pets. Judith, the eldest, was the one most able to benefit, but both girls still loved animals, and were still very good with Lynn and Teddy. They had been brought up to love and respect animal life, and never annoyed or teased them. The twins' reaction to the children was still the same. Lynn loved small children to the extent of idolising them. Teddy's bad temper, on the other hand, like her mother's often got the better of her, and I continued to keep an eye out when she and Caroline were together.

If anything, this trait of Teddy's had become worse, as I noticed one day shortly after we had moved into the bungalow. At school lunchtimes and breaks, the field at the back of the house filled with children, who got into the habit of coming right up to the fence bordering our garden, calling out to the dogs and thrusting their arms through the chain links. Lynn loved this, and would let the children pet and fondle her, but to my amazement Teddy began barking fiercely at them. Not only was she barking, but was seriously trying to bite their waving arms! Straight away I built a second fence within the outer one, to avoid any harm being done.

I racked my brains to think what could be causing the aggression. Was it insecurity, caused by that early separation from Lynn, when she was sent away to live on her own? I noticed that her short temper had got slightly worse since Lassie died, so it could have been a coping trait. Or was it a hereditary trait coming out in her? The new responsibility of acting as 'mother' to Lynn, and seeing herself as my main protector, might have triggered an instinctive response. I could not get to the bottom of what was causing it, but to be on the safe side, as we had to do with Lassie we took extra care to see that she was not put in the position where she might bite or attack someone.

Already quite old when Lassie died, the twins were now ten. Eight years had gone by since our departure from the farm. As with Lassie, I often wondered whether they would come into season but, unlike Lassie, who eventually obliged, they never did. I had often been told that sterility was to be expected in identical twins. Not only were these two identical, they were also the offspring of a possible hybrid, making the chances of a litter even more remote. Now, of course, they were too old to breed. By this strange quirk of nature, they were to be the end of the line.

Once again, I fell to thinking about the nature of

their grandfather. Was he dog – or fox? I had come to be slightly less adamant about my conviction that he had been a fox, yet many of the characteristics of Lassie, the first generation of his offspring, had been undoubtedly fox-like, and I could not forget them. The answer would never be known. A strange and inexplicable story, you might say but, nevertheless, true to the facts as I knew them, and verified by any others who saw Lassie.

The uncanny resemblance of the twins to their mother continued to increase as they became older, as photographs bear out. Their close 'mental link' with each other also became more acute. Perhaps the best record of the telepathic process that had once seemed to link all three dogs, was now made startlingly evident, one summer's evening. Coming home from work one day, I found Teddy critically ill. She had been unwell for several days, but not badly so, and each day I had left her to her own devices, hoping that on my return she would be recovered, as so many creatures do. Now, she had suddenly declined, and was literally at death's door!

I rushed her to David Hopkins, who, after making his examination, told me he would have to operate on her immediately. I listened anxiously whilst he told me what he would have to do to her. She was suffering from the fairly common ailment of an infected ovary. Bitches die very quickly from septicemia when they get this, and so he intended to perform an emergency pymetre on her – the equivalent, in human terms, of a hysterectomy – and remove the whole of her womb, tubes and ovaries. It was a serious operation that healthy young dogs usually recover well from. Teddy had been caught in time; but her age was against her.

I left Teddy in his hands, confident that she would be

all right, and drove home. The operation took place at seven o'clock that evening. On arrival at the bungalow, I was amazed to notice Lynn's reaction. Almost precisely at seven she began to behave very oddly, pacing restlessly up and down the kitchen. Jean and I thought that she wanted to be let out, and obliged her. Moments later she wanted to come in again – then out, then in. As the hours wore on, her restlessness grew worse. She seemed to have a problem knowing where to sit, or indeed whether to stand or sit. Next, she began quivering, and then began to foam at the mouth, and finally heaving, as though she wanted to be sick. This heaving and retching continued until about ten o'clock, when David rang from his surgery to say that Teddy's operation was completed. Teddy was awake, but was alarmed and fretting, and needed to be collected that night.

Climbing into my van, I rushed to the surgery, to find Teddy swathed in bandages about her middle, and in a very weak condition. Overjoyed at the operation's apparent success, I returned home with the patient, driving slowly so as not to jolt her. At the very moment I carried her into the house, Lynn ceased her strange symptoms. We had exchanged their separate baskets in the kitchen for one larger, single basket, where both twins now slept together, and I carried Teddy to this and laid her gently down inside it. I stood back to watch, as Lynn jumped in beside her. She instinctively realised that her sister had been seriously ill, and calmly began to comfort her, washing her face and neck. I was left shaking my head in wonderment.

This 'telepathy' was not finished, though. Next morning I awoke, pleased to see Teddy sitting up in her basket and looking much brighter. But I was now concerned to find that Lynn appeared to be unwell. She was soon showing exactly the same symptoms of distress that her twin had done, just twenty-four hours earlier! Convinced that she had the same illness, I rushed her to surgery and, sure enough, she too underwent an emergency pymetre – and it was now Teddy's turn to show symptoms of empathetic distress. In her weakened condition, this was really alarming to see. Fortunately, her distress too ended as her twin's operation finished.

Both dogs were operated on by David personally. He told me that he had never come across anything quite like it before, although he had long administered to the twins and originally verified their identical status. When I brought him Lynn, he was at first struck by her similarity, which had increased with age, to Teddy, whom he had just operated on, then was staggered by her identical illness. I reminded him of the twins' controversial history, and the story of their mother, and he listened intently, slowly nodding his head and confining himself to the occasional "Erhm". Finally, he was as convinced as I that Lynn's illness had been brought on by grieving about Teddy. Being now more used to these coincidences, I was not so surprised as he was, but once again I was struck by the unusualness of these two very special dogs. It was then that David wrote his article for the British veterinary journal, acknowledging their special status and bringing them yet more fame.

Lynn's wound healed very quickly, but not so Teddy's, whose stitches became septic. On my lunchtimes, when I checked and fed the animals, I powdered Teddy's nasty, wet wound, and comforted her as best as I could. One day, I entered the kitchen to find the two of them unusually quiet. I sensed that they were in trouble and had been waiting for me to arrive. Teddy was sitting very still in her basket. Beneath her was what at first I took to be a piece of rope. Then, to my utter horror, I realised that her stitches had burst. Her guts had pushed out through the wound beneath her, and her long, trailing intestines were spilled out, covered with hair, and dull with dust and dirt.

It is not often that I can be put into a panic, but this was one of those times. Teddy was sitting motionlessly, evidently aware that further movement would put her in worse danger. What could I do for the best? After forcing myself to think, finally I acted.

"Now stay there!" I admonished her, as I rushed about to find a washing-up bowl and a bottle of antiseptic. Filling the bowl with warm water, I poured in a very small drop of the domestic disinfectant – just enough to kill any germs, but not to burn her – and with difficulty managed to insert a piece of clean paper beneath her and her entrails. Then, painstakingly, I cleaned her gut, inch by inch, feeding it back inside her as I went. It took me more than an hour to get every little bit back inside, and I was exhausted from holding my breath and running with sweat at the end of it. Returning to work that afternoon was out of the question, and after I had finished I wrapped her tightly in a bandage and took her straight back to the vet's. She was anaesthetised, cleaned up and re-stitched. This time a clip was put on her, to make sure that the same thing could not happen twice!

Although the healing was a very long in the happening, the incision eventually did heal nicely and, amazingly, there were no further problems. After recovering from their ordeal, both Lynn and Teddy had new leases of life, taking full advantage of the garden, which was big and interesting enough for them to have small adventures. They were intrigued by the aviaries and their contents, frequently sending the birds off in wild, screeching flights with their inquisitive nuzzlings, or attempting to round up the fowls. Like Lassie, they never tried to harm them.

The two made excellent guard dogs, warning off strangers who came to the door, and guarding both bungalow and van with the same efficiency as had their mother. The only slight worry in these later periods of their lives continued to be Teddy's unpredictability.

Over the next few years, life continued happily. Judith and Caroline, who had been small when Lassie died, and had been forbidden even to try and touch her, were now both old enough to take an intellectual interest in her story, and loved me to relate her life to them. On some bedtime occasions I would tell them the whole story, beginning with the shooting of the little blue collie, who had strayed once too often into man's affairs. At other times they were delighted by the adventures in Laurel Wood, or to hear again the episode of the bull, or about the night my torchlight caught Lassie within the circle of foxes. Having not got to know Lassie themselves, they never failed to tire of listening to me talk about her.

Wherever we went, we took the dogs along too. They had none of the intransigence of their mother, and we went equally to town or country, even, once, on holiday to North Wales, in a caravan belonging to a friend of my mother's. Mother hired it fairly regularly for her own use, but on this occasion Jean and I booked it. The site, beneath the cliffs at Conway Morfa, was particularly lovely, right at the sea's edge in the sand dunes, and overlooking the white limestone headland of the Great Orme. The cliff-top walks, and the countryside inland of hills, high heather moors and the wide Conway river valley, made for marvellous rambles with the dogs, who much preferred them to our walks along the beach. They never entered the water, and preferred grass to sand. Even so, we would occasionally all stroll along the shore, when they would run along the sea's edge, tantalised by the inrushing waves. The children, of course, loved the beach, so I would find myself taking the dogs to the wilder places that I had always loved, and whilst they padded sedately around, I would daydream of how life might have been under different circumstances. Mostly, the twins played quietly, or slept in the long sunny hours, and I found myself thinking often of Lassie, and of how she would have enjoyed herself in these rich, new pastures. I fancied that in her old age I could have persuaded her to come with us – the thought of her foxy-red form loping across the purple moors under bright summer skies, was a particularly pleasant daydream. But in those grim days at Broken Cross, where she ended her life, such luxuries were unaffordable.

Always ready to please, affectionate and totally obedient, were the twins, and it was difficult to realise they were now fourteen years of age and fast becoming old ladies. I continued to see Lassie reborn in them, as daily they continued to grow more like her with their fabulous, fiery coats and well-kept appearances. As had been the case with Lassie, a slight silvering at the muzzles was the only indicator of their advancing years.

Quite suddenly, for no apparent reason, Teddy one day began to lose weight. Despite every veterinary care, she developed kidney failure. She became weak, and showed no sign of improvement, until I despaired that once again the inevitable must happen. Eventually, she was only able to walk with great difficulty. On a hot, sunny lunchtime from work I found her lying in the garden in her favourite spot, beneath an old oak tree, with Lynn standing quietly nearby. Teddy could not rise at all. Knowing instinctively that this was the end, I called David. We deduced that she could go on no longer in this state, and poor Teddy was put painlessly to sleep just where she lay, under the tree. A little sigh, and she was gone.

That same evening I made a sad return to Laurel Wood, and buried Teddy in a small grave to the right of Lassie. She was wrapped in a blanket, placed in the ground, and her grave marked in the same way as I had marked Lassie's. She was at rest with her mother, no longer able to feel the pain and distress of her illness.

Poor Lynn was the survivor, and felt very much alone despite everything we tried to do for her. For some time we were very worried about her state of mind, as she was very morose, and often to be found lying on the spot where Teddy had died. It distressed me to find her there, and I would call her away, but moments later she would return to lie in that very same place. I began to fear that she was broken-hearted and pining fatally for her sister, from whom she had never been parted for more than a few hours since their enforced separation as puppies. That reminded me of how she had been the one to suffer most, at least mentally, at the time. Then, in February of 1976, she received unexpected company.

One snowy, wintry day, Jean and I, on a shopping

trip to a Manchester store, took a short cut back to the parked van, and found ourselves passing along Tib Street, the area that was then famous in the city for its pet shops, which is now part of the Northern Quarter. As Jean tried desperately to drag me away from the exotic birds on display, all at once our eyes were attracted – as they were meant to be – by a lonely, brown mongrel terrier puppy sitting by itself in the sawdust. She was cut off from us by a pane of glass, but was just begging for us to buy her!

I had not intended to buy another puppy whilst Lynn was alive, but this appealing little soul went straight to our hearts, and she was purchased for the then princely sum of ten shillings! As you can imagine, the puppy also went straight to our daughters' hearts, and signalled another new era in our lives. Actually, we had not really bought it for ourselves, but to 're-home' it, as the puppy had looked so forlorn in the pet shop. But we were inevitably captivated by her.

I had never owned a terrier before, and called this one Sally. Much to our surprise, Sally was just what our old dog needed to pull herself round. Quite the reverse of resenting the puppy, which I had feared might be the case, she took an immediate interest in her, not only washing and playing with her, but taking her into her own basket, and protecting her like a real mother would have done. It was a delight to behold the two of them together – the young and the old, especially when the old had a new lease of life. There was now no question of moving Sally on. Once again, I breathed a sigh of relief and looked forward to at least a little more love of life for Lynn and, by extension, for us.

Where before Lynn had been a humble dog, now she began to push herself forward a bit more, and required more attention. Though over fourteen years old she was still a remarkable dog. Unfortunately, she had begun to grow deaf, although in every other respect she was still very alert, and her fiery-red coat was a constant reminder to me of her mother.

I had first noticed her deafness with the arrival of Sally. The puppy would come to the door and make scratching noises in her attempt to get in, but it was only when she barked that Lynn would hear and take notice. When the terrier barked, Lynn would begin to bark too. After the long period of solitude and silence she had endured after Teddy's death, this was indeed music to my ears. She continued to be a good guard dog, now backed-up by Sally's keener hearing.

Sally, like Lassie and the twins had been, was a super-intelligent puppy who required no house training, and who quickly grew up into a strong, healthy dog. She was a funny little soul, in that she objected to being left behind after we had gone to work. She would not go so far as to damage things or tear anything, but would pull the cushions off the chairs and settee, and pile them in the middle of the room, as a sort of protest. When we came home, we would find this enormous mound in the centre of the room. It was a habit she continued until she was two years' old.

Uneventfully and happily, the months rolled by, and slowly, almost imperceptibly, Lynn took to sleeping more often during the day. One evening, when she had slept for most of the day and was still asleep on her rug in front of the fire, I noticed her old forehead wrinkling and relaxing, and her dim eyes fluttering sightlessly behind their closed lids. A slight whimper escaped her throat. Reaching down from my chair I ran my hand along her fine flank. She quietened at once, and I wondered just what had been going through her mind. Perhaps she was dreaming of Lassie, her wild mother, or the woods and the long walks we used to take, racing in pursuit of rabbits with Teddy, or even perhaps of the young man she had so long adored and depended on.

Some nights later, out walking with Sally and I, Lynn collapsed on a grassy verge. I stooped down to her, and tried to coax her up.

"Come on, girl," I said to her in encouragement. She feebly wagged her tail but simply could not find the strength to rise. Finally, I gathered her up in my arms – she was a big dog, and had become the heaviest of them all – and carried her until I grew tired. Gently setting her down, I tried again to urge her to walk. Wearily, she rose to her feet, and walked slowly home with me.

After examining her the next day, David told me he thought she had suffered a mild heart attack. I had expected this news, and sorrowfully began to prepare myself for the inevitable conclusion, towards which she was now heading.

Within a week, Lynn had another, stronger, attack. One morning, taking the dogs with me in the car on some errand, Lynn crumpled-up on the front seat. She went over on her side, without a sound, and went into a kind of coma. As calmly as possible, I turned the car around and drove straight back home. As soon as I touched her to lift her out, I could tell she was dying. I carried her lovingly to the garage where I knew there was a piece of carpet, and gently laid her down. Even as I did so, she gave a little shudder and died.

When her end came, it was, literally, the end. For the third time, I made the journey to Laurel Wood, on the same sad mission. As I drove there I felt terribly dejected. There had been three deaths and three burials in the same few years. Mother had also recently lost a new corgi, Cindy, who she had acquired just after leaving the farm, and her pet cat, and I was worrying for her, too.

I had left the bewildered Sally at home with the family, and drove there in silence, heavily conscious that in the back of the car, wrapped in a blanket, lay a small bundle – all that remained of my glorious youth.

Miraculously, Laurel Wood was still largely intact, though the houses that I had seen in the process of being erected six years ago were now up, and a new school was operational. The hustle and bustle of ordinary life had crept almost, but not quite, up to the little wood. I laid Lynn beside Lassie and Teddy, to Lassie's left side, in the peace of the quiet wood, so that the two daughters symbolically were separated physically from each other but joined, as they had once been in their mother's womb.

Now they were all together again, resting peacefully in the still unchanged and enchanted wood. A lump came in my throat as I stood by the three graves. There, in my mind's eye, I could not help but see a young beautiful princess lying out on the tree above the pool's reflecting surface, just as she had used to do over twenty years before. Could time really have passed so quickly? The lifetimes of the three dogs had spanned almost twenty-four years. Now, there being no further offspring, the line from the wildwood had come to an end. Lassie and her two daughters were gone, and it would take me a long time to get used to the barrenness of life without them.

Picking up my spade, and taking a long, last look at the still scene, I quietly walked out of Laurel Wood for the last time, and headed for home.

Lassie had taken her true identity with her, unrevealed, to the grave. There could be no scientific proof in support of, or against, her being a hybrid. But though I have come to regret that I had not tried harder to find ways of having her tested, at the time I thought the approach I took was right. Lassie had been born into a wild world, of a wild mother – and probably an even wilder father. In life she had retained much of her wayward will and yet had, in the end, after my long boyhood struggles with her, returned home from the wild to be with me. Our love, and the relationship that had arisen from that love, in those still hot days of lingering youth, was what counted for us.

Although the final curtain on the saga of Lassie and her twins had fallen, and their magical presence gone, they would not, could never be forgotten. I must not look back, I thought to myself, in my many moments of sorrow and grief. I should look forward to the future, by sharing her story. Perhaps, when time had erased some of the painful memories of youth, one day I would sit down and start to write it.

About

John Roberts Warren was born at Pool End Farm, Tytherington, East Cheshire in 1934. He is still living in Cheshire and enjoys a hobby of poultry keeping.

Philip Snow BA is well known for book illustrations, and latterly, writings, about the natural world. He has contributed illustrations or covers to well over seventy books, and many magazines, prints, cards, leaflets, reserve maps et cetera, and to exhibitions in London, Wales and venues in various countries including the Royal Academy's *British Art* show in the Gulf States.

His work is found in many private, and several public and royal collections, including HRH Prince Charles, USAF, Welsh Assembly and Sheik Suroor of Abu Dhabi. He has recently both written and illustrated the critically acclaimed *Light & Flight – Hebridean Wildlife & Landscape Sketchbook* (Brown & Whittaker, Mull), *Tall tales from an Estuary* about his Anglesey home, and the controversial Creationist book *The Design and Origin of Birds* for DayOne Books, in the UK and USA.

www.snowartandbooks.co.uk

Other Titles

Colin Wilson: Philosopher of Optimism
by Brad Spurgeon

Fifty years after publication of *The Outsider*, writer and
philosopher Colin Wilson sums up his philosophy of
optimism and refutation of pessimism. As well as clearly
outlining his thinking he also talks about his fiction
and his writings on criminology and the occult. In this
extended interview, published in 2006 and conducted
at Wilson's home in Gorran Haven, near St Austell,
Cornwall, UK, International Herald Tribune journalist
Brad Spurgeon provides a fascinating portrait of one
of our overlooked national treasures. Accompanied by
essays chosen by Wilson.

ISBN 978-0-9552672-0-8
150 pp
Paperback
RRP £9.99

Jackson Pollock the Musical
by Roger McKinley

Who was Jackson Pollock? Driven genius, misunderstood drunk, the most influential, elusive and provocative artist of the modern world? *Jackson Pollock the Musical* is a tragi-comic, imaginary musical journey to discover the nature of the greatest American painter of the 20th Century, his death by car crash and his continuation in the Underworld. With eighteen original songs – ranging through traditional spiritual, folk, bebop, swing, music hall, free jazz, concrete and early electronic/experimental audio – *Jackson Pollock the Musical* is a libretto for a musical based on the life and times of this Abstract Expressionist painter. By Northern Irish author and artist Roger McKinley.

ISBN 978-0-9552672-1-5
170 pp
Paperback
RRP £9.99

Please order from your local bookseller or direct from the publisher at *www.michael-butterworth.co.uk*